Connecting the West

TONAPAH 2003

To Bobbie,
Happy Ghost Town Hunting!
Best Regards,
Shawn Hall

D1737421

Connecting the West

*Historic Railroad Stops and Stage Stations
of Elko County, Nevada*

SHAWN HALL

 University of Nevada Press, Reno & Las Vegas

University of Nevada Press, Reno, Nevada 89557 USA

Copyright © 2002 by University of Nevada Press

All rights reserved

Manufactured in the United States of America

Library of Congress Cataloging-in-Publication Data

Hall, Shawn, 1960–

Connecting the West : historic railroad stops and stage stations of

Elko County, Nevada / Shawn Hall.

p. cm.

Includes bibliographical references and index.

ISBN 0-87417-499-6 (alk. paper)

1. Railroad stations—Nevada—Elko County—Guidebooks.

2. Historic sites—Nevada—Elko County—Guidebooks.

3. Elko County (Nev.)—History, Local.   I. Title.

TF302.N3 H35 2002

385.3'14'1979316—dc21

2001008689

First Printing

09   08   07   06   05   04   03   02   5   4   3   2   1

To

HOWARD HICKSON

A dear friend and mentor

A Museum Expert Extra-Ordinaire

Contents

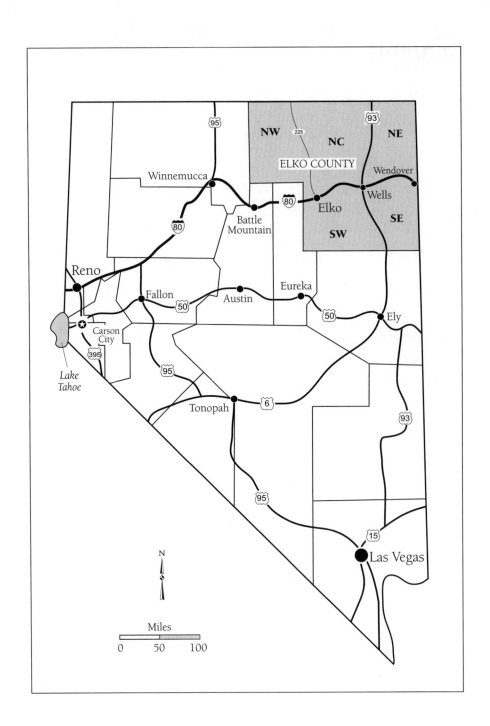

NW 225 NE
NC
ELKO COUNTY
95   93
Wendover
Winnemucca   Wells
80   Elko
Battle   SE
Mountain   SW

Reno
Fallon   Eureka
Austin   Ely
50   50
Carson
City
395
6
Lake   Tonopah
Tahoe
95

93

95

N

15
Las Vegas

Miles
0   50   100

Preface

When I first started research on this book in 1986, I never envisioned the depth and breadth of the undertaking. Many times over the past years, I had felt I was finally done with the research and ready to start writing, only to find additional sources of information. Once the writing phase began, the fun of whittling down and organizing well over one thousand pages of notes into a readable and understandable format began. Finally, after eight years of work, the final product has arrived. Although I have written other books, the two books on Elko County have been the most challenging of my career because of the huge scope they encompass. Almost three hundred historic sites, ghost towns, stage stations, railroad towns, ranches, mining camps, and forts were covered. This meant that for the book to be publishable, it would have to be divided into two sections. The first part contained only ghost towns and mining camps, while this subsequent volume covers railroad stops, stage stations, valleys, and other historical sites not covered in the first volume. Some sections are duplicated in this volume because they satisfied criteria for both books. This volume basically covers the historic sites not covered in the first volume but some have been completely eliminated.

It has been an enjoyable experience traveling around the county, meeting and talking with residents, and visiting each and every site. This has involved almost fifteen thousand miles of travel to reach and investigate every corner of the county. Being a camper at heart, I found the beauty of Elko County to be overwhelming at times. While I had visited different areas over the years, it wasn't until I moved to Elko that I had the time to truly enjoy all of the wonders that the county has to offer.

I have tried to present as accurately as possible a history of each historic site in Elko County. However, with any book this size, and with all of the historical information presented, errors can appear despite the intensive scrutiny that the script has undergone by me and local history buffs. If the reader finds something questionable, please don't get upset; rather, contact the author so corrections can be made in future reprints.

There are a couple format changes from my previous books. Endnotes have been added so interested readers can find additional information in the sources cited.

One disappointment is the amount of vandalism to the historic sites covered firsthand. Buildings have been destroyed to see if anything is in the walls. Foundations and sites ruined by overzealous bottle hunters. This is inexcusable and shouldn't be tolerated by anyone who witnesses such vandalism. Let the proper authorities know when our historic sites are being threatened. I hope that my children will have the opportunity to enjoy the historic sites of this county as much as I have, but unless some respect is shown by local residents, visitors, and federal agencies, there won't be anything left for anyone to see.

Many of the historical sites discussed in this book are on private property. Please respect all private-property signs and contact the owner. Most of the time, a simple request for permission is all the property owner is looking for. I hope everyone enjoys visiting the many places in Elko County as much as I have. While I no longer live in Elko, I treasure the memories acquired during my four years there. While some remembrances are tainted, the ones I chose to keep strong in my mind are the good ones. Enjoy the book and get out and visit Elko County, one of the most beautiful areas in the western United States.

Acknowledgments

First and foremost, I have to thank my daughter, Heather. It was very special to have her share my travels visiting the many historic sites in Elko County.

I would also like to offer my special thanks to my parents, Albert and Lorraine Hall. They continue to be supportive of my endeavors and it is very difficult being almost three thousand miles away from them.

Special thanks to Howard and Terry Hickson. Through Howard's guidance, I was able to learn the intricacies of museum management. He and Terry, more important, are close and dear friends and I am deeply indebted to them for their friendship. I also thank my friends in the history field for their assistance and support: Bob and Dorothy Nylen, Wally Cuchine, Bill Metscher, Gloria Harjes, Phillip Earl, and Doug and Cindy Sutherland. My best friend, Bruce Franchini, continues to be an important part of my life. While we see each other a lot less these days, our times together playing mountain Frisbee golf and camping are among my most enjoyable and memorable moments.

Many other people and groups have been instrumental in making this book a reality, through their "true" friendship and/or assistance with historic information: BeBe Adams, Matilde Griswold Allen, Delmo Andreozzi, the Barrick II basketball team, Robin Boies, Louise Walther Botsford, Robley Burns, Llee and Mary Chapman, Arthur Clawson, the late William E. Clawson Jr., P. J. Connolly, the Desert Sunrise Rotary, the Elko Chamber of Commerce and its board of directors, Rick Fleishmann, Fred Frampton, Helen Fullenwider, Cliff Gardner, Meg Glaser, Norman and Nelda Glaser, Steve Glaser, Lee Hoffman, Art and Cora Holling, Thomas and Irene Hood, Lori Kocinski, Gregg Lawrence, Irene Davis Linder, Lorry Lipparelli, Peter Marble,

Carole and Frank Martin, Joe McDaniel, the late Dr. Leslie Moren, Joe Nardone, Dan and Karen O'Connor, Dennis Parks, Edna Patterson, Jim Polkinghorne, Tony and Ellen Primeaux, Elizabeth Pruitt, Jerry Reynolds, Diane Beitia Rice, Pauline Riordan, Billy Robb, Jane and Ray Schuckman, Gertrude Sharp, Paul and Carol Siegel, Ed Strickland, Lanny and Terry Tron, Christina Ulm, Paul Walther, Jack and Francis Wanamaker, Barbara Wellington, Helen Wilson, and Bob Wright.

I will always treasure the "true" friendships that I forged during my four years at Elko, and thank you for making me feel welcome.

Northwestern Elko County

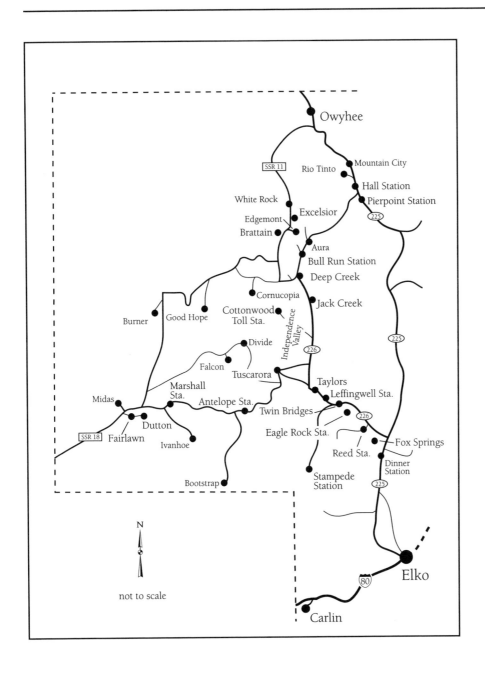

Owyhee

Mountain City

SSR 11   Rio Tinto

Hall Station

Pierpoint Station

White Rock   225

Excelsior

Edgemont

Brattain

Aura

Bull Run Station

Deep Creek

Cornucopia

Jack Creek

Burner   Good Hope   Cottonwood
Toll Sta.

225

Divide

Falcon   226

Tuscarora

Taylors

Marshall
Sta.   Leffingwell Sta.

Midas   Antelope Sta.

Twin Bridges   226

Dutton

SSR 18   Eagle Rock Sta.   Fox Springs

Fairlawn

Ivanhoe   Reed Sta.   Dinner
Station

Stampede
Station   225

Bootstrap

N

not to scale

80   Elko

Carlin

Antelope Station

DIRECTIONS: *14 miles southwest of Tuscarora, via old Nevada 18.*

Antelope Station was a horse-exchange stop on the Tuscarora to Battle Mountain Road during the 1870s and early 1880s. Jack Gaston ran the stagecoach line, and W. S. Freeman served as stationmaster. Freeman, a native of Massachusetts, died of consumption at Tuscarora in December 1880. The stagecoach line was unable to compete with the Elko to Tuscarora stage and folded in 1882. The station was torn down later that year, and nothing remains at the site.

Brattain

DIRECTIONS: *Located on the SN Ranch, 3 miles southwest of Edgemont.*

Brattain was a short-lived post office that opened on July 16, 1904, with Lee Faison as postmaster. The office served local ranches but did not produce enough revenue to justify its continued existence and closed on March 14, 1906, forcing local ranchers to travel to Edgemont for their mail.

Bull Run Station
(Golden City)

DIRECTIONS: *Located 2½ miles south of Aura on Nevada 226.*

Bull Run Station was a station and horse-changing stop on the Mountain City branch of the Northern Stage Company, which ran from Tuscarora to Mountain City. Bull Run was the first stop north of Deep Creek; the fare from Tuscarora was $2.50. During the 1870s, Benjamin Haws and his family built and ran a small hotel here.

With the mining revival that created Aura and the formation of the camp at Bull Run, the station became an important one. It was the drop-off point for supplies destined for Bull Run, and a small settlement developed around the station. In the belief that Bull Run would continue to boom, a townsite, named Golden City, was laid out at the confluence of Bull Run and Deer Creek, near the station. However, before any actual construction began, the project was given up.

When Bull Run faded during 1907 and 1908, the need for the station vanished. Combined with the end of the Aura boom, the Mountain City branch of the stagecoach line was abandoned. Only a couple of cabin logs mark the site, located where the road to Bull Run heads west.

Cottonwood Toll Station

(Golconda)

DIRECTIONS: From Spanish Ranch, go west on a gravel road for 8½ miles to Cottonwood Toll Station.

Cottonwood Toll Station was a horse-exchange stop and fare collection point on the toll road built by William Ford in 1873 around the west slope of Silver Peak to Cornucopia. The road ran from Taylor Canyon to the boomtown of Cornucopia; Cottonwood was the last stop before the rugged climb to Cornucopia. Ford later built a branch of this road connecting to the Deep Creek road on the east side of Cornucopia. Woodruff and Ennor bought the toll road in 1874. Cottonwood was known as Golconda during this period.

While the town of Cornucopia prospered, Cottonwood was in operation as a stage stop. The stagecoach line was taken over by Smith Van Dreillen in 1875, but when the Cornucopia boom ended in the late 1870s, the stage route was moved to run through Deep Creek rather than Cottonwood and Cornucopia. The station was not used after that, and now only the stone walls of the station and horse barn mark the site.

Deep Creek

DIRECTIONS: From Jack Creek, on Nevada 226 go north 5.8 miles to Deep Creek.

Deep Creek served as a stagecoach station from the 1870s to the 1890s. Mining activity at Cornucopia, Bull Run, Columbia, and Blue Jacket kept a constant flow of goods going through Deep Creek. The main stagecoach line through Deep Creek Station, located at the confluence of Deep Creek and Chicken Creek, was the Northern Stage Company, which ran the Mountain City–White Rock Road. Deep Creek was where the road from Tuscarora split, one branch running to White Rock and the other to Mountain City. Fare from Tuscarora to Deep Creek was $2.50. The station, which served both as a stage and freight stop, was run for many years by Dick and Lena Young.

After the stage stop ended in the 1890s due to lack of business, a couple of small ranches operated along Deep Creek. A small school was built in the 1920s at the Ken Reed Ranch. Mary Myers served as schoolteacher, but by 1934, there were only three students and the school closed in 1935. Today, one old ranch house remains, but only foundations mark the station site. Most of the Deep Creek area is now part of the IL Ranch.

House of Bessie Read in Deep Creek. (Ruth and Roy Roseberry collection, Northeastern Nevada Museum)

Dutton

DIRECTIONS: *Located 5 miles southeast of Midas, 1.1 miles west of Squaw Valley Ranch.*

Dutton was a post office located on a ranch near Midas. The office opened on June 20, 1907, and operated until September 30, 1913. With the growth of Midas nearby, the Dutton office was no longer needed. During Dutton's six years of operation, its postmasters were Charles Dorsey, Jonathan Webb, and Harry Petriell.

Eagle Rock Station

DIRECTIONS: *Located on the south side of Nevada 226, 8 miles west of the junction with Nevada 225.*

Eagle Rock Station, located between Reed Station and Twin Bridges Station, was a stop on the Elko-Tuscarora stagecoach line. It was built in 1875 by Smith Van Dreillan, who used the station as an overnight and meal stop. The fare from Elko was $4.50. The station was run by N. Nelson until he sold it in October of 1896. Nelson later bought a ranch near Island Mountain.

During the next few years, there was a series of owners, including W. F. Mahoney, Reid, Stewart, and M. E. Frenchy Gaillard. By 1910, Jess Snider was the owner, and the station served only as a horse-changing stop. In February 1916, snow around Eagle Rock Station was so deep that mailman Roy Primeaux had to haul the mail wearing snowshoes. With the arrival of automobiles and trucks in the 1920s, there was no longer any need for the station, which fell into disuse. Today, a foundation marks the site.

Excelsior

DIRECTIONS: From Deep Creek, take road west for 5.8 miles. Take a right turn and follow the road for approximately 10½ miles to White Rock Creek. Hike along the creek to the east to find remnants.

Excelsior was a post office that operated from July 18, 1871, to March 12, 1872, with Aaron Van Ulick as the only postmaster. Van Ulick later served as the Tuscarora Mining District recorder and later as the Elko County recorder.

The post office was on White Rock Creek where placer deposits were being worked. A camp of about twenty men formed around the mines, but only a couple frame buildings were built before being abandoned. Once the placer mining stopped, the post office closed, and mail for prospectors was received at the White Rock Post Office. A couple of collapsed dugouts mark the site.

Fairlawn
(Squaw Valley)

DIRECTIONS: From Midas, go southeast on old Nevada 18 for ½ mile. Bear right and follow for 1 mile to Fairlawn.

Fairlawn was a post office in Squaw Valley on the home ranch of the Nevada Land and Cattle Company. The post office, housed in the company store, opened on June 14, 1888, with Thomas Parkinson as postmaster. The company had been grazing cattle in the area since the early 1880s, and built the Willow Creek dam and reservoir in 1884. In addition, a ten-mile telegraph line was strung to the ranch.

In 1887, Nevada Land and Cattle built a two-story ranch house, complete with furniture imported from England. A store opened at the ranch under the management of E. G. Weth, who also served as the Nevada Land and Cattle Company's accountant. Weth, a native of England, served the company and lived in Squaw Valley for many years. The post office remained open until June 30, 1904, when it was moved to North Ranch in Humboldt County. Herbert Guernsey and Richard Richie also served as postmasters.

The Golconda Cattle Company bought the ranch and nearby Kelley Creek Ranch in 1905. Shortly afterwards, the ranch house burned. In 1948, E. G.

Weth died in England at the age of eighty-five. His daughter honored his final wish, scattering his ashes in his beloved Squaw Valley. The ranch is still active today and is part of the Ellison Ranching Company's holdings.

Fox Springs
(Oldham Station) (Fox Station)

DIRECTIONS: From Dinner Station, go north on Nevada 225 for 1 mile. Turn left and follow for 2½ miles to Fox Springs.

Fox Springs, located between Dinner Station and Reed Station, was an overnight and meal stop on Smith Van Dreillen's Elko to Tuscarora stagecoach line. A man named Fox built an eight-team barn and a small house to serve as the station.

Fox Springs also became the assembling point for cattle roundups along the Lone Mountain range. Cattle were driven to Fox Springs, and sorted before winter. In the 1880s, D. E. Hooten bought Fox Springs and ran the station until 1911.

Ed Oldham, who had sold Dinner Station, took the station over from Hooten and homesteaded 160 acres to start the Fox Springs Ranch. He built a seven-room house, covered with redwood shingles, to house his large family. In addition, a building was moved from Dinner Station to serve as a storehouse. Edward and Kate Oldham's son, Charles, was killed during World War I when his ship, the *Lake Moor,* was torpedoed and sunk.

With the arrival of the automobile, the need for stations along the Elko-Tuscarora road ended. The Fox Springs Ranch has continued to operate and is still in the Oldham family, now owned by John Oldham. Original buildings remain amid newer structures. The site is on fenced private property.

Hall Station

DIRECTIONS: Located ½ mile south of Mountain City on Nevada 225.

Hall Station was a stagecoach station active during the 1860s in the early days of the Cope rush and was located just south of Mountain City. The station was run by Joe Hall, who also owned a store in Mountain City. Once Mountain City became well established, the station was abandoned. Nothing remains of the station today.

Independence Valley

DIRECTIONS: *Independence Valley is a river valley that stretches from Tuscarora north to Jack Creek.*

Independence Valley, from which the headwaters of the Owyhee River flow, was named by a group of soldiers passing through the fertile valley on July 4, sometime in the 1860s. Farmers and ranchers have prospered in Independence Valley for more than 125 years. P. J. "Old Jack" Harrington started the first ranch in the valley; nearby Jack Creek was named in his honor. John Byrne, from Ireland, came to the area in 1871 and his wife, Amanda Jane Rader Byrne, was the first non-Indian woman in Independence Valley. Their daughter, Eva Edna Byrne Rizzi Smith, born on December 30, 1871, in a tent, was the first non-Indian baby born in the valley.

By 1871, five ranches operated in the valley, and many more started during the ensuing years; the largest was Spanish Ranch. The Tuscarora boom at Tuscarora increased farming and ranching in the valley. Three hay ranches (Beard, Lancaster, and Shoecraft) provided food for livestock and horses used on the stage and freight lines. Mahan's farm supplied dairy products for stores in Tuscarora. A school opened at the Byrne Ranch in the 1870s. Nevada governor Lewis Rice "Old Broadhorns" Bradley, a friend of the Byrne family, often visited Independence Valley.

The Independence Valley school moved from ranch to ranch as one family would run out of children to support it. By 1883, the school had twenty-one students; a school still operates in Independence Valley with kindergarten through eighth-grade classes. Above that grade, students go to the Elko schools, with the children normally boarding with families there. Some of the early teachers who served in the old one-room schoolhouses were A. C. Stoddard, W. H. Schmidt, Charlotte Bacher, Edith Fleming, May Foley, and Elizabeth Asmus.

The Clawson family deserves mention in the history of Independence Valley. The Clawson family ranched and farmed in the valley since before 1900, and consumers in Tuscarora eagerly sought their farm goods. The Clawsons also ran the biggest freighting outfit on the Elko-Tuscarora run, also hauling to mining camps like Edgemont, Bull Run, and Aura, where they had mining interests. In 1910, the family bought the Griffeth Ranch for $3,500, whose ranch house had been moved from Tuscarora. Marion Clawson, a child at that time, later became director of the Bureau of Land Management in 1948. The Griffeth Ranch was sold to Bertyn Williams in 1915 for $10,500, and the Clawsons left the valley.

The most important ranch in the valley was the Spanish Ranch, established in 1871 by Pedro and Bernardo Altube. The brothers were Basques who came to Independence Valley after first ranching in California. Pedro was very tall and was known as Palo Alto, "Tall Pine," by his vaqueros. Palo Alto, California, where he had a large ranch, was named in his honor. Once established at the Spanish Ranch, the Altubes employed Shoshones from the Duck Valley Reservation to haul logs and build a house, bunkhouses for the vaqueros, a storehouse, and a blacksmith shop.

By the 1880s, the Spanish Ranch was one of the largest and most prosperous in Elko County. The Altube brothers were respected gentlemen and held the honorary title of Don. They were always fair to their men; for years the Altube family received thankful letters from former workers. The Altubes always bought their supplies from local farmers, which the farmers appreciated. In October 1884, the main ranch house burned; only a trunk containing family papers was saved. A new house was soon built.

The devastating winter of 1889–1890 was particularly harsh for the Altubes, and most of their cattle died. They began the process of rebuilding their herd; they renamed the company the Palo Alto Land and Livestock Company. Around 1900, the son of one of the Altube brothers, Jules, took over the management of the ranch, and Bernardo and Pedro moved back to California. Pedro died in 1905 at age eighty-six and residents of Tuscarora and Independence Valley were sad to know that they would no longer hear his familiar greeting: "Hey, son-of-a-bitch, my friend, take a drink with me."[1] In 1960, Pedro was elected to the Cowboy Hall of Fame. Bernardo died in 1916 at age eighty-five.

In 1907, all of the Altubes' holdings, except for the Taylor Canyon horse ranch, were sold to H. G. Humphrey, William Moffat, Peter Garat, and Lewis Bradley. Jules Altube owned the horse ranch until he sold out in 1918. The estate, sold in 1907, consisted of twenty thousand sheep, twenty thousand head of cattle, two thousand horses, and four hundred thousand acres of land.

In 1913, the Union Land and Cattle Company was organized, adding the Spanish Ranch to their vast holdings. The ranch was used to raise hay for all of the operations, which consisted of forty-five thousand head of cattle running all the way to Lovelock. During the summers, five hundred men were employed haying one hundred thousand acres between Jack Creek and the ranch, using fifty mowing machines and twenty-five hay rakes. The superintendent of operations was George Calligan, a huge man more than six feet tall and weighing 350 pounds, whom few workers questioned.

The Spanish Ranch was a stop on the Northern Stage Company's daily route, with a fare of $1.50 from Tuscarora. In 1915, A. W. Sewell relocated his grocery store from Tuscarora to the Spanish Ranch. The store was run by Ben Trembath, and Robert "Doby Doc" Caudill was hired as bookkeeper. Eventually, Sewell's grocery store chain grew to seventy-three stores.

In 1920, Doby Doc was arrested and charged with misappropriating funds from the Union Land and Cattle Company. Doby Doc had been keeping a second set of company books, but these books were written in a cryptic backward fashion that no one could decipher, and so the charges were dropped. Caudill was released and the shortages thereafter ended. The Sewell store burned in August 1923 at a loss of $40,000 and was not rebuilt.

The Union Land and Cattle Company went bankrupt in 1925, at which time John G. Taylor and E. P. Ellison bought the Spanish Ranch division. The property was divided, Taylor taking the northern Allied ranches and Ellison taking the Spanish Ranch. The Ellison Ranching Company became the parent company. Claude Barkdull was hired as foreman in 1929, and he and his wife, Frankie, stayed at the ranch until retiring in 1962.

A one-room schoolhouse was built in 1932; the first teacher was Edna Garralda. Other teachers included Ruth Roseberry, Helena Archibald, Sadie Andrae, Dorothy Gavin, and Anna Reed. The school operated until 1962; the school building was restored by the Ellisons and friends in 1977. Other old buildings still at the ranch include the cookhouse, originally a drugstore in Tuscarora, the original blacksmith shop, and the main ranch house. The Ellison Ranching Company still operates the ranch and many other ranches in the area.

Independence Valley continues to be a prosperous ranching area. In addition, many clear creeks tumble down from the surrounding mountains to flow into the Owyhee River. Before the advent of downstream dams, it was a common sight to see spawning salmon swimming through the valley. A drive up the valley provides historic sites and many scenic views.

The Woodward family in
front of their house and
hotel, 1890s. (North-
eastern Nevada
Museum)

Jack Creek

(Anderson) (Jackson)

DIRECTIONS: *Located 15½ miles north of Taylors on Nevada 226.*

Jack Creek was named in honor of its original settler, Jack Harrington, who homesteaded in the area in 1868 and spent the rest of his life ranching at Jack Creek. Jack Creek was soon added as a stop on the Northern Stage
Company's line from Tuscarora to Mountain City, with a fare of $2 from Tus-
carora.

The Jack Creek area was the prime source of wood for Tuscarora for firewood and mine timbers. From 1877 to 1892, an average of twelve thousand
linear feet of firewood and two hundred thousand feet of mine timber were
harvested each year. Some limited mining interest in the Jack Creek area occurred during the 1870s when a local rancher, Chesley Woodward, who had
settled at Jack Creek in 1869, staked a number of claims and formed the
Woodward Mining District in May 1877. However, nothing was ever produced, and Woodward abandoned the claims in 1878. Woodward and his
family operated a ranch, store, restaurant, and rooming house at Jack Creek
for many years.

In June 1879, the Jack Creek School District was organized and Nevada
Hardesty Griswold, then seventeen years old, taught ten students. A settlement of about twenty people had formed at Jack Creek, and a few other
ranches were homesteaded in Jack Creek Canyon and nearby areas to the

north and south. For many years, there were two schools in the Jack Creek area, each with about ten students.

Because of the number of families in the area and the lack of a proper gathering place, Harrington built the Jack Creek Opera House in November 1880. Despite its elegant name, the building was more of a barn with a stage rather than an actual opera house, but the local residents enjoyed the entertainment and camaraderie shared there.

In 1884, the Jack Creek population had grown sufficiently that Harrington was named justice of the peace, Clay Hardesty was selected constable, and R. D. Lamham was chosen as road superintendent. A voting precinct was established and local resident Charles Woodward served as the voters' registry agent. Jack Harrington died in 1886, and his ranch and stage stop were purchased by Frank Culver in April. Culver built a lodge for travelers and fishing parties, promising, "Clean beds and good meals will be the rule."[2] Many people from Tuscarora and Elko came to Jack Creek to fish and hunt on weekends.

In 1889, the era of two schools ended at Jack Creek when Jack Creek School District Number 22 was abolished in May, and the Jackson School District Number 40 was formed. The residents turned the abandoned Jack Creek School into a dance hall.

In 1890, the townspeople applied for a post office named Jackson. On June 25, the post office, with William Clawson as postmaster, was established there. However, the postal establishment order was rescinded on March 10,

The Jack Creek Guest Ranch in 1960. The building is the original Woodward house. (Tony and Ellen Primeaux collection, Northeastern Nevada Museum)

1891. Some postal histories incorrectly place the Jackson post office in the eastern part of Elko County at the Jackson mine north of Tecoma. However, Clawson's son, William E. Clawson Jr., related information that his father, who had been the Jackson postmaster, lived at Jack Creek after selling his ranch in Independence Valley. Also, the *Tuscarora Times-Review* reported the birth of William Clawson's son at Jack Creek in November 1890.

In December 1897, the schoolhouse was seriously damaged by a fire started by sparks from the wood stove. The students had an extended Christmas holiday while the school was repaired.

In August 1898, the Tuscarora-based Dexter Mining Company began construction of a hydroelectric power plant on Jack Creek. The old Defrees Mill in Taylor Canyon was dismantled for use in building a boardinghouse and bunkhouse at the power-plant construction site. The power plant was completed in January 1899, with power lines strung to the forty-stamp Dexter Mill that crushed the ore in Tuscarora. The final phases of construction had been delayed by heavy snowfall. The three thousand–foot pipeline that brought creek water to the generators was buried in ten feet of snow. Water was brought first from Jack Creek to Chicken Creek by flume, then entered the pipe and dropped four hundred feet to the plant to turn the electric generators. More than nine hundred horsepower was generated. The power plant cost $50,000 to build.

The power plant brought many new residents to Jack Creek and a new store, owned by Christian Anderson, opened in August 1899. By 1900, the population of the Jack Creek area was 74. On April 2, the Anderson post office opened, with Anderson himself as postmaster in his store. Anderson also owned Taylor Station, located in Taylor Canyon near Tuscarora.

In June 1903, J. R. Plunkett, a relative of *Tuscarora Times-Review* publisher W. D. Plunkett, was hurt at Jack Creek while loading sheep. His startled horse threw him under a moving wagon. He had no broken bones, but the newspaper reported that he was not happy with his horse.

The population shrank drastically once the power plant was operating efficiently, and most workers had moved back to Tuscarora. The Anderson post office closed on September 30, 1905. The power plant was completely refitted and enlarged in 1910. In June 1911, the plant was struck by lightning, burning out transformers, which were quickly repaired.

Ranches in and around Jack Creek were gradually bought by Basque immigrants. By the 1920s, Jack Creek had become a Basque community. Balbino Achabal ran the old Harrington Ranch, opening the Jack Creek Guest Ranch in 1943. Other Basque ranchers included Ysidro Urriola, Vincente Bilbao, Andres Inchausti, Joe Saval, and Feliz Plaza. Plaza also ran the Jack Creek store, owned by the Urriola family. Despite Prohibition, the store also featured a bar serving bootleg whiskey and home-brewed beer. The upper floor of the two-story building was rented to travelers and sportsmen. Urriola also had a small service station, a necessity in such a remote area.

Dances were a popular diversion at Jack Creek. Because trips to Elko were rare, most shopping was done by catalog. With the arrival of school buses, children from Jack Creek were bused to the Independence Valley school, and the Jack Creek school was closed. Teachers at the two Jack Creek schools through the years included Imogene Warder, Florence Meyers, Mary Divine, Helena Achabal, Rose Sherman, Ennah Bowen, Katie McCarty, and Barbara Long.

Jack Creek remains a popular recreational destination, with local fishing being some of the best in Elko County. Although the owners changed, the so-called Jack Creek Resort remained open until the 1980s, providing lodging, food supplies, and gas for sportsmen and campers. Eunice and Loren Wilder bought the property in 1961, and although Loren died in 1976, Eunice still lives in the area. Hank and Wendy Ispisua ran the business for their relatives until it closed in the early 1990s.

A number of ranches still operate in the area. The "resort" is closed but could be reopened in the future. Foundations mark the site of the power plant, and parts of the flume are still visible.

Leffingwell Station

DIRECTIONS: *Located on the south side of Nevada 226, 2 miles southeast of Taylors.*

Leffingwell Station was the northern terminus for the Elko and Independence Toll Road, built in 1873. The road originated from just north of Dinner Station. The Elko and Independence road ended at the Carlin and Idaho Toll Road. Leffingwell Station served both roads for only a couple of years. When both toll roads folded, the station was abandoned. Subsequent stagecoach lines used either Eagle Rock or Taylors as their stations. Nothing is left at Leffingwell today.

Marshall Station

DIRECTIONS: *From Tuscarora, go south, then west, on old Nevada 18 for 20 miles to Marshall Station.*

Marshall Station served as a stage station during the 1870s on Willow Creek. It was a stop on the Charles Haines stagecoach line to Battle Mountain. Hubert Bancroft mentions the station in his book, *History of Nevada,* but the only other known reference to Marshall Station is in the Elko County Recorder's *Miscellaneous Records* books. The station was most likely abandoned in the early 1880s when most of the Tuscarora stage lines to Battle Mountain stopped running. Nothing is left of the station today.

Owyhee
(Duck Valley) (Number One Settlement)

DIRECTIONS: *Located on Nevada 225, 95 miles north of Elko.*

The name Owyhee was given to the area by two Hawaiians who worked with the Hudson Bay Company. The name was the original phonetic spelling of "Hawaii" before the pronunciation was corrupted by white settlers. Before Owyhee became a reservation for the Western Shoshone and Northern Paiute tribes, Owyhee Meadows served as a stop on Hill Beachey's Elko-Idaho Toll Road, beginning in 1869. The odyssey of these two tribes being settled at Owyhee was a drawn-out affair punctuated by terrible hardships.

The Shoshone, or Newe, tribe had signed the Ruby Valley Treaty of Peace and Friendship on October 1, 1863, and it was ratified on June 26, 1866. However, little was done to accommodate the tribe's needs, and only minimal efforts to find a place to relocate the tribe were made. Exposure to diseases carried by settlers devastated the Shoshone, and the federal government did little to improve conditions. One white man, Levi Gheen, stood out in his attempts to help the Western Shoshone.

As early as 1870, the tribe had requested that Duck Valley be established as their new home. President Rutherford B. Hayes did not sign the order granting the tribe this land until April 16, 1877. Despite great promises, it had taken fourteen years for the federal government to fulfill its part of the treaty. However, the tribe's problems were not over.

The Western Shoshone Agency was initially run by a dishonest agent who kept most of the government goods for himself, creating more hardship for the Shoshones. John Mayhugh Sr. became the replacement agent in 1882, but many Shoshone had already left because of the harsh conditions. In 1883, the Shoshone were ordered to move to Fort Hall, but they protested, joined by local settlers. The objections were heard this time and the order was rescinded in 1884. At the time there were three hundred residents in Owyhee.

As a result of the successful protest, the reservation was established, and the town of Owyhee began to grow. The town was the terminus of the daily Owyhee stage with a fare from Elko of $14. In 1881, $1,800 had been spent to build a one-room school, and an additional school was built in 1884. The schools had twenty-five students. It was difficult to retain teachers in Owyhee. Most came from the East and once they arrived in Owyhee, quickly left. The *Duck Valley News* began publication on March 24, 1886. The newspaper was a family affair with John Mayhugh Jr. serving as editor, and his parents working as reporters. The newspaper apparently did not survive for even a month.

During the 1880s, the Northern Paiutes, under Chief Paddy Cap, were added to the reservation. On July 13, 1889, a post office opened at Owyhee (Austin Bender, postmaster) but closed on December 31, 1890. By 1893, the schools had more than fifty students, and Owyhee had a population of six hundred.

There was a lot of discord on the reservation because of the limitations put on the Shoshones and Paiutes by the federal government, most of which seemed intended to destroy the native culture and traditions. Traditional dances and feasts were prohibited, and the tribes could not use their native language, wear ceremonial blankets, or have the traditional long hair. The reservation straddled the Nevada-Idaho border, which meant the tribes had to comply with the laws of both states. Mining in the area also caused problems because settlers could mine but Indians could not. Ranchers also filed on existing water rights that supplied the reservation, which led to constant water problems that were not solved until Wildhorse Reservoir was built in 1937.

The Owyhee post office reopened on December 15, 1899, and has remained open ever since. Telephone service reached Owyhee in September 1904. The Taft Proclamation of July 1910 not only increased the size of the reservation, but also attempted to address the water problems by guaranteeing water rights for the reservation from Mary's River. However, the proclamation did not help; much of the reservation turned into a dust bowl. In the early 1900s, the Swayne School, named for F. A. Swayne, was built to replace the schools from the 1880s. In 1914, a hospital was built.

During the 1920s, Elko County attorney Milton Badt discovered that the government had not been paying the $5,000 annual fee promised by the Ruby Valley Treaty. Some money had been paid in the early years of the treaty, but was given to overseers who did not turn it over to the Indians. When this was discovered, the Shoshones and Paiutes refused to take the federal government's money, considering themselves independent. They dealt directly with horse and cattle buyers, were seldom cheated, and were greatly respected for their livestock-raising abilities.

In the fall of 1931, a new Owyhee School was built and had 120 students. In 1946, high school classes were added to the school. The completion of the Wildhorse Dam and reservoir in 1937 greatly helped the reservation, not only because of the additional irrigation water, but also because of income generated from recreational use of the reservoir. The operation of the reservoir has always benefited the reservation, although attempts have been made to take control of the reservoir from the reservation. Today, Owyhee has a population of about 1,200, and continues to be a thriving agricultural community. The high school's sports teams have been successful, winning a number of state titles.

Pierpoint Station

DIRECTIONS: *From Mountain City, go south on Nevada 225 for 5½ miles to Pierpoint Station.*

Pierpoint Station, located south of Mountain City, was a short-lived stop on the Elko and Idaho Toll Road. In 1870, it also served as the northern terminus for the short-lived Johnson Toll Road, which ran to Bruno City, ending at Friend's Station. However, the station was abandoned when the Elko and Idaho Toll Road ceased operations. Subsequent stage lines did not use the station and nothing remains at the site.

Reed Station
(Stewart Station) (Willow Creek Station)

DIRECTIONS: *From Dinner Station, go north on Nevada 225 for 4.2 miles. Turn left onto Nevada 226 and follow for 4 miles. Take a left exit and follow for 2 miles to Reed Station.*

In 1875, Willow Creek Station was established to serve Smith Van Dreillan's Elko to Tuscarora stagecoach line as a meal and overnight stop, but Dinner Station received the majority of the business. Henry Reed, who had originally come to Elko County in 1865 after serving in the Civil War, purchased the Willow Creek Ranch in 1879 after leaving Pleasant Valley to start his own ranch.

After Reed bought the ranch, the stop became known as Reed Station. Some historical sources list Reed Station and Eagle Rock Station as being the same, but Eagle Rock was a separate station a few miles west of Reed Station. After Van Dreillan folded his line, Reed Station continued as a stop for other stagecoach lines, and it was common for two hundred horses and twenty-five teamsters to stay at the station overnight.

A school operated at Reed Station during the 1880s. The station was the main shipping point for years for all supplies heading to the mines on Lone Mountain a couple of miles away.

Reed was known for his fast trips in his wagon with his horses, Dynamite and Danger. No one would travel with him when he was in a hurry. In 1888, the Reeds built a large white house at the station. Reed later served as an Elko County commissioner. In June 1900, in a double wedding, Reed's sons Marshall and Addison got married at the ranch.

Reed died in 1906, and soon afterward Robert Stewart and his half brother, John Carter, bought the ranch and station. In 1910, the partnership dissolved. Stewart took over Reed Station, and Carter moved to the other part of the property at South Fork. The stage was still running to Tuscarora. The fare to Elko from Reed Station, now called Stewart Station, was $3.50.

With the emergence of the automobile, the station declined until it was no longer needed. Stewart lived at the ranch until 1919, when he moved to Pleasant Valley. Stewart continued to run the property until he sold it in 1947 to M. E. Gaillard. In September 1938, a water pipeline was built from Stewart Spring to the new mill being constructed at the Rip Van Winkle Mine on Lone Mountain. Stewart was paid $25,000 for half of the water flow from the spring.

Since the 1960s, Reed Station has had many different owners and continues as an active ranch today. However, most of the buildings on the ranch are modern, with only a couple from the early days of Reed Station.

Stampede Station

DIRECTIONS: *From Nevada 226 at Twin Bridges, take a gravel road south 14 miles to Stampede Station.*

Stampede Station was used as a horse-changing stop on the Tuscarora to Carlin road during the 1870s. Its exact location is unknown except that it was near a good-flowing spring on the west side of Lone Mountain. The facility was also used as a drop-off point for supplies heading to the miners scattered around Lone Mountain.

Taylors

(Taylor Canyon)

DIRECTIONS: *From Dinner Station, go north on Nevada 225 for 4.2 miles, then go west on Nevada 226 for 17.6 miles to Taylors.*

Taylors, named in honor of Taylor Postlethwaite, was a stop on the Van Dreillan stage. A bed and two meals at Taylors cost $2.50. During the Cornucopia boom of the early 1870s, a new stagecoach line joined the Tuscarora stage line at Taylors. The DeFrees Mill, built in 1875 to treat ore from the Tuscarora mines, was located at Taylors. The mill was sold in August 1880 at a sheriff's sale to W. J. Urton for $971 but was little used.

In 1898, the Dexter Mining Company of Tuscarora built a power plant using water from Niagra Creek. The plant generated ten thousand volts, and a power line was strung to the Dexter Mill. The old DeFrees Mill was dismantled for use as a boardinghouse and bunkhouse next to the power plant. These facilities were used until a more efficient facility was built at Jack Creek, where the water supply was more reliable.

A number of ranches are located at the mouth of Taylor Canyon, owners including Ben and Nona Trembath, Rube Kilfoyle, Bing Crosby, and Willis Packer. Today, a bar and some cabins cater to both local residents and sportsmen. The remains of the DeFrees Mill are east of the cabins.

Twin Bridges

DIRECTIONS: *Located 5 miles east of Taylors on Nevada 226.*

Twin Bridges was located between Taylors and Eagle Rock. It was not a stop itself, but rather the point where the Carlin-Tuscarora stagecoach line joined the road used by the Elko-Tuscarora stage. Twin Bridges was also the name for the area where the Denver-Shepherd Toll Road crossed the South Fork of the Humboldt River.

North Central Elko County

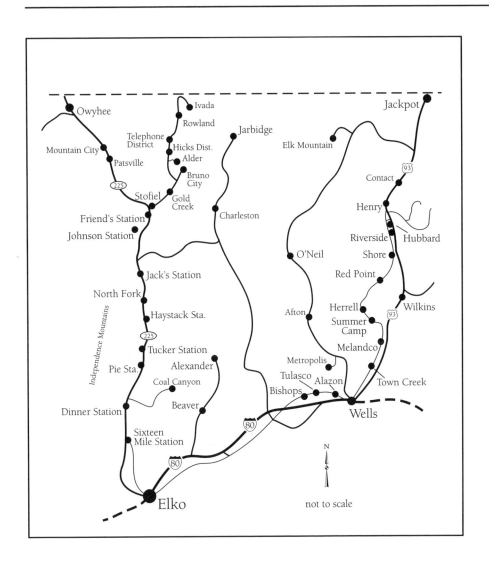

Owyhee
Ivada
Rowland
Mountain City
Telephone District
Jarbidge
Hicks Dist.
Alder
Elk Mountain
Patsville
Bruno City
225
Stofiel
Gold Creek
Contact
93
Charleston
Henry
Friend's Station
Johnson Station
Riverside
Hubbard
Shore
O'Neil
Jack's Station
Red Point
North Fork
Independence Mountains
Haystack Sta.
Afton
Herrell
Wilkins
225
Summer Camp
93
Tucker Station
Alexander
Melandco
Pie Sta.
Coal Canyon
Metropolis
Tulasco
Alazon
Town Creek
Dinner Station
Beaver
Bishops
Wells
80
Sixteen Mile Station
80
N
Elko
not to scale

Alazon

DIRECTIONS: *3.3 miles west of Wells and 1.1 miles north of I-80.*

Alazon was established in 1909 when the Southern Pacific Railroad realigned its route between Deeth and Wells. Alazon became the junction of the Western Pacific and Southern Pacific Railroads; the railroad built a section house and workers' houses here. As many as twenty people lived at Alazon at times, and a small school opened during the 1910s, which remained in operation until 1938 when the Alazon school district consolidated with the Wells school district. Alazon also served as a telegraph station; it was the first railroad stop west of Wells. During the spring of 1942, floods plagued all of Elko County including Alazon. Residents in the small town were completely cut off for a few weeks after the only road to Alazon washed out.

Murder struck the little town in October 1948 when Richard Stewart, a section worker, was shot to death by Richard Boudreau at Mineral Springs, north of Wells. John Moschetti, manager of the Thousand Springs Trading Post at Wilkins, discovered Stewart's abandoned, bloody car and his body nearby. Circumstances surrounding the murder remain murky. Stewart and Boudreau had been friends, and no motive was ever established. Boudreau, also known as Dick Days, was found guilty and sentenced to death on December 17, 1942. His sentence was reduced to life imprisonment when Stewart's mother pleaded for mercy on Boudreau's behalf.

Alazon continued to serve the Southern Pacific until August 1956. The railroad moved its offices to Wells as part of an economic consolidation. At the time, three telegraph operators and their families were living in company houses at Alazon. This was the end of Alazon, and all remaining structures were removed during track reconstruction. Nothing is left of Alazon.

Alexander

DIRECTIONS: *From the Devil's Gate interchange on I-80, 15 miles east of Elko, head north on a gravel road for 19½ miles to Alexander.*

Alexander is incorrectly described as being in the Tuscarora area in some sources. Although there was an Alexander family in the area for a time, the Alexander post office was located about twenty miles northwest of Deeth. The office opened at the ranch of Charles Alexander, five miles north of Devil's Gate Ranch on the north fork of the Humboldt River on May 25, 1895. Alexander served as postmaster. The mail arrived by stage in Alexander via Deeth and Beaver on Monday and Friday and left on Tuesday and Saturday. The carrier for the route was paid $1,500 per year. The post office served more than twenty ranches over a thirty-mile radius. The next-nearest post office was in Deeth, a day's horse ride away. However, Alexander grew tired of running the post office. In December 1900, the office was moved five miles east to another ranch near the headwaters of Pole Creek. Julia Hardesty was postmaster until the office closed on July 31, 1901.

Beaver

(Devil's Gate Ranch)

DIRECTIONS: From Elko, go east on I-80 for 15 miles to the Devil's Gate interchange. Go north on a gravel road for 12 miles to Beaver.

Beaver was a post office established to serve ranches in the Devil's Gate area. The office opened at the Bello Ranch on January 10, 1896, and was on the Deeth-Alexander mail route. John Burns was the first postmaster but was replaced by Louis Bello in 1898 after Burns left the area. Felippe Carillo took over as postmaster in 1906 and worked until the office closed on April 15, 1908.

In addition to the demand for mail service, there was a local need for a school because the nearest school was in Deeth. In 1903, the North Humboldt School District was established, and a one-room school was built with Annie Dewar as the first teacher. The school was active through the 1910s, when declining enrollment and the rise of car and bus use made it more efficient to bus students to Deeth. Other North Humboldt teachers included Agnes Brown, Jessie McIntosh, and Lola Slater.

A number of ranches are still in operation in the area, including the Devil's Gate Ranch, established by Dan Murphy, a prominent Elko County rancher, in the 1870s. Murphy had already built a ranching empire in the North Fork area with its headquarters at Rancho Grande. After Murphy's death in 1882, his daughter Diana and her husband, Morgan Hill, took over the ranch. The ranch was sold in 1922 to J. J. Hylton, a popular businessman from Hylton (Jiggs), who had a vast empire of cattle, sheep, and flour mills throughout the West. However, the empire eventually collapsed and Hylton declared bankruptcy in 1925. A receivership company, the Hylton Ranching Company, ran Devil's Gate until 1943. The ranch has passed through many subsequent owners and is still in operation.

Many nineteenth-century buildings remain on area ranches. One structure near the Bello Ranch may be the old schoolhouse.

Bishops

DIRECTIONS: From Welcome interchange on I-80, go north 4 miles, crossing the railroad tracks.

Located about ten miles west of Wells, Bishops was one of the original construction camps for the Central Pacific Railroad, established in 1869, and a section house and boardinghouse were built. However, once this initial phase of construction was completed, the camp moved east and Bishops became a siding on the railroad. In March of 1872, Frank Hunter was killed in Bishops when he was crushed by the wheels of a caboose after having fallen off a freight train.

More violence occurred in June 1881 when two section men had a heated argument. Arthur Malvin tried to shoot Thomas Lovejoy. Lovejoy crushed Malvin's head with an iron wedge. The killing was ruled justifiable homicide.

Although there was no post office at Bishops, mail was brought from Deeth twice a week. During the early 1880s, Bishops's population was about thirty-five. In 1882, the first ranch in the Bishops area was organized by a man named Flannigan. The Hardesty family bought out Flannigan in 1887. Morris Badt, a prominent Wells businessman, purchased the ranch in 1900 and established the U7 brand.

The Bishops School District was organized around 1900. The Bishops school was at the Franklin Ranch and had students from the Cory and Cazier Ranches on Trout Creek. Birdie Drown Winchell was the first teacher, and the school was used until the 1920s when the district was combined with the Wells district. Wells teachers included Effie Johns, John Cazier, Dollie Blevins, and Delia Webb.

These ranches are still active today, but the Bishops railroad siding is gone. When the track was realigned, what little was left of Bishops was destroyed.

Dinner Station

(Coryell's) (Dorsey's) (Weiland's) (Winters's) (Oldham's) (Parks's)

DIRECTIONS: Located on Nevada 225, 23 miles north of Elko.

Dinner Station, known by many names during its history, was the most important stop on the Elko to Tuscarora stage road; the station also served stages heading to Mountain City. The first station was a wood frame building built by Alex Coryell in the late 1860s to serve as a stop on Hill Beachey's Elko to Idaho route. The property was sold in May 1870 at a sheriff's sale to John Dorsey for $12.70.

Members of the Oldham family in front of Dinner Station, 1907. (Tony and Ellen Primeaux collection, Northeastern Nevada Museum)

During the 1870s, there was a constant flow of traffic through the station, including Van Dreillan's Elko-Tuscarora-Cornucopia-White Rock stage. The fare to Dinner Station from Elko was $3. In addition, Dinner Station was the terminus for the North Fork-Gold Creek Stage Company, a triweekly stage run by Will Martin.

In 1880, the station complex was purchased by J. H. Weiland, who ran an unofficial post office. He distributed mail locally and made sure mail was transferred to the proper stages. In 1884, the station burned down, but by October, Weiland had built a new two-story stone station that was "the handsomest and most comfortable wayside hostelry in the state of Nevada."[1] Fred Wilson, a freight-line operator from Tuscarora, sold subscriptions to help Weiland raise money to rebuild the station. The new station had on one side a kitchen, dining room, living room, and two bedrooms for the staff. Three double bedrooms and two single rooms for guests were on the side nearest the road.

A controversy developed with Weiland and the Elko-Tuscarora stagecoach line in October 1886. The stagecoach line ordered Weiland to pay $0.50 per person in addition to providing free board for stage employees. In protest, Weiland stopped serving dinner to passengers, so the stagecoach line moved the dinner stop to Reed Station. Within a couple of months, a compromise was reached, and Weiland was providing full service by the end of 1886.

In July 1888, Weiland opened a saloon and a small store next to the station house, and a school opened in 1889 with Fannie Grant teaching. The station house burned again in September of 1890. Tuscarora residents raised more than $500 to help Weiland refurbish the station. Because the stone structure was undamaged, reconstruction was quickly completed. While the station was closed, operations were run out of other buildings at Dinner Station.

There is an interesting story about foreign visitors stopping at Dinner Station for a meal: "It was the custom during summer for the plates to be set out on the table upside down so flies couldn't walk on the side where food was to be served. The serving dishes were passed, and the foreigners piled the food onto their plates, which were still upside down. They apparently believed that upside down plates were a western table custom."[2]

Weiland became ill in May 1900 and died of influenza. He had been born in Pittsburgh, Pennsylvania, had first come to Elko in 1876, and served in the Nevada Assembly in 1894. He left a wife, four sons, and four daughters. One son, Alex, took over operation of the station. In 1900, forty-five people lived around the station. Mrs. Weiland sold the station to Frank Winters in October 1901. The new boom at Jarbidge led to an increase of traffic, and Winters hired two Chinese cooks to handle the additional travelers.

Winters had a reputation for helping unfortunate travelers. Walt Davidson, a Swede, was traveling to Mountain City from Minnesota to join his brother, Jack, and had run out of money when he boarded the stage at Elko. He had only cheese and crackers to eat, and during the stopover at Dinner Station, he went behind the corrals to eat his lunch. Winters saw this and invited him inside to eat. He asked Walt if he was Jack Davidson's brother. On hearing that he was, Winters shook his hand and squeezed a $5 bill into Walt's hand, saying, "You can pay me back when you have it." Davidson never forgot this generosity and cried whenever he told the story.

Ed Oldham bought Dinner Station in 1905. The station could serve as many as seventy-five travelers for lunch, and could house twenty people overnight. The barn held seventy-five horses. Oldham charged $0.50 per person for meals and lodging and continued to run the store and saloon. The Oldham family eventually sold Dinner Station to Tom Parks and moved to Fox Springs, also a stop on the Elko-Tuscarora stage line.

A substantial ranch had grown up around Dinner Station. With the coming of the automobile, the need for the station diminished. In 1915, Joe and Frank Yraguen bought the ranch and station. From 1918 to 1924, the complex was managed by Gertrude and Tom Eager, who also ran a stagecoach line from Dinner Station to Gold Creek, carrying passengers, mail, and freight. Ninety horses were housed in the big barn. The school at Dinner Station was active into the 1920s and teachers included Mattie Keith, Mayme Delaney, Irene Suttle, Lila Welshows, and Adolphine Finck.

The Moffat Company bought Dinner Station in the 1940s. E. L. Cord bought it in 1960. David and Marion Secrist purchased the station in 1972 and extensively renovated the station house. The station was later sold to Frank and Phyllis Hooper, the current owners. In October 1991, the station again burned, resulting in extensive damage. The Hoopers restored the building, completing the project in 1994.

Friend's Station

DIRECTIONS: *Located 2 miles south of the junction of Nevada 225 and Gold Creek Road.*

Friend's Station was established in 1869 as a stop on the Elko and Idaho Toll Road. It also served as a terminus in the early 1870s for the short-lived Johnson Toll Road, which ran to Bruno City and rejoined the Elko and Idaho Toll Road at Pierpoint's Station. The station was run by Samuel Friend, who also ran the Bruno Toll Road in the early 1870s.

Friend's Station was also a stop on the Island Mountain stage road, part of a Smith Van Dreillen–operated stagecoach line. Van Dreillen built a large stable during the early 1870s that held thirty horses. The stable burned in July 1875 and was not rebuilt. At that time, Friend's Station ceased to exist, and nothing is left to mark the site.

Haystack Station

DIRECTIONS: *From North Fork, go south on Nevada 225 for 9 miles to Haystack Station.*

Haystack Station was one of the original stops on Hill Beachey's Elko-Idaho Toll Road during the 1860s. The station was an overnight and dinner stop. A small station house was built along with a stable for twenty horses.

When Beachey's empire collapsed in the 1870s, the toll road closed, and the station was abandoned. A ranch was founded at the site in 1873 and became part of the extensive Morgan Hill holdings. The ranch is still active today. A couple of buildings remain, but the station house has long since disappeared.

Henry

DIRECTIONS: *From Contact, go south on U.S. 93 for 5 miles to Henry.*

Henry was a depot and water station on the Oregon Short Line. The railroad established the station in 1925, named for Henry Harris, a popular black foreman for the Sparks-Harrell cattle empire. Harris had come from Texas where he served as a cook for Nevada Governor John Sparks. After mov-

Oregon Short Line depot and water-tank structure at Henry. (Photo by Shawn Hall)

ing to Elko County, he became respected and admired for his knowledge of the cattle industry.

A couple of ranches operated near Henry, using the depot for shipping cattle. Because of the many children on nearby ranches, a school operated at Henry during the 1930s and 1940s. By the time the Oregon Short Line was abandoned in 1978, the area had been deserted. The small depot, joined by the water pump and tower, remains today amid a stand of trees.

Herrell
(Harrell)

DIRECTIONS: *From Wilkins, follow the former railroad grade southeast for 6 miles to Herrell.*

Herrell, as it is usually incorrectly listed (it was intended to be named Harrell), was a signal station and switching yard for the Oregon Short

Line. The station was named for Jasper and Hardy Harrell, partners in the Sparks-Harrell cattle outfit. Jasper Harrell sold his partnership in 1883 and purchased mining property at Spruce Mountain.

Because of a cartographer's typographical error, the station has always appeared as Herrell, rather than Harrell, which was intended. The station was established in 1925. In addition to the common railroad buildings, Herrell included a triangular sidetrack, or wye, for turning and storing helper engines needed to assist trains up the grade from the valley below. The buildings were dismantled when the railroad was abandoned in 1978. Concrete foundations and the roadbed of the wye today mark Herrell's location.

Hubbard

DIRECTIONS: *From Contact, go south on U.S. 93 for 10 miles to Hubbard.*

Hubbard was a stop and signal station on the Oregon Short Line Railroad beginning in 1925. The stop was named for Smith Hubbard, who had established a nearby ranch in the 1870s. In 1933, the Civilian Conservation Corps, or ccc, a government program that gave people work during the Depression, built Camp Hubbard here. By 1938, fifteen buildings had been constructed including a large mess hall for the two hundred men, aged eighteen to twenty-three, assigned to the camp, most of whom had come from a similar camp in Sparta, Illinois. U. S. Army First Lieutenant Edward Clark was the camp's commanding officer. Dr. Olif Hoffman, also the doctor at the Warm Creek ccc camp, provided medical services.

The *Wells Progress* supplied the camp with complimentary newspapers. The Camp Hubbard Ranch baseball team formed in 1933, playing games against other ccc camps. Home games were played in Wells. The men of Camp Hubbard accomplished much, including extensive road building and paving in the region. The buildings were removed after the camp closed in the early 1940s. The Hubbard railroad stop was abandoned when the Oregon Short Line was abandoned in 1978. Only foundations today mark the railroad stop and ccc camp. Hubbard Ranch is still operating and is owned by the Boies family.

Jack's Station

(Vega Ranch)

DIRECTIONS: From North Fork, go north on Nevada 225 for 8 miles to Jack's Station.

Jack's Station was established as a stop on the Hill Beachey stagecoach line in the 1870s. Later, the station was used as a stop for the North Fork-Gold Creek Stage Company. The driver was Will Martin of North Fork; the fare from Elko to Jack's Station was $7. During the mining activity at Gold Creek, Jack's Station enjoyed a lot of business and a saloon was opened, complete with gaming tables.

A. M. McAfee and his wife bought Jack's Station in the late 1880s and built a large house. McAfee was a prominent resident of Tuscarora, served as a county commissioner, and had substantial mining interests at Bullion. In August 1899, the McAfees sold the ranch and station consisting of four hundred acres of land, a stable for twenty-six horses, a two-story house, a lumber house, and a well. The sale advertisement mentions, "the house is pretty well furnished. One can always make a few dollars for meals, hay and pasturage for horses."[3] The selling price was $800, $400 less than the McAfees had paid for it.

After the stagecoach line stopped running, the stable was moved to another ranch on Spring Creek. Jack's Station was purchased by Manuel Vega in 1903 and has been known as the Vega Ranch ever since. During the 1920s, the Island Mountain School operated at the ranch in a small building known as "the Hut." The teacher was Leona Gilbertson Harris, and her students were mainly the Vega children.

Manuel Vega and his wife, Anna, ran the ranch for many years. Manuel died in 1954; Anna died in 1978. The Vegas had many children: Guy, Jule, Aldo, Manuel "Dude," Aldo Lee, Diana, Evelyn, Anna, and Della. Manuel is owner of Vega Construction in Elko. The ranch is still in the Vega family, and a number of original buildings remain.

Johnson Station

DIRECTIONS: From Wild Horse, go south on Nevada 225 for 4 miles. Turn right and follow the dirt road for 1 mile to Johnson Station.

Johnson Station was first a way station on the Cope Road and later a stop on Will Martin's North Fork-Gold Creek stage line. This station should not be confused with another station located on the Johnson Ranch, north of Wells, which was run by Bues Johnson. Fare to the Cope Road station from Elko was $7.50. The station, the last stop before Gold Creek, was run by William Johnson.

The initial Johnson Station was located on Walker Creek in 1869, but the Cope Road was later moved. Johnson and his wife, Catherine, relocated eight miles south and established a new ranch and station at the present site of North Fork. Most information available concerns the Johnson Station located at North Fork.

At the Walker Creek station, Johnson built a couple of log buildings for the station itself and for stables. These buildings were removed when the Johnson family relocated. Today, the original site on Walker Creek is part of an active ranch, but nothing remains to mark the station.

Melandco

DIRECTIONS: From Wells, go north on U.S. 93 for 13 miles. Turn left on the road and follow it for ½ mile to Melandco.

Melandco was a stop and signal station on the Oregon Short Line beginning in 1925. The name was an abbreviated form of the Metropolis Land Company and was so named because it was the siding nearest the Bishop Creek Reservoir and part of the company's great plans for the area. All buildings at the site were removed when the railroad ceased operation in 1978. Concrete foundations mark the site.

Foundations in Melandco. (Photo by Shawn Hall)

The Johnson Ranch at North Fork in 1948, owned at that time by Bing Crosby. (James and Larry Monroe collection, Northeastern Nevada Museum)

North Fork

(Johnson Station)

DIRECTIONS: *From Dinner Station, go north on Nevada 225 for 28 miles to North Fork.*

The first signs of a settlement at North Fork began in 1870 when William and Catherine Johnson moved from the original Johnson Station, located on Walker Creek, and reestablished the station at North Fork on the newly completed Cope Road. A daily stagecoach passed through Johnson Station, which had a thriving business feeding and lodging travelers. The Johnsons had eight children, five of whom were born at the ranch in North Fork. One child, William, died in December 1877, a few months before their last child, Lillian, was born. A couple of other families came to the North Fork area during the late 1870s, including the John Walker family. North Fork's population in 1880 was thirteen, which included Catherine Johnson and her six surviving children, all under the age of twelve.

A number of ranches formed, and large cattle outfits like the Morgan Hill Company and the Murphy Cattle Company used the range. The larger ranches were created by consolidating the many smaller ranches throughout the North Fork Valley.

A small town formed at North Fork, which became the social center for the scattered ranches. George Pratt moved to North Fork, and later his brother-in-law, Richard Morse, joined him; the pair established a freight business to Tuscarora and Midas. Morse, with his wife and five children, settled on Morse

Creek where he built a sawmill, producing mine timbers for Tuscarora. The ranch stayed in the Morse family until 1948.

By the time a post office opened at North Fork on January 17, 1889 (Dollie Shearer was the first postmaster), a hotel, saloon, grocery store, stage station, and school already existed, and seventy-five people were living in and around North Fork.

In the 1890s, Manuel Larios built a new stage station that offered good meals, lodging, and a stable. A small store featured wine, liquor, and cigars. Henry Van Dreillan began running a stage from Elko to Gold Creek in 1897, which passed through North Fork. The stage also carried mail; the fare from Elko was $4. In March 1897, the Bowles Lumber Mill opened to provide lumber for the boomtown of Gold Creek to the northeast.

In June 1900, J. D. Franklin began operating the triweekly North Fork-Gold Creek Stageline, with North Fork as the home base for the line. This stage connected with the Tuscarora-Elko Stage at Dinner Station. Because of the extensive ranching industry in North Fork Valley, the North Fork Cattle Association formed; meetings were held in the Domingo Hall at North Fork. The population in North Fork Valley was 122 in 1900.

At the Johnson Ranch, across the road from the businesses at North Fork, a family built a new two-story house. Until completion of the house in 1901, the family had lived in log buildings from the 1870s. In 1906, Bill Mahoney built a large stone building containing a store, saloon, and stagecoach stop.

The North Fork post office was located in the new Johnson home, which

Remains of the stone store in North Fork. (Photo by Shawn Hall)

also served as the lunch stop for the Elko-Mountain City stagecoach. After Catherine Johnson died in 1908, two of her children, Lillian and Emery, took over the ranch and other operations, and Lillian became the North Fork postmaster in 1909, a position she held for thirty-five years until the post office closed on June 30, 1944.

In 1912, Lillian married Chester Laing, and the couple bought out Emery's interest in the ranch and businesses. Percy Royals and Chester Laing then ran the store and built a dance hall next door. The North Fork School, sometimes called the Harrison School, was initially in a log cabin on the Johnson Ranch; it later moved to a room of the new Johnson ranch house. The original school later became part of the Robert "Doby Doc" Caudill collection that was featured at the Last Frontier Village in Las Vegas, a tourist attraction consisting of a collection of buildings and artifacts. The location of the school has been a mystery since its sale after Caudill's death. Teachers who taught at the school included Mattie Keith, Blanche Plumb, Martha Gee, Mabel Mason, Merle Mues, and Edith Billings.

Two other schools served other parts of the North Fork Valley. The North Humboldt School, where teacher Flo Reed received $120 a month to teach seven students, was located at the McKnight Ranch during the 1920s. The school was a twelve-foot-by-twelve-foot adobe building with very thick walls. In 1932, the Mahala School opened at the Tremewan ranch and was active for a number of years.

As the years passed, the stagecoach lines stopped running, but the store and saloon survived because of increased automobile traffic. In the 1930s, Chester and Lillian Laing built a new store, the North Fork Mercantile, next to their ranch. In August 1934, Wallace Frost and Earl McCullough robbed the store of clothes, whiskey, bacon, and saddles and were later arrested for the crime. The store, which was the last business in North Fork, burned to the ground while leased to Joe and Alice LeGarza and was not rebuilt.

Despite the decline of the town of North Fork, ranching continued to be important in the North Fork Valley. During the early 1940s, Newt Crumley Sr. bought many of the ranches in the valley including the Kearns, Evans, Bellinger, Saval, Truett, and Tremewan ranches. In July 1947, he sold all the ranches except the Saval ranch to Bing Crosby, who had been named honorary mayor of Elko in 1948. Crosby combined the ranches into one large ranch, the Bing Crosby, or px, Ranch, and spent as much time as possible at the ranch with his family. John and Doris Eacret managed the Crosby ranch.

In June 1948, Crosby also purchased the Johnson, or Laing, ranch from Chester and Lillian Laing, who had retired to Elko. In September 1949, Crumley sold the Saval ranch and retired from the cattle business. In December 1953, the Johnson ranch house was destroyed by fire. Crosby ran the px Ranch until November 1958 when he sold his holdings in North Fork to Edward and William Johnson, and Earl Presnell, for more than $1 million.

Although the ranches have changed hands over the years, the area continues to be a prosperous ranching district. At North Fork, the stone store still stands, but the dance hall has collapsed. For years, a house made of bottles stood at North Fork, but it is now gone. A huge barn marks the location of the old Johnson Ranch. A number of foundations and other ruins remain at North Fork, next to a Nevada Department of Transportation maintenance station.

O'Neil
(O'Neill)

DIRECTIONS: From Wells, take Metropolis Road north for 13 miles. Go past the Metropolis turnoff and continue north for 24 miles to O'Neil.

Although O'Neil referred to the specific location of a post office, the name generally refers to the entire area in the O'Neil Basin. The O'Neil family first came to Elko County in the mid-1880s after being run out of White Pine County because of their illegal ranching practices. Initially the family continued these illegal practices in their new home.

Four O'Neil brothers (James, William, Richard, and Charles) carried on the family tradition of expanding their own cattle herd by taking cattle from other ranchers' herds. This practice had led to their father's death at the hands of a mob in White Pine County. The O'Neil family was known for its ornery disposition. Not long after their arrival in Elko County, the four brothers were caught killing cattle from the Mason and Bradley outfit:

> There was considerable excitement last Friday over the arrest of W. T. and R. C. O'Neil on a charge of killing cattle belonging to Mason and Bradley. Deputy Sheriff Gleason was in the act of locking the two brothers in the branch jail when a man rushed out of the rear of a group of buildings and, raising a shotgun, fired at the boys. A sister of the O'Neils who saw the man coming with the gun, rushed in front of her brother, Will, and received a bad wound in the ankle. The front of Dick O'Neil's coat has a number of buck shot holes in it. As soon as the man fired, the boys left the officer and went home for their rifles, saying they would protect themselves. The man who fired at them got on a horse and left the country.[4]

The entire family, regardless of gender or age, was so intimidating and dangerous that juries and judges were continually intimidated into acquitting the O'Neils of rustling, brand alteration, and the attempted murder of a constable. Nobody wanted to stand in their way and become an enemy of the O'Neil clan. They were ruthless, and hired many gunmen to protect their range; there was no tolerance of anyone trespassing in the O'Neil Basin. Over time, however, the O'Neil family changed and eventually became a family of respected ranchers.

A post office opened at the O'Neil ranch on August 17, 1894, with Richard O'Neil as postmaster. The office closed on February 8, 1897, but reopened on May 17, 1898, and remained in operation until January 25, 1925. James O'Neil was postmaster the entire time. Occasional problems arose for the post office because of its isolation. One example occurred in February 1903 when Edward Burrows, a mail carrier employed by the O'Neils, lost one foot and the toes on the other foot due to frostbite after becoming stranded in a snowstorm.

By 1900, forty-eight people lived in the O'Neil area. In 1904, William, James, and Charles O'Neil and William and James Capell formed the O'Neil-Capell Land and Cattle Company. William Capell had married the O'Neils' sister. By 1910, the company's herds had grown to ten thousand cattle and one hundred and fifty sheep. Ironically, the O'Neil family, who earlier drove sheepherders off their range, was now one of the largest sheep outfits in the state.

Some of the southern O'Neil holdings, including the old Hardesty Ranch, were acquired by Horace Agee in 1910. Agee and the O'Neils had been at odds for years, and the O'Neils had hired men to injure or kill Agee, without success. Agee organized the Ox Yoke Livestock Company, which later consolidated with the Steptoe Livestock Company in 1915. The original O'Neil ranch was made the company's base, which the O'Neil family did not like. The company went out of business in 1932 due to the Depression. A telephone line to Tobar was completed in 1914; why the line went to Tobar instead of the closer town of Wells is unknown. In April 1915, the O'Neil brothers bought out the Capells for $250,000 and became sole owners of the O'Neil Company.

Cattle and sheep prices dropped dramatically in the early 1920s, which spelled doom for the O'Neil empire. Another blow was the death of William O'Neil in January 1920. In April 1925, Sheriff Joe Harris sold the ranch and holdings to Wells Fargo for $248,000 to pay off the family's debts.

The O'Neils then moved to California. Richard, a former president of the cattle company, died in May 1926 and was remembered as "A great friend to all, who never turned away a plea for a grubstake for miners and was always a friend of the sheepherder and cattleman."[5] James died in August 1926. The O'Neil brothers had succeeded in turning their bad reputation into one of high respect among residents of Elko County.

A school opened in 1932 near the old Helsley Ranch and operated for a number of years. The O'Neil Basin continues today as an important ranching area and numerous pre-1900 buildings are left on the scattered ranches in the basin.

Pie Station

(Pie Creek) (Milk Station)

DIRECTIONS: *From Dinner Station, go north on Nevada 225 for 8 miles to Pie Station.*

Pie Station, or Milk Station as it was first called, was a stop on Hill Beachey's Elko-Idaho toll road beginning in 1869. A German baker ran the station; hanging in front was a sign with "Piecake" written on it. Gradually the station became known as Pie Station.

Once the Beachey line had folded, the station was abandoned, but was re-established by J. H. Weiland in 1897 to serve the Gold Creek stagecoach line. After Weiland's death in 1900, his son Aleck took over the station, which was permanently abandoned in 1907 when the Weiland family left the area.

Well-weathered, low adobe-type walls are all that is left of Pie Station. A horse barn located nearby is of more recent origin.

Red Point

DIRECTIONS: *Located 3 miles north of Wilkins on the former Oregon Short Line right-of-way.*

Red Point, situated between Herrell and Shores, was a stop and signal station on the Oregon Short Line beginning in 1925. Archie Bowman named the location for a prominent red formation located on an adjacent hill. Because of its location, Red Point was a busy cattle-shipping point. When the Oregon Short Line ceased operations in 1978, the buildings and tracks at Red Point were removed. Today, concrete foundations and wood rubble mark the site.

Riverside

DIRECTIONS: *From Hubbard, go south on U.S. 93 for three miles to Riverside.*

Riverside, located near the present-day Boies Ranch, was a siding and depot for the Oregon Short Line from 1925 to 1978. During the construction of the railroad, a small temporary town was built at Riverside to accommodate construction crews. Once the line was completed, the buildings were removed and only concrete foundations remain.

Shore
(Shores)

DIRECTIONS: *Located 6 miles south of Hubbard on the old Oregon Short Line.*

Shore, located between Hubbard and Red Point, was a stop and signal station on the Oregon Short Line, named for George Shore, a local rancher. The stop is sometimes incorrectly listed as Shores. Only concrete foundations of the water tower and signal shack mark the site.

Sixteen Mile Station
(Dorsey Station)

DIRECTIONS: *Located 16 miles north of Elko on Nevada 225.*

Sixteen Mile Station, first known as Dorsey Station, was briefly used as a stop on Hill Beachey's Elko-Idaho toll road during 1869 and 1870. In 1875, Smith Van Dreillen started the Elko-to-Tuscarora stagecoach line. The station was renamed Sixteen Mile due to its distance from Elko, and was a meal and overnight stop. Sixteen Mile Station was the first stop on the line from Elko; fare from Elko was $2. There was also a small ranch at the station. A new route built in the 1880s over Adobe Summit led to a great reduction of traffic along the old route through Sixteen Mile Station; only some freight traffic continued to use that route.

In August 1886, Frank McPheters found a pile of sagebrush, used as fuel wood, burning next to the station and was able to put it out before the building was affected. It was noted that the new stagecoach company did not use the station. In April 1899, Johnny McComb and his family moved to the station, running it and the ranch for many years. McComb was also a stagecoach driver to Tuscarora. In June 1912, Bill Doyle, a helper on George Williams's freight team, was killed when he fell off a freight wagon and was run over by three other wagons.

With the coming of the automobile, Sixteen Mile Station was used less and was eventually abandoned. In 1928, the station building, then owned by Robert Burwell Stewart, but unused for years, caught fire and was destroyed. Only scattered debris and a faint foundation mark the site.

Stofiel

(Butlers) (Wildhorse)

DIRECTIONS: Located 19 miles south of Mountain City on Nevada 225.

Stofiel was named for Walter Stofiel. He first came to the area in the 1870s and got involved in mining at Island Mountain with Emmanuel Penrod, one of the original locators of the Comstock Lode. Stofiel married Penrod's daughter, Lydia, in 1877. In 1880, the Stofiel family moved to Bellevue, Idaho, but returned a couple of years later, establishing a small ranch and stage station near the future site of Wildhorse Reservoir.

The boom in Gold Creek turned the Stofiel stop into an important shipping point for supplies heading to the mining camp. A post office opened at Stofiel on June 11, 1891, and remained open until July 15, 1897. Lydia Stofiel served as postmaster until she died of pneumonia in January 1897. After Lydia's death, Walter Stofiel raised their three children.

In 1897, Henry Van Dreillan began a stagecoach line from Elko to Gold Creek with a fare from Elko of $5. Stofiel moved away after 1900, and died in Los Angeles in May 1905. The Butler family ran the stage station until it was no longer needed in the 1910s.

Construction of the Wildhorse Dam in 1936 brought many workers to the area. The dam was completed in January 1937 and dedicated on September 6, 1937. Besides providing irrigation water for ranchers and farmers, the reservoir was a recreation site, and a couple of businesses opened near the reservoir. The Wildhorse post office operated from July 3, 1945, to February 28, 1948, with Josephine Ford as postmaster. Wildhorse Reservoir continues today as a popular destination for water recreation and fishing. A store and gas station are located nearby.

Summer Camp

DIRECTIONS: Located 4 miles northwest of Melandco on the former Oregon Short Line right-of-way.

Summer Camp, located between Melandco and Herrell, was a stop and signal station on the Oregon Short Line from 1925 to 1978, used mainly to ship cattle. Only concrete foundations of the small depot and water tower remain.

Ranch house near Summer Camp. (Photo by Shawn Hall)

Town Creek

DIRECTIONS: *Located 7 miles northeast of Wells on the former Oregon Short Line right-of-way.*

Town Creek, located between Wells and Melandco, was a stop and signal station on the Oregon Short Line, run by the Union Pacific Railroad, from 1925 to 1978. Only concrete foundations of the small depot mark the site.

Tucker Station

(Idaho Ranch Station) (Ganz Creek) (Gaunce Creek)

DIRECTIONS: *From Dinner Station, go north on Nevada 225 for 10 miles. Turn left and follow a dirt road for ½ mile to Tucker Station.*

George Ganz established a station on the Beachey and Wines Elko-Idaho Toll Road in 1870. A tall, narrow two-story station house was built, and overnight lodging and meals were provided. The station was later taken over by Bob and Sally Tucker. Sally, known as Aunt Sally, was the daughter of Emmanuel Penrod, one of the original locators of the Comstock Lode. Aunt Sally was known for her salty language.

Over the next thirty years, a number of other stagecoach lines used Tucker

Station. Henry Van Dreillan's Elko-to-Gold Creek stage ran through Osino and rejoined the main Gold Creek road at Tucker Station. In 1897, Will Martin established the North Fork-Gold Creek Stage Company, which ran from Dinner Station to Gold Creek. In August 1901, Sally Tucker died at the station at the age of seventy-five. Bob Tucker remained at the station until the early 1910s, by which time stages no longer ran.

Farther up Ganz Creek, W. F. Mahoney started a sheep operation in the 1890s. By 1908, he ran more than twelve thousand sheep over a wide area and had earned the moniker of "Sheepman of Eagle Rock." Mahoney had other interests outside of his ranch and was instrumental in making Elko's Commercial Hotel successful, after he and his partners purchased the old Humboldt Lodging House. He also ran a saloon in North Fork for many years. The Mahoney Ranger Station in Jarbidge was named in his honor. Mahoney sold his ranch to Guy Saval, whose brothers ran a sheep outfit at Jack Creek. Saval, with Pedro Jaurequi, ran the Telescope Hotel in Elko.

Today, the old Saval Ranch is still an active operation. At Tucker Station, an adobe-type foundation is all that is left of the station.

Remaining walls of Tucker Station. (Photo by Shawn Hall)

Tulasco

DIRECTIONS: From Wells, take I-80 west for 3½ miles. Head north on a gravel road for 1½ miles to Alazon. Then head west, following the railroad tracks for 4 miles to Tulasco.

Tulasco was a siding station on the Central Pacific Railroad beginning in 1869, but was relocated to its current location in 1909 when the Southern Pacific Railroad realigned its tracks between Deeth and Wells. The Southern Pacific built a sectionhouse and water tank at Tulasco.

In 1912, Tulasco became the terminus for the railroad spur built to Metropolis, and a small depot, saloon, and restaurant were built. When the spur was abandoned in 1925, Tulasco became a siding again, housing only a section crew. In June 1936, section head George Johnson was killed when he stepped in front of a train; L. B. Fairchild, the gang foreman, was hurt in the same incident.

During the summer of 1946, there were many problems with the section gang. In two separate fights among gang members, George Ruffin and Murphy Corley were killed.

Today, Tulasco serves the former Western Pacific and Southern Pacific Railroads (now both part of the Union Pacific) as a signal station and siding. All that remains of the town of Tulasco are the concrete foundations of the sectionhouse and water tower. The old railroad roadbed for the Metropolis spur lies to the east of the foundations; piles of broken bottles mark the spot where the saloon once stood.

Wells

(Humboldt Wells)

DIRECTIONS: Located 50 miles east of Elko on I-80.

Humboldt Wells became an important stop on the California Emigrant Trail during the 1840s because of the area's lush meadows and deep, clear springs, a rarity on the Nevada part of the trail. This gave pioneers and their animals a chance to recover before embarking on the toughest part of the journey to California.

The town of Wells originated with the arrival of the Central Pacific Railroad in February 1869. Little development occurred at Wells at first; a post office opened on July 17, 1869, but closed on February 7, 1870. It wasn't until September 1869 that the railroad placed a boxcar as a passenger and freight station at Humboldt Wells. This station was located at the old Humboldt Wells, located one mile west of the present town. The first resident was Bob Hamill, who served as both the railroad agent and the express agent for Wells Fargo.

During the summer of 1869, the railroad established Humboldt Wells as a freight division point and helper station. This led to the construction of large railroad facilities, which required moving the facilities one mile east to the more spacious area of the current town of Wells. The first business, a saloon, opened at the new townsite on Christmas Eve 1869. The Bullshead Saloon, housed in a log building, was built by H. R. Renshaw and William Humphries. In 1870, the town of Wells began to develop, and a general store, hotel,

Overview of Wells, circa 1910. Dr. Olmsted's house is at the lower right. (Mrs. Austin Peltier collection, Northeastern Nevada Museum)

livery stable, and telegraph office soon opened. Partners Badt and Cohn built the first brick building in town, a twenty-five-foot-by-one hundred–foot store that featured a sugar cellar, coal oil cellar, and warehouse.

Wells became the main shipping point for mines at Spruce Mountain, Victoria, Dolly Varden, and Cherry Creek, as well as for farmers and ranchers in Starr, Ruby, and Clover Valleys. Stage and freight roads emanated from Wells during the 1870s. The post office reopened on February 18, 1871. Due to demand, a one-room schoolhouse was built in 1872 and was soon expanded to two rooms. An old locomotive bell summoned students to school every morning.

The Elko County commissioners changed the town's official name from Humboldt Wells to Wells in 1873. By this time, Wells had a population of about three hundred and a sizeable Chinatown, most of whose residents had helped build the Central Pacific Railroad. The first of a number of devastating fires struck Wells on March 31, 1877. The fire, which started in a building adjacent to the Hamill and Meigs store, destroyed most of the town, but the rebuilding process began as soon as the ashes cooled.

By 1880, the population of Wells dropped to 244. The town always relied almost completely on freight and ore shipping and thus went through many ups and downs over the years depending on the state of these industries. The devaluation of silver during the 1880s caused a drastic slowdown in the mining industry, which in turn led to tough times in Wells. A fire in February 1881 was another setback for the town. This fire started in a barbershop run by Richard Richardson and spread east, destroying a large part of the business district. Only the fireproof buildings of E. H. Griswold, and Hamill and Meigs, kept the fire from spreading west. Businesses that burned included J. M. Surface's saloon, W. T. Van Namee's store and restaurant, and E. T. Greenberg's brewery.

During the 1880s, Wells shrank to about 150 residents, but the growth of Ely, to the south, in the late 1880s helped revive Wells, because Wells was the nearest railhead to Ely. In February 1887, a company planned to build the Wells–North Elko and Idaho Central Railroad from Wells north to the Idaho border. Hopes were high until the railroad company demanded that Elko County provide a bond to cover any additional money needed once construction of the railroad began. This proviso ended all mention of the proposed railroad.

Another fire in April 1880 burned the O'Neil Hotel and a business run by Adolph Fish, but this fire did not spread.

The disastrous winter of 1889–1890 temporarily crippled the local livestock industry around Wells. The Central Pacific Railroad charged cattlemen exorbitant rates to ship hay and to scatter it along the railroad right-of-way to feed the starving cattle. Morris Badt saved many of the local ranches after this terrible winter by obtaining loans from the Bank of California, and as a result ranches in the Ruby, Clover, and Starr Valleys resumed operation. His efforts on behalf of the ranchers forged an enduring, strong relationship between the Badt family and the ranchers.

The cycle of ups and downs continued for Wells during the 1890s. A revival of the Cherry Creek mines in the early 1890s brought additional business to Wells, but in 1896, Wells lost its position as a railroad freight division termi-

Main Street, Wells, 1880. (Anita Cory collection, Northeastern Nevada Museum)

nus, although it continued as the western terminus for helper engines. In May 1896, the *Wells Index* became the first newspaper in Wells, but Phil Triplett ran the paper for only three months before the paper folded. In 1897, Reverend J. S. Donaldson opened the Presbyterian church; prior to this, church services had been held in the schoolhouse.

On March 19, 1897, George Ferguson and George Vardy founded the *Nevada State Herald,* a weekly newspaper that cost $2 per year. Phil Triplett returned to Wells and bought the paper in 1901, continuing to run it until his death in 1921. His son, Charles, then took over and ran the paper until the end of publication in October 1933.

By 1900, Wells's population had grown to 543, and businesses in the town included Bullshead Hotel (Wes Johnson), Allen Hotel (George Allen), San Marin Restaurant (Mrs. M. E. Allen), Quilici Store, Coryell and Smith Meat Market, A. W. Goble General Merchandise Store, Morris Badt and Company Store, J. R. Nuttall Store, and blacksmith and wheelright Frank Jeanney. Fraternal organizations included the Good Templars and Knights of Pythias. In addition, the Wells Dramatic Club performed plays in the Good Templars Hall.

The Quilici brothers' store was very popular, particularly because the owners had a generous attitude toward ranchers and residents who were going through difficult times. One example is Pete Itcaina, a prominent Elko County sheep rancher, who needed supplies but was short of money. The Quilicis told him that as long as they had groceries on the shelves, he could have them. Itcaina never forgot their generosity and when his fortunes rose, he continued to buy his goods from the Quilicis even when he could have purchased them cheaper elsewhere.

Another setback for Wells was the completion of the Nevada Northern Railway in 1906. The ore business that helped to sustain Wells now went by this new railroad to Cobre to the east of Wells, which led to tough times for the residents of Wells. Business picked up when the Western Pacific Railroad was completed in 1908. The Bank of Wells opened in 1911 with Mel Badt, son of early resident Morris Badt, as president. The bank was a great asset for the community.

The Wells Commercial Club, a forerunner of the Wells Chamber of Commerce, was organized in 1912. A new high school was completed in 1914. A school newspaper, the *Mirror Reflections,* began publication, and was renamed the *Leopard* in the 1940s. The first graduating class in 1916 was Robert Weede, Nevada Cazier, and Kenyon Olmsted. In January 1922, one of the oldest businesses in town, the San Marin Restaurant, was sold to John DiGrazia, the beginning of a long DiGrazia legacy in Wells.

In February 1923, the Quilici Store, the largest in Wells, was destroyed by fire. The residents formed a bucket line, saving the threatened Pershing Hotel. A new Quilici Store quickly opened in the old Sugar Bowl Bakery building.

During the 1920s, a Wells baseball team competed in the professional Humboldt Valley League.

One of the biggest days in Wells history was February 15, 1926, when the Oregon Short Line (OSL) Railroad, owned by the Union Pacific Railroad, officially arrived at Wells. The railroad right-of-way had actually been completed a couple of months earlier. Fifteen hundred people attended the celebration of the railroad's arrival. The first OSL train had two engines, a baggage car, seven Pullman cars, and two private cars, containing many dignitaries. To cap off a great day, the Wells High School basketball team beat its rival, Metropolis, for the first time in three years.

Another big event was the municipal incorporation of Wells in May 1927. The vote was very close, and the measure passed by only nine votes. The first city council consisted of George Toombs, J. W. Felts, and Albert Supp. H. H. Coryell, a longtime resident, was elected the first mayor, but died in April 1928. Before becoming mayor, Coryell had served as president pro tem of the Nevada Senate for forty-four years. Coryell had formerly owned Dinner Station, located north of Elko. After his death, his wife became the first female member of the city council.

In December 1927, Wells received special honor when the town became a part of the first rural electrification system in Nevada. The power was supplied by a hydroelectric plant at Trout Creek, built by H. H. Cazier. He established the Wells Power Company, later purchased by the Wells Rural Electrification Company. Wells's fortunes were kept alive by its reliance on the railroad and

Interior of M. Badt and Company Store in Wells, 1890s. (Gertrude Badt collection, Northeastern Nevada Museum)

the ranching industries. This was aided when the Oregon Short Line instituted daily passenger train service in March 1929, but soon the Depression hit. A major blow for the town during the Depression was the closure of the Wells Bank, run by George Wingfield, in 1932.

The Depression also killed off the well-established *Nevada State Herald* in October 1933. However, the new weekly *Wells Progress* began publication under the guidance of Ed Shirton on June 26, 1936. Charles Triplett, former owner of the defunct *Herald,* bought the *Progress* in 1940 and the Triplett family published the paper until 1977.

By 1936, Wells had a population of about three hundred. Businesses at Wells included Pyper's Cash Market, Supp Brothers Garage, Toomb's Garage, Wells Hotel and Cafe (George Murao), Simon Grocery, Capitol Club (John and Joe DiGrazia), Shroeder Pharmacy, Quilici Store, Western Hardware and Lumber Company, Tuttle Coal and Feed Yard, and the Nevada Theater.

In November, the old grammar school, used until 1914, was sold to the American Legion and Veterans of Foreign Wars to serve as a meeting hall.

Dr. A. C. Olmsted was honored by the Knights of Pythias in February 1937 for his forty years of service to the community. Olmsted deserves special mention because he had a great impact on Wells and its citizens. He came to Wells in 1897 and set up a private medical practice, but also served as the company doctor for the railroads served by Wells.

Olmsted, also the town veterinarian, was often called late at night to travel to places like Wendover, Montello, Cobre, and Shafter. Olmsted's passion, however, was baseball, and he managed the Wells team in the Humboldt Baseball League. Olmsted had a kidney condition during the last years of his life but never refused to see a patient. Olmsted died on June 14, 1943, at the age of seventy-two, a valued member of the Wells community.

Another fire struck Wells in March 1937, destroying the Western Lumber and Hardware building and its lumber. Only a great effort and a favorable wind kept the main business district from burning. The cause of the fire was arson, following an unsuccessful attempt a few days earlier. In May 1937 a volunteer fire department was organized in Wells with Carl Supp as the first fire chief. During the same month, a new Catholic church was completed.

In 1938 and 1939, a movement began to split Elko County into two counties, with Wells intended to be the county seat of new Ruby County. Wells residents had felt slighted by rival city Elko for years and finally formed a Committee on County Division. Proponents believed that if a new county was formed, property taxes would drop 46 percent. The Elko newspapers responded with fury, referring to the taxpayers in the eastern part of the county as "the south end of an Equus Caballus going north," stating that the new county should be called Shirttail County. Eventually, the furor died out, mainly because of Elko County legislation that required a two-thirds vote of the county's residents to split the county.

In March 1940, the property of the defunct Wells Bank (which included the bank building, grazing lands, and twenty-two thousand shares of the Missouri-Monarch Consolidated Mining Company at Spruce Mountain) was sold to Leo Quilici for $2,000. In 1943, Quilici also purchased the Wells Hotel. The Ely-Wells bus line began operating in July 1941 on the same day that the Nevada Northern Railway discontinued passenger service from Cobre to Ely.

The economy of Wells slowly turned to tourism for survival. Fires continued to plague Wells. In August 1943, the Western Pacific depot was destroyed at a loss of $20,000. A temporary station was set up in an outfit car until a new station was completed. In September, J. A. Donelly bought the Overland Hotel from J. H. Wein for $20,000, and W. C. Wilson sold the Golden Rule Store to Harry Bradley in 1945.

During World War II a number of young men from Wells were killed in action, including Norvin Davis, Daniel Remick, Clarence Collins, Louis Simon, and Robert Curtiss. Returning veterans Carl and Matt Smith opened Smith's Grocery Store, and Charles Nannini opened the Eagle Club in 1946.

The local Lions Club was organized in 1946. The same year, the federal government pledged $100,000 for the construction of a Wells airfield, named Hattie Field, after the wife of Senator McCarran. The Humboldt Baseball League was re-formed, consisting of eight teams. There were three teams from Wells, the most successful of which was the Harold's Club Gamblers, who won the title in 1948. Wells was especially proud in 1947 when the high school basketball team won the state title; Horace Smith and Bob Morrow were named to the All-State team. An economic boost came from the opening of a new bank, the First National, in May 1947, and the reopening of the Nevada Theater by George Goble in November.

A homicide occurred in Wells in March 1948. Rhea Morning, wife of the Reverend Richard Morning, was murdered in the Wells Manse by Laszlo Varga, who was later captured in Petaluma, California. He claimed he had an accomplice, Joseph Basda, who looked like Varga and had identical fingerprints, who forced him to kill the woman. The jury did not believe Varga's story, finding him guilty. The court sentenced him to death in the state's gas chamber. No motive was ever established for this crime.

Increasing tourist traffic led to the opening of two new motels, the El Rancho and the Wagon Wheel. The owner of the Wagon Wheel, John McDaniel, also mayor of Wells, was killed in a head-on collision in December 1949 in which five occupants of the other car were also killed. McDaniel had originally homesteaded in Tobar during the 1910s before coming to Wells.

Wells residents were pleasantly surprised to have a celebrity in town during May 1951 when Rita Hayworth stayed at the Shellcrest Motel and ate

Albert Supp, George Toombs, and Carl Supp inside their garage in Wells, 1920. (V. W. Birdzell collection, Northeastern Nevada Museum)

breakfast at the Skyway Cafe before continuing on her trip. In July, the Golden Rule Store was sold, this time to H. E. and Charles Read of Mountain City, who also had stores in Mountain City, Owyhee, and Eureka.

As elsewhere, a setback for the Wells economy came with the arrival of diesel locomotives, which eliminated the need for the helper engines for mountain grades that Wells provided. Fortunately for its economy, Wells no longer relied as heavily on the railroads as it had in the past, and the impact was minimal. A political surprise took place in 1952 when local resident Tom Mechling upset Alan Bible for the Democratic Party nomination for the U.S. Senate. Although Mechling lost to George Malone in the general election, his surprise defeat of Bible in the primary made him a local hero.

In January 1955, the Hinds Shell Station was completely destroyed by an explosion and resulting fire. Part of an adjacent motel also burned, and the concussion from the blast broke $15,000 worth of glass in nearby businesses.

Many remnants of Wells's early days were torn down over the next twenty years. The Southern Pacific's 65,000-gallon water tank was dismantled and moved to Myers Station, south of Lake Tahoe, in 1959. The old high school, which had been replaced in 1953, was sold for $1,950 to Thomas McCrary, who tore it down and used the materials to build a new house. The school's cornerstone, laid in 1914, contained many relics, including a copy of the legislative act issuing bonds for the school's construction, and copies of the *Nevada State Herald, Elko Free Press,* and *Elko Independent.* The first eight students in 1914 were Bert Brandis, Nevada Cazier, Zanzie Connolly, Glen Firth, Edwin Lambert, Kenyon Olmsted, Jesse Turner, and Dolly Woolverton. Gerald Kerr was principal.

The Allen Hotel, a stately two-story stone and brick structure, was torn down in 1973. The Presbyterian church, built in 1897, was completely restored in 1966. The Wagon Wheel Motel and Restaurant were torn down in 1978. The Wells Grammar School, built in 1931, was demolished in 1978 to make way for a new school. The Ranch House Casino and Restaurant burned in 1980, killing four patrons and resulting in a loss of $1 million.

The closure of the Oregon Short Line railroad in 1978 ended Wells's direct association with railroading, although Union Pacific trains on the former Western Pacific and Southern Pacific mainlines still rumble through town without stopping.

The venerable *Wells Progress* ended publication in September 1989. During the last few years of publication, the newspaper tried many different approaches and local editions in an effort to increase subscriptions. During 1985, there were four different papers: *Wells Progress, Jackpot Progress, Wendover Progress,* and *Carlin-Eureka Progress.* Later, the number shrank to two: *Wells Progress* and the *Carlin-Eureka-Jackpot-Spring Creek-Lamoille-Wendover* edition. By 1986, only the *Wells Progress* was left, although the *Elko County Progress* was produced briefly in 1987.

There have been many prominent Wells residents over the years, and some deserve particular mention in this history. Horace Agee came to the Wells area in the 1890s and built a ranching empire that included the Ox Yoke and Steptoe Livestock companies. Agee was also involved in freighting to Contact and Spruce Mountain. Agee married Esther Tuttle, and the couple built a house in Wells. He was also on the Elko County School Board and was a strong supporter of creating Wells High School in 1914. He was instrumental in the Wells Bank reorganization in 1922 and was the bank's president until 1930. Agee also managed the Adams-McGill cattle company in Ely from 1925 to 1930. During the 1930s, he served in the state legislature, and was also on the state tax commission. Agee retired to Wells in the 1940s, building an apartment building on the foundation of his old house, which had burned in 1919. Agee died in 1952 and is buried in the Wells Cemetery.

The Badt family has had an influence on Wells since the 1870s when Morris Badt first opened his store. His sons—Herbert, Selby, Milton, and Melville—all had impacts on Wells and Elko County. They all were involved in business and had mining interests in Spruce Mountain and elsewhere. While his brothers maintained the family business, Milton became a lawyer with an office in Elko. Milton served as president of the Nevada Bar Association in 1933 and 1934, but his crowning achievement was being elected to the Nevada Supreme Court in 1947. Milton was unchallenged in elections and was reelected four times, one of the most respected jurists in Nevada history. He served on the court for nineteen years, most of them as chief justice. Milton Badt died in 1966.

Albert and Carl Supp operated the Supp Brothers Garage for years, but were inventors and adventurers at heart. The brothers had their own airplane, a Varney biplane, but their flying career was cut short when Albert crashed the plane in April 1927. They also built the first glider in the county, which was pulled by a Ford Model A.

During the early 1920s, the Supps developed the first snowmobile in the United States. The first snowmobile was small and could not carry many passengers. The Supps built a larger model, using an airplane engine, which could reach a top speed of ninety miles per hour. When the snowmobile was dismantled, a movie company bought the engine and propeller, using them to blow sand and dust during the filming of a movie in Utah. During their years at the garage, the Supp brothers also built their own automobile. Although the car was not a practical model, a family member said it was a lot of fun making it.

Another beloved resident was Jean McElrath, who spent most of her life in Wells. When she was sixteen, she fell off a hay wagon, damaging her spine. This eventually led to severe arthritis, and by 1938 she was unable to walk. As a further complication, McElrath lost her sight in 1950. However, McElrath was a determined person and didn't let these problems deter her from producing a weekly column, "Tumbleweeds," in the *Wells Progress*.

McElrath also served as the Wells correspondent for the *Elko Free Press, Nevada State Journal,* and *Salt Lake Tribune*. She did all this by having a complete news desk operation surrounding her bed. As a tribute, the University of Nevada honored her as a Distinguished Nevadan in 1965. She also wrote a book, *Aged in Sage,* a collection of her stories about the Wells area. McElrath died in October 1967, but her spirit still lives on through her articles and written memories.

When Interstate 80 was completed, replacing U.S. 40, which ran through the middle of Wells, the town was bypassed. Since then, new businesses have opened next to the highway, about a mile from downtown, but Wells continues to be a vibrant community. With Interstate 80 and U.S. 93 crossing in Wells, the town has a constant flow of vehicles through it. Wells offers a full complement of modern services such as motels, RV parks, restaurants, casinos, stores, and a golf course.

Much of Wells's new development has been outside the downtown area and has had an impact on the downtown business district. A downtown redevelopment plan provides for the restoration of the historic district along the railroad tracks. The old bank building is included, and there are hopes that after restoration, the former bank will house a local museum. Many historic buildings remain in Wells, and although they are in various stages of deterioration, these landmarks can be brought back to life.

Wilkins
(Thousand Springs Valley)

DIRECTIONS: *From Wells, go north on U.S. 93 for 26 miles to Wilkins.*

Long before Wilkins became a stop on the Oregon Short Line railroad in 1925, the Thousand Springs Valley was an active ranching area. As early as October 1870, a station was built in the valley to serve the Toano-Boise stagecoach line. During rainy periods, the valley became a muddy quagmire, making it difficult for the heavy freight wagons to pass through. However, completion of the Idaho part of the Oregon Short Line in 1884 ended the need for the stage and freight line to Idaho, and it folded.

A short-lived mining district, the Rough and Ready, was established in 1870 after some promising galena ore float was discovered. The Mayflower, Buttercup, Good Friday, Hillside, and Elko mines operated. However, the district, located seven miles from Wilkins, never produced and was abandoned the next year. William Holbert reopened the mines in 1885; again, little was produced. At the same time, John Bourne Jr. and Sr. were working the Jane Day, Mountain View, and Hillside mines.

In 1886, John Sparks and John Tinnan consolidated many of the small ranches in the valley, creating the base of their large ranching operation. A few years earlier, Jasper Harrell started the Winecup and HD Ranches, but Harrell sold his holdings to Sparks and Tinnan in 1886 for $950,000. Harrell used the money to open several mines on Spruce Mountain. In 1891, after the disastrous winter of 1890–1891, Tinnan sold his part of the cattle company to Andrew Harrell, son of Jasper. The Sparks-Harrell Company now controlled virtually all of the ranches in the valley. Sparks later sold his share to Harrell so he could begin a career in politics. Sparks was elected governor of Nevada in 1902, serving until his death in 1908. Harrell died in 1907; ownership of the cattle company passed to the Vineyard Land and Livestock Company in 1908.

At the same time, B. B. "Bush" Wilkins, a former bartender at Wells, began a ranch in the Thousand Springs Valley. In February 1911, Wilkins was sick in bed when a drunken Joe Ford broke into the house and confronted Wilkins. Wilkins shot and killed Ford; the homicide was ruled self-defense.

The Utah Construction Company took over the Vineyard Company in 1921. In 1925, the Oregon Short Line branch to Wells was completed, and the railroad built a small depot and water station near the Wilkins Ranch. The branch line became an important cattle-shipping point for the valley. A school periodically operated at the HD and Winecup Ranches from the 1910s through the 1930s. After the Utah Construction Company folded, its holdings were bought by Russell Wilkins and Martin Wunderlich.

Oregon Short Line water station and depot at Wilkins. (Photo by Shawn Hall)

In the 1940s, a hotel, store, and service station opened on U.S. 93 near the Winecup Ranch. It was owned by the ranch and managed by John Moschetti. The gas station was the first Phillips 66 station in Nevada, which Wilkins developed into a full-service truck stop, with a mechanic on duty twenty-four hours a day and twelve employees in all. The Wilkins post office opened on July 1, 1948, with Moschetti as postmaster. Tom Bowers took over the Thousand Springs Garage in 1950, enlarging the facility. In 1952, Russell Wilkins died while riding a train to Salt Lake City. Much of his property was broken up. The Winecup Ranch and the complex at Wilkins were sold to actor Jimmy Stewart and his partners Kirk Johnson, Arn Ehrheat, R. E. Harding, and Sue Harding Knott for $700,000.

The Wilkins post office closed on April 12, 1963, when Moschetti left the Thousand Springs Trading Post. Over the years, Moschetti had operated the Wilkins businesses under a percentage agreement with the current owner of the Winecup Ranch. However, when Bill Addington bought the ranch in 1962, this arrangement did not work. The operation deteriorated without Moschetti's supervision after he left Wilkins. The motel burned down a few years later, and some of the other buildings were damaged in another fire shortly afterward.

Today, only the heavily vandalized shells of the buildings are left. At the Wilkins siding, which was abandoned in 1978 when the Oregon Short Line ceased operation, the depot and water station still stand amid old corrals. The siding is a couple of miles west of U.S. 93. The Winecup Ranch and other ranches still thrive in the area. A kiosk commemorating the California Emigrant Trail, which ran through the valley, stands next to the road to Winecup Ranch, giving a short history of the trail in the local area.

Northeastern Elko County

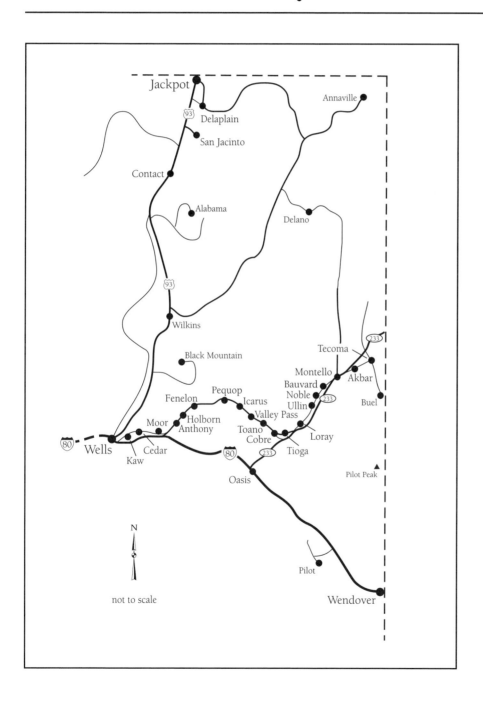

Jackpot

Annaville

93 Delaplain

San Jacinto

Contact

Alabama

Delano

93

Wilkins

233

Tecoma

Black Mountain

Montello

Akbar

Bauvard

Pequop

Noble

Fenelon

Icarus

Ullin

233

Buel

Valley Pass

Moor

Holborn

Anthony

Toano

Loray

80

Cobre

Wells

Cedar

Tioga

Kaw

80

233

Pilot Peak

Oasis

N

Pilot

not to scale

Wendover

Akbar

DIRECTIONS: 3 miles northeast of Montello on Nevada 233.

Akbar was a Southern Pacific Railroad signal station, the first station east of Montello. A signal station was not a scheduled stop on a railroad, but just a maintenance station manned by a crew member who took care of the signal lights. A small sectionhouse was the only structure built at the site, and is long since torn down.

Anthony

DIRECTIONS: From Moor, just north of I-80 east of Wells, take a gravel road northeast 3 miles to Anthony.

Anthony is a signal station on the Union Pacific Railroad (formerly Southern Pacific Railroad) and also a nonagency (not associated with one particular railroad company) siding on the Salt Lake Division, located between Holborn and Moor. The only known mention of Anthony in historical documents is in November 1939 when Lawrence Bishop, a transient, was found dead in a Southern Pacific ice car. No one was ever arrested for the crime. Only a signal shack and small sectionhouse were built at Anthony, both of which are gone, and only a concrete foundation marks the site.

Bauvard
(Banvard) (Old Montello)

DIRECTIONS: From Nevada 233 in Montello, take a gravel road paralleling the railroad track southwest 3 miles to Bauvard.

Bauvard, shown incorrectly on some early maps as Banvard, was established by the Southern Pacific Railroad in 1904. The town was an engine terminal for trains traveling on the newly completed Lucin Cutoff, built by the Southern Pacific Railroad across the Great Salt Lake in Utah east of Montello. The railroad built a number of buildings to house railroad workers and shops for engine repairs. In addition, the railroad constructed a depot, sectionhouse, and water tanks. Houses were brought by train from Terrace, Utah, which had been cut off from the Southern Pacific mainline by the Lucin Cutoff. A post office opened on June 4, 1904, with Wes Johnson as postmaster.

Within a couple years, the Southern Pacific moved the facilities at Bauvard to Montello, where it had built a new division point complete with a seven-stall roundhouse. All buildings were removed, and the town of Bauvard ceased to exist. The name lived on for a while because, despite being in Montello, the post office retained the Bauvard name until it was changed on February 27, 1912. Once the town was moved, local residents referred to the site as Old Montello, and only cellars and scattered lumber now remain.

Cedar

DIRECTIONS: *Located 5 miles east of Wells.*

Cedar was a small depot and signal station on the Central Pacific Railroad (later the Southern Pacific Railroad and now the Union Pacific Railroad). It was primarily a fueling station for wood-fired steam locomotives, but also had a winter telegraph station and sectionhouse. John Dorsey operated woodcutting crews here during the 1870s, and also ran a small store and Wells, Fargo & Company office. Tempers sometimes flared on the crews. In February 1879, two men, John Dempsey and Allen Bickford, were attacked and killed by Noley Campbell, who turned himself in and claimed he killed the men with an ax in self-defense because Dempsey and Bickford had shot at him. At trial, the jury believed Campbell, and he was found not guilty.

By the 1880s, Cedar had lost its importance. Dorsey closed his store, and the Wells Fargo office was moved. The small depot remained open but served few passengers and was primarily used as a livestock shipping point. In May 1906, tragedy struck Cedar when Southern Pacific engine 2402 was climbing the grade at Cedar. The engine exploded, killing the engineer, L. F. Zimmerman, and fireman, M. S. Irwin. The engine's boiler was blown two hundred feet away, but the trucks of the engine stayed on the tracks. During an earlier stop in Montello, Irwin had complained that the engine seemed faulty. Southern Pacific investigators believed that Zimmerman was already dead by the time the engine exploded, because when rescuers reached the accident site, Zimmerman's body was cold while Irwin's was warm. The investigators concluded that Zimmerman had been killed when he hit his head on a water pipe when leaving Montello. However, they couldn't explain why Irwin, the fireman, didn't then operate the locomotive.

Cedar later served as a water stop and not much else. With the coming of diesel locomotives in the 1940s, Cedar's valuable function as a water and wood fuel stop ended. The station was abandoned by the Southern Pacific in 1948, because Cedar no longer had sufficient passenger or freight traffic. The station was dismantled, and today only scattered rubble and a couple woodcutter dugouts mark the site.

Cobre

(Omar)

*DIRECTIONS: From Oasis, take Nevada 233 northeast for 7 miles. Turn
left and continue for 1 mile to Cobre.*

Cobre, originally named Omar, was a station on the Elko division of the Southern Pacific Railroad. The actual Omar station was located
some distance to the east, but when Cobre was picked as the terminus for the
Nevada Northern Railway, most of the town's buildings were moved to the
new townsite at Cobre. Omar did not achieve prominence during its history
until work was begun on the Nevada Northern Railway in 1905.

Because of the link with rich copper mines in the Robinson district in
White Pine County, the railroad terminus was named Cobre, Spanish for copper. Grading for the railroad under the supervision of W. H. Wattis reached
Cobre in September 1905 with actual railroad construction beginning from
Cobre in November 1905. Cobre experienced a boom in 1906 because of the
significant amount of work in laying track, with all supplies coming through
the town. The Western Pacific Railroad moved its construction headquarters
from Winnemucca to Cobre.

In February, Cordelia Spencer opened the Pioneer Hotel in Cobre, and a
post office opened on March 12 with Spencer as postmaster. In 1907, Spencer
sold her hotel and other holdings in Cobre to Horace Kelley for $25,000.
While growing, Cobre developed a reputation as a violent town. In June 1906,

an insane man, R. A. Harlon, fired three shots at J. F. McBride, owner of a saloon. Harlon missed, but McBride didn't, and his three shots killed Harlon. The death was ruled justifiable homicide.

Another incident in August 1907 also involved a local drinking establishment. Two masked men robbed the J. C. Hillman saloon of $1,200. The saloonkeeper, G. B. Gilliam, drew his gun but was shot through the head and died. The sheriff hired local Indians to track down the men. One man they pursued was killed but proved not to be one of the killers. The posse continued unaided, but the killers were never caught. Investigators believed that Gilliam recognized his killer as an ex-convict from when he had been a tough prison guard, or turnkey, at the Washington State Prison. Gilliam and Hillman had previously received three letters warning them that their lives were in danger.

In 1908, Hillman sold his saloon to Horace Kelley, who then owned most of the businesses in Cobre. Hillman decided to concentrate on his mining interests in Six-Mile Canyon, ten miles west of Cobre, where he joined with J. A. Smith and organized the Cobre Lead Mining Company. A number of buildings were constructed at the mine, but the mining activity lasted only a short time.

By 1910, Cobre boasted a population of sixty, and businesses included a hotel, store, mercantile company, and a couple of saloons. Cobre had reached its peak. Although ore trains—carrying primarily copper ore—from Ely kept coming through Cobre, passenger and other freight traffic gradually declined.

Passenger and freight depots at Cobre, 1930s. The Southern Pacific tracks are in the foreground; the Nevada Northern tracks are behind the water tank. (Mel and Mae Steninger collection, Northeastern Nevada Museum)

The remaining residents, however, required construction of a school in 1915. The first teacher was Amy Parker, and the school stayed open through the 1930s. In December 1921, the town was shocked when postmaster George Hall was arrested for embezzlement and issuing money orders with no funds in the office. He had lost money in a local poker game and wrote money orders so he could keep playing. Hall was replaced by Mayme Mitchell. The post office closed on May 31, 1927, but reopened on June 10, 1929, with John Toyn, owner of the Cobre Hotel, as postmaster.

As early as 1937, Cobre was labeled a ghost town even though twenty people still lived there. In 1930, a large pumice deposit was discovered one and one-half miles north of Cobre, but the Cobre Minerals Corporation was not organized until summer 1936. Extensive development began, and plans were made to build a large mill. The company, based in Detroit, claimed it had the only true deposit of pumice in the United States. The *Wells Progress* declared, "Ghost Town of Cobre to Become Important Manufacturing Center of State."[1]

Construction on a $500,000 mill, built by the Bowers Building and Construction Company of Salt Lake City, began in late 1937. About a dozen buildings were built near the mill, and the pumice mined was used for a variety of purposes including acoustic plaster, synthetic travertine, marble, tile shingles, building blocks, and fire bricks. The mill was completed in May 1938 and was 218 feet by 60 feet, with a daily capacity of 150 tons. Fifteen men were employed, with the number rising to nearly 100 by the end of summer. The company held to a strict policy of hiring only men from Nevada. The housing built for employees had baths, showers, toilets, and electric lights. However, despite the high hopes, demand for pumice was small, and the operation shut down after a few years with only a small profit to show for the effort.

Cobre returned to its past ghost-town status with only a handful of people residing in the town. The rise of automobile and truck use ended the need for the Nevada Northern Railway, except for hauling copper ore. Daily passenger service to Ely ended in 1938, and all passenger service was discontinued in July 1941. In November 1948, the Southern Pacific Railroad abandoned the Cobre station, and the Cobre Mercantile Store took over the handling of any railroad business. Cobre's end came on May 31, 1956, when the post office closed. Postmasters over the years included Horace Kelley, Andrew Bennett, Ethel O'Neil, Ralph Druehl, Glen Johnson, Frances Anderson, Eugene Danforth, Julia Wunder, and Sarah Betteridge.

The Nevada Northern Railway continued to use Cobre as a shipping point until the 1980s, but the trains rumbled through a dead town. As late as 1980, a couple of original buildings remained but now only foundations exist. The only structure remaining is a cinder-block engine house built during the last years of the Nevada Northern Railway. At the pumice mine, extensive mill foundations and other ruins mark the site.

Contact Inn, which included a hotel, bar, and store, 1961. (Tony and Ellen Primeaux collection, Northeastern Nevada Museum)

Contact
(Contact City) (Salmon City) (Salmon River)
(Kit Carson) (Porter) (Portis) (Alabama)

DIRECTIONS: *From Wells, take U.S. 93 north for 51½ miles to Contact.*

Although Contact did not achieve major significance until after the turn of the century, the first discoveries took place in 1870 when James Moran found gold in Contact. However, no production took place at this time. In 1872, a prospecting party of three men (Hanks, Lews, and Noll) located a number of new deposits on China Mountain, which led to the opening of other mines by the end of 1872 including the Pocohantas (Henry Prosser), Golconda (J. H. Means, J. A. Hicks, and S. W. Wessels), Dunderberg (Means, Hicks, and Wessels), and Virgin (B. J. Virgin). Four separate but adjacent mining districts were organized: Salmon, Kit Carson, Porter (Portis), and Alabama. Mines in the Kit Carson district were the Juniper (A. C. Minear, H. A. Noll), Montezuma (Robert Parsons), Edith (W. J. Hanks, C. W. Servis), Morningstar (Parsons, Noll, Minear), Polar Star (Servis, Hanks), and Sioux (Servis, Hanks). Servis also served as district recorder. All of the mining districts were later consolidated into the Contact Mining District.

Although a town did not develop at this location, a small hotel was completed in April 1874 that served as a stop on the Toano and Idaho Fast Freight Line. In 1876, a Southern Pacific Railroad official found other deposits on China Mountain, and many Chinese workers were hired to work the mines on a commission basis. The most prominent of the early mines, the Boston, shipped copper ore to Swansea, Wales, until 1880.

During the early 1880s, new mines continued to open but had little sustained production. In the Kit Carson district, the Reverend Goode and Exchequer Goode were opened by Thomas Cochran and John Mitchell, and L. F. Wrinkle worked the Cedar, Nevada, and Stormy mines. In the Porter district, W. J. Hanks and P. H. Jackson opened the Arizona mine, and relocated the Boston, Albany, and Harper mines. The Porter (H. A. Noll), Utah (W. J. Hanks), Dividend (E. D. Boyle), California (Boyle), and Juniper (Boyle) mines were also active. The Stevens Gold and Copper Mining Company owned the Ontario, Michigan, Erie and Elko mines. In the Alabama district, the Lizzie (Dwight Thourot) and Emily (P. A. Dwight) were being worked. The Salmon River district mines were the Domingo, Blue Jay, Manhattan, and Riverside (Cochran and Mitchell), Chester (Dwight), and Wonder (C. O. Akin). Despite this flurry of activity, little was produced, and most mines had given up by the end of 1883. The area remained essentially abandoned until 1887.

In 1888, the Delano group of claims, which eventually became one of the most productive in the Contact district, was located by Hickey, Delano, Ayres, and Hechathin. In 1889, two men, Warwick and English, located the Brooklyn mine, and by 1891, two other mines (Empire and Copper Queen) had also begun production. By 1895, Contact mines employed seventy miners, and the extensive prospecting around Contact continued to be rewarded by new discoveries. In 1896, David Bourne, later known as the "Father of Jarbidge," located the Mammoth mine, and the Bonanza mine was discovered by Colemen, Moore, and Thompson. Coleman later became rich after discovering the Father De Sinet property in the Black Hills.

In January 1897, 100 men were employed in the Contact area, and by April 1897, the number of workers had grown to two hundred. A post office, with Eugene Shields as postmaster, opened in Contact on February 6, 1897. There were a number of mines being worked, including the Blue Bird, Jackrabbit, Reliance, Yellow Girl, and Delano. The Salmon River Mining Company (S. P. Kemper, president) was formed by twenty miners who contributed $100 each for the purpose of building a fifty-ton smelter, which proved unsuccessful and processed only fourteen tons from the Bluebird mine before closing. This was a heavy blow to the area, and many people left soon afterward. In February 1898, the Delano property was bonded to an English syndicate for $65,000, but nothing came of it. By 1900, population had dropped to eighty-five and only five residents were left by 1905.

A slow revival began in late 1905, which led to Contact's first real boom. A new town formed just south of the original townsite, which had contained only a few buildings, including a school, with Flora Vincent as teacher. A stagecoach line to Twin Falls, Idaho, began service in September 1906. The new town was named Contact, a mining term meaning the contact zone between two types of rock, such as the granite and porphyry in the district. The United States Mining and Smelting Company came to the district in 1907. By 1908, Contact's population was three hundred. In February 1908, the Contact Power and Milling Company in Seattle bought many claims and immediately planned to build a $200,000 concentrating plant with its own power plant.

Prospects looked so good that in April 1909, three townsites were platted: Contact, Contact City, and East Contact. Two companies, the Western Townsite Company (Mose Jones) and the Contact City Townsite Company (Henry Smith), developed the townsites and Smith declared Contact the "Butte City of Nevada."[2] The most developed site was Contact City, which contained 15 buildings. Among the three townsites, 450 lots were sold by 1915. The 35-room Contact Hotel (Etta Bruneau), built from local granite, was completed in August. A number of saloons, including G. L. Collins's Mint Saloon and Restaurant, the Palace Saloon and Northern Saloon (Lewis Pratt), and the Blue Ribbon Bar (Ole Haas), a barber shop (William Hankins), and the W. A. Kent General Merchandise Store also opened. Kent was called the "Pioneer Merchant of Contact," and was beloved by Contact's residents.

A promotional newspaper, the *Contact News,* began publication on May 20, 1915, but details about the paper are scarce. Nevada history books do not mention the paper, and its existence was unknown to modern historians until a copy of the third issue was given to the Northeastern Nevada Museum in Elko. This issue reveals little about the paper but appears to have been printed by the Western Townsite Company. The publication was short-lived and apparently did not survive the summer.

In 1910, the Nevada Copper Mining, Milling, and Power Company, based in Tecoma, bought out the United States Smelting Company. The Contact Company was renamed the Contact-Seattle Copper Mining Company, and the two organizations controlled virtually all the mines in the district.

Due to demand, a triweekly stage to Rogerson, Idaho, began in April 1910. Another newspaper, the *Contact Miner,* began publication on March 20, 1913. J. V. Marshall served as editor and owner of the Miner Publishing Company. The paper, which was staunchly Democratic, cost $2.50 per year. In December 1915, Marshall sold out to E. H. Childs, who printed only a couple of issues before ending publication.

In August 1914, the Nevada Copper Company began construction of a 100-ton copper-leaching plant, with Henry Smith as manager. Coincidentally, Smith had sold the land for the plant, which was completed in late 1915. Most of 1915 was spent developing four mines (Delano, Champ Clark, High Ore, and Copper Shield), and only $2,300 was produced. In 1916, the Contact-Seattle company's Delano mine produced almost all of the $181,000 mined, keeping the operation solvent.

Mines in Contact produced ore, primarily copper ore, from 1916 to 1958, a tremendous record of consistency. In 1918, the Vivian Tunnel Company began work on a new mine, a Sutro-type tunnel to help drain water from the Contact mines and provide an easier method of ore removal. However, this proved too expensive and was abandoned before completion.

Although there was consistent production from 1916 to 1919, the 1920s proved to be the decade that put Contact on the map. In September 1922, the Three in One Mining Company announced plans to build a $2.5 million smelter fifteen miles south of Contact. However, the plan was an investor scam, and the smelter was never built.

Despite this, Contact continued to prosper. In 1923, H. A. DeVaux, head of the Contact Sewerage Company, constructed a number of new buildings, including a two-story, thirty-room office building, built from Contact granite. By 1924, the town was abuzz when construction on the Union Pacific Railroad's Oregon Short Line, which ran from Rogerson, Idaho, to Wells, Nevada. A jail was completed in March and was full every weekend.

With great fanfare, the $110,000 three-story, fifty-room Fairview Hotel opened on May 24, 1924. One of the owners, H. A. DeVaux, provided fireworks, and W. G. Greathouse, Nevada secretary of state, was guest of honor. The hotel was owned by the Contact Construction and Investment Company, with Robert Weir as president. In July, the Gray Mining Company, of which the Vivian Tunnel Company was a subsidiary, began to work the Vivian Tunnel once again and hoped to quickly complete the twenty thousand–foot tunnel.

A new newspaper, the *Nevada-Contact Mining Review,* began publication on November 22, 1924, and was operated by Mark Musgrove, former mining editor of the *Nevada State Journal.* The newspaper was published by the

Nevada State Herald in Wells, but Musgrove never paid the *Herald* for the printing, changing *Herald* editorials from praise for the Contact paper to reports on how the paper was a blight on the newspaper business. Musgrove moved the printing job to a plant at Filer, Idaho, in January 1925, but the paper was taken over in June by Leslie Fox, who also ran the *Kimberly (Idaho) Tribune*. Despite the new ownership, the paper folded in September.

On March 11, 1925, the first construction train of the Oregon Short Line arrived in Contact, and a depot was built below the town next to the Salmon River Falls. Regular service began within a month. Meanwhile, the Fairview Hotel had suffered hard times and went into receivership in September. It was initially sold at a tax sale for $1,525 to Robert Weir Jr. (the owner's son), but this ruse was discovered and the sale was disallowed. At another tax sale in October, the hotel was purchased by J. L. Newland for $2,700. The hotel burned on May 31, 1926, in only thirty minutes.

The chief business in Contact by the end of 1926 was the Fred Johnson Merchandise Store, with branch stores in Wells and Montello. A new two-room school was built in 1927 for forty students. Flo Reed, who taught at many Elko County schools, served as teacher of the Contact school from 1927 to 1930. Marguerite Patterson Evans was the school's last principal and the only teacher in the high school, which closed in 1934, although it was sporadically used during Contact's revival periods. In the 1920s and 1930s, two separate schools operated. The grammar school was in the original building from 1927, while the high school occupied a former pool hall.

The advent of Prohibition in 1917 did little to lessen the thirst of Contact's populace. Bootleg activity was prominent in the mountains of the area. It was said that more people bootlegged than lived in the town during the 1920s. The biggest operation was a place called Heaven's Delight. In town, the products were sold at a speakeasy named Hell's Delight. Virgil Church recalled, "There were six major moonshine operations in Contact from 1917 until the repeal of Prohibition in 1932. Those were just the big outfits. I was a moonshiner. Hell, everybody in town was a moonshiner, making grain whiskey in their cellars."[3]

John Detweiler echoed these sentiments: "My father was justice of the peace here for years. He was never a bootlegger or moonshiner. Said he couldn't risk the chance; said they'd throw away the keys to the jailhouse if the judge was ever arrested. But hell, he was the No. 1 supplier of everything needed to make the whiskey. Dad hauled in all the coal, barrels, wheat, and sugar to supply the moonshiners. Dad had the slot machine concession in town and would always take me with him when he collected the money from the slots at Hard Rock Tilly's sporting house at the south end of town. As long as I was with him, mother figured dad would not get in any trouble."[4]

In 1930, a new Contact townsite was laid out. Power for the town came

One of the more impressive ruins in Contact is this old stone store. (Photo by Shawn Hall)

from the power plant the Vivian Tunnel Company had built. Contact's population was 260, but the town's best days were past. In October 1931, the property and buildings of the Gray Mining Company were put up at a tax sale, but a lack of bids forced Elko County to buy the property for $956, despite the appraised value of the property being $37,000. In January 1932, the property was again put up for sale to satisfy tax liens, but again Elko County ended up buying the property, this time for $1,124. By 1935, Contact still had two general stores, a hotel, two saloons, a post office, and a school, but the population had shrunk to one hundred.

Most of the remaining residents were supported by the Works Progress Administration, or WPA, a New Deal program that hired unemployed workers during the Great Depression. A depressed copper market plagued the town, and mine production continued to shrink. Despite the slowdown, an Episcopal church, St. Agnes Chapel, was completed in June 1936. In August 1942, the church was destroyed by a fire that started in the L. C. Bugbee Mercantile Store when a kerosene burner in a refrigerator exploded. There was little water to fight the fire, and the Bugbee building, which housed a store, restaurant, hotel, bar, and service station, was completely consumed. The fire spread to the church and also burned a number of houses before being put out.

Mines in the Contact area did not revive until 1943, when wartime demand for copper raised prices and made copper mining profitable again. The Marshall Mining Company (Maurice Marshall, president) began working the Delano mine and developing a new prospect, the Marshall mine. At the same time, W. C. Lewis and Charles Whitcomb began development of their land, named the Bonanza Property. Fire affected Contact again in May 1947 when a service station, bar, store, and dance hall, all owned by Ed Henzinger, were completely destroyed at a loss of $40,000. In November 1947, Contact elected a mayor for the first time, Ray King. Despite renewed optimism, the Contact revival had faded completely by 1947. From 1943 to 1946, Contact mines produced eight hundred thousand pounds of copper, but from 1947 to 1951, only seven thousand pounds were mined. Another fire in August 1951 destroyed the last hotel, formerly owned by Contact Mayor Ray King.

Contact's last revival began in 1952 when the Marshall mine was renamed the Nevada-Bellvue mine, and extensive work began. However, this activity was insufficient to maintain Contact as a passenger stop on the Oregon Short Line route, and the station closed in December 1952. The depot building was later moved to Lee, southwest of Lamoille, where it still stands.

A strange occurrence took place in March 1953 when seventy-year-old Thomas Williams shot and killed seventy-two-year-old J. R. "Tex" Hazelwood. The two men had feuded for years. Since the 1920s, Tex had developed a reputation around Contact and nearby ranches of the Union Cattle Company, where he was labeled as "one stave short of being round." He roamed the area, living in caves or crude willow shelters, and his reputation for being strange prevented him from working for any of the local ranches. He achieved the height of his notoriety when he developed a new way to rustle cattle. Hazelwood fashioned shoes that had cow hooves on the bottom. Puzzled cattlemen couldn't figure out how, even in deep snow, their cattle were disappearing without any human footprints nearby. Tex was finally caught and spent a couple of years in prison. After his release, Hazelwood returned to the Contact area where he continued to be a problem. It was because of his orneriness and shenanigans that Hazelwood eventually was killed while sitting in his pickup truck in Contact. The shoes used in his cattle rustling are on display at the Northeastern Nevada Museum in Elko.

The Nevada-Bellvue mine, still owned by Maurice Marshall but leased to the American West Exploration Company, produced substantial amounts of copper between 1952 and 1957. Copper ore, which was still shipped by rail from the Contact siding despite the railroad depot closure, was sent to the smelters at Garfield, Utah. The revival ended abruptly in 1957 when the price of copper collapsed. The Nevada-Bellvue had produced virtually all of the two million pounds of copper mined in Contact from 1952 to 1957. No significant production has taken place since. In total, the Contact district produced 5.8 million pounds of copper, 360,000 pounds of lead, 127,000 ounces of silver, 18,000 pounds of zinc, and 1,200 ounces of gold.

By the time the Contact post office closed on August 31, 1962, the town was virtually empty. Postmasters who served included James Dwight, Mary Reed, Albert Carpenter, Adam Schmidt, Isaac Reed, Wyatt Kent, James Marshall, Ferdinand Johnson, Stella Klitz (who died while postmaster in 1951), and Isabella Wright.

The Sunshine Mining Company, Exxon Minerals, and Homestake Mining Company undertook further exploration in the 1980s, but since then no other work has been done. A few residents still live in Contact, mainly working in Jackpot or for the Nevada Department of Transportation (NDOT) at the Contact Maintenance Station.

In the oldest part of Contact, located just north of the highway maintenance station, are the rock walls of one of Contact's first stores. In the main town of Contact, west of U.S. 93, old houses remain, mixed in with newer mobile homes. An impressive concrete building, which served as the Community Social Hall, dominates the townsite. Many social functions, in particular dances, were held there, and the walls were covered with grandiose murals of the developers' fanciful visions of what Contact was going to be. The old school, now a residence, remains, a cemetery is located nearby, and in the hills around Contact, many reminders of its mining heyday abound. The rails of the Oregon Short Line were torn up after the railroad ceased operation in 1978.

Delaplain

DIRECTIONS: *From Contact, go north on U.S. 93 for 13 miles. Turn right on a gravel road and continue for 1½ miles to Delaplain.*

Delaplain began as a station on the Union Pacific Railroad's Oregon Short Line route, named for an employee of the railroad. The railroad built a small depot and several other buildings, including a boardinghouse

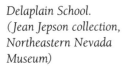

Delaplain School. (Jean Jepson collection, Northeastern Nevada Museum)

for section crews. Because of Delaplain's central location among local ranches, a school was built there in 1927. The Delaplain School District formed in July 1927, and the first students were Donald, Frank, Harry, and Byton Williams, Gordon Sigman, and Charlotte Teeters. The students rode horses to school, but with the advent of school buses, the children were sent to school in Contact, and the Delaplain school closed.

Delaplain was not an important station on the Oregon Short Line, and the railroad buildings were dismantled even before trains stopped running in 1978. Only concrete foundations are left today.

Fenelon
(Otego)

DIRECTIONS: *From Moor, take a dirt road adjacent to the railroad tracks east, then northeast for 10 miles to Fenelon.*

Fenelon, also known as Otego, was a water stop and signal station, first on the Central Pacific Railroad, and then after 1899, on the Southern Pacific Railroad (now the Union Pacific Railroad). While it was part of the Central Pacific, the stop was known as Otego. During the harsh winters, railroad workers at Otego gave notice to approaching trains of snowbound trains farther up the line.

A small station building, used only during the winter, housed a telegraph

Stone foundation in Fenelon. (Photo by Shawn Hall)

office. A couple of buildings for railroad workers were also built. In March 1874, a broken rail threw a passenger train from the tracks. The coach turned over in a ditch, and several people were injured. When the Southern Pacific took over the line from the Central Pacific in 1899, a day telegraph was added.

By the turn of the twentieth century, about twenty people lived in the area and a half-dozen buildings stood. Disaster struck at Fenelon in December 1900 when two trains collided head-on. One train, headed by engine 1751, was supposed to wait at a red signal but ran through it, striking a train led by engine 1800 and killing that train's fireman, Charles Duncan, immediately, and brakeman, Timothy Kennedy, who died shortly after. Kennedy had married Catherine Palmer a year earlier, and his last words were, "Tell my wife I still love her."[5]

In 1902 and 1903, the Southern Pacific rebuilt portions of the former Central Pacific rail line, including the line through Fenelon. In October 1902, there was a serious confrontation between the Greek railroad crew and the construction subcontractor, J. C. Sullivan. In the ensuing exchange of bullets, Sullivan was seriously injured and the Greek crew was fired. During 1903, the new road crew organized a baseball team that played against other Elko County teams.

Once reconstruction of the line was finished in the fall of 1903, Fenelon ceased to exist. The railroad removed the buildings, and Fenelon ceased functioning even as a signal station. Only foundations, including the brick water tank holder, and scattered debris mark the site today.

Holborn
(Independence)

DIRECTIONS: From Moor just north of I-80 east of Wells, take a gravel road northeast for 7 miles to Holborn.

Holborn, a signal station on the Southern Pacific Railroad, was established during the reconstruction of the former Central Pacific Railroad line during the early 1900s. Holborn's only significant event occurred in July 1951 when James Foster fell out of a coach car and was killed by an oncoming passing train.

Independence, originally located one mile south of Holborn, was a locomotive water stop on the Central Pacific before Holborn was constructed. A couple of buildings were built at Independence to house a section crew. Only scattered debris and broken glass now mark the Independence site.

Just past the site where Independence once stood, on the old CP railroad bed abandoned by the SP when they took over the line, is an excellent example of the Chinese crews' meticulous work in constructing the railroad: a water culvert under the railroad right-of-way is carefully constructed with square-head nails. Only the concrete foundations of the Independence sectionhouse are left at Holborn.

Drainage culvert built by Chinese railroad workers under the Central Pacific tracks at Independence (later known as Holborn). (Photo by Shawn Hall)

Icarus

DIRECTIONS: From Cobre, go northwest on a gravel road for 10 miles to Icarus.

Icarus was a signal station on the Southern Pacific Railroad, named for an imaginary country where perfect communism existed, not for the Greek myth of the same name. In February 1903, a train wreck killed Southern Pacific engineer Fred Stokes. One train struck a broken rail, and its last two cars derailed. Then, a following train slammed into the derailed cars. Two engines, a dynamo, or power plant, and two mail cars were thrown into the ditch. Stokes's body was found crushed under the locomotive's tender. No structures were ever built at Icarus.

Kaw

DIRECTIONS: Located 2 miles east of Wells.

Kaw, located between Wells and Cedar, served both the Southern Pacific Railroad and Western Pacific Railroad (both now part of the Union Pacific Railroad) as a signal station. At one time, a water tank and sectionhouse were built, but only foundations are left today.

Loray
(Luray) (Leroy)

DIRECTIONS: *From Cobre, return Nevada 233 north 4 miles to Loray.*

Loray was a station on the Central Pacific Railroad and later on the Southern Pacific Railroad. However, the station had few passengers and was used mainly to ship wood cut nearby for railroad use. Woodcutting crews lived in housing next to the tracks. In May 1875, a near tragedy occurred near the station when two freight trains collided, wrecking three engines. Twenty-five cars were thrown off the tracks, and brakeman William Cassin and conductor Snyder were seriously injured.

Copper ore was discovered in the early 1880s about three miles south of the railroad, and in 1883, A. P. Shively (also the district recorder) organized the Loray Mining District. During the next few years, the Shively and Wilson (Shively, James Wilson), Castle Park (Shively), Stokes (William Stokes, Wilson), Queen of Sheba (Shively, David Kay) Birthday (Wilson), Ruby Chief (Wilson), and King Fisher (Wilson) mines were worked, although little was produced until after the turn of the century.

In March 1907, twenty tons of copper ore were shipped from the Anderson property, where R. P. Christian was in charge of operations and eight men were employed. A copper and silver strike was made on the Will Porter claim in May 1908, and Kellough and Lang discovered the Lillian mine in July 1908, but only intermittent ore was produced from the district's mines until 1958.

From 1908 to 1958, producing mines included the Alabama, Jay Bird, Pickup, Maybelle, Castle Peak, Lost Hope, Silver Bell, Silver Star, and New Deal. The Delno Mining and Milling Company worked a few of the mines from 1928 to 1936, producing $62,215. The two biggest production years were 1945 and 1946, when Charles Roberts reworked old tailings and recovered more than $69,000, primarily from the Maybelle mine discovered by Walter Long in 1934.

During the 1930s and 1940s, most of the miners lived at the Loray railroad siding, where a school operated for a number of years. Total value of mining in the Loray district is $191,000, which includes 480,018 pounds of lead, 28,802 ounces of silver, and 25,883 pounds of copper.

Mining remnants abound on both sides of the mountain east of Loray, including gallows frames, shafts, and a converted Ford Model T used as a hoist. At the Loray siding, where at one time a dozen buildings stood, only foundations and scattered debris are left.

Montello

(Bauvard)

DIRECTIONS: Go 23 miles northeast on Nevada 233 from the Oasis interchange on I-80.

Present Montello was created in 1904 when the Southern Pacific Railroad built the Lucin Cutoff across the Great Salt Lake of Utah. Long before the town of Montello formed, the area was the site of a train robbery, a rare occurrence in Elko County and Nevada history. In January, a Central Pacific engineer stopped his train when he saw a red flashing light on the Montello water tank. Masked bandits pounced on the engineer and crew, tied them up, and locked them in a railroad shack. The bandits headed to the Wells Fargo express car, where messenger Aaron Ross was protecting the shipment. Ross refused orders to come out and barricaded himself in the car where, despite being hit by three bullets, he continued to defy the robbers.

Another train approached the Montello siding; the robbers met it and ordered its crew to continue. With guns at their heads, the crew could do little but comply. The robbers returned to work on the express car, and when they again tried to force their way in, Ross shot one. The robbers then tried to smash the express car by ramming the engine into it, but fears of another train's arrival caused them to abandon the attempt. The only booty taken was $10 found in the conductor's wallet. With a reward of $1,250 for each of the robbers, it was easy for Sheriff Henry Taber of Elko to assemble the posse.

Overview of Montello, 1937. (Mel and Mae Steninger collection, Northeastern Nevada Museum)

The first two robbers, Orris Nay and Frank Hawley, were wounded and captured in Utah County after a shootout on January 28, 1883, and the pair told the posse where the rest of the gang was hiding. The other three robbers, Sylvester Earl, Erastus Anderson, and Frank Francis, surrendered without incident when confronted by the posse, which was armed with dynamite and a small cannon. All five captured robbers were taken to Salt Lake City.

The prisoners were returned to Elko in February and all pleaded guilty. Nay, Hawley, and Francis received fourteen years in prison, while the two teenagers, Earl and Anderson, received twelve-year sentences. The express car messenger, Aaron Ross, was treated as a hero for refusing to surrender to the robbers and received rewards from the Central Pacific Railroad and Wells Fargo. The rewards for capture were divided among the seventeen men of the posse, each receiving $350.

The town of Montello was later created in 1904 by the Southern Pacific Railroad during the construction of the Lucin Cutoff, east of Montello, in Utah. The first train came through the town on March 4, 1904, and houses were moved to Montello from Kelton and Terrace, Utah. Montello replaced Terrace as the main railroad division point, plunging the town of Terrace into oblivion.

Montello was initially known as Bauvard, the same name of the old siding located three miles to the southwest. Bauvard's post office was transferred to the new town, but the name was not changed to Montello, which in Shoshone means "rest," until February 27, 1912. The railroad built a large hotel, which burned down in 1908, and complete railroad facilities at Montello. A small Chinatown developed because many of the Chinese crews were based at Montello, and the forty Chinese residents supported a store and joss house, or Chinese house of worship.

In July 1904, O. T. Hill finished construction on an eight-room house, storeroom, and lodging house for Wes Johnson, who also opened a general merchandise store. In October 1904, part of the new library was used as a school, with Ethelyn Allen teaching ten students the first year. A separate schoolhouse was built in 1906. In 1907, the Utah Construction Company (UCC) purchased the Vineyard Land and Livestock Company's vast holdings. Montello, because of its convenient location to the railroad and their ranches, was made the headquarters. The company ran a store in Montello for many years, and the original store, with the UCC logo on it, still stands in Montello.

From 1904 to 1929, Montello's population approached eight hundred. The town also served as a supply point for the mining camp of Delano, located to the north. The Southern Pacific's monthly payroll reached as high as $1 million in 1915. A new school was built in 1910. Teachers serving the school during the next decade included C. I. Bonham, M. D. Hunter, Helen English, Matilde McQuisiton, Olive Burgess, and Alma Nichol. The old school was moved downtown and converted into the town's amusement hall, run by the

Montello Amusement Corporation. The Montello Mercantile Company was incorporated in July 1912. A new jail was built by A. C. McGinty during the spring of 1916, replacing the original jail, made of railroad ties, from which a prisoner could escape by removing a tie or two.

During the 1920s, Montello began to decline. A major blow struck the town in October 1925 when a large fire, started by an exploding coffee urn in the Nelson Cafe, burned the business district, destroying the Wes Johnson store, the Nelson Cafe, the Bryant Pool Hall, the post office, and the home of A. R. Cave. In addition, the Utah Construction Company was broken up and sold. One part of the holdings, the Gamble Ranch, continues to operate as one of the largest ranches in Elko County. The ranch was sold in 1950 for $3 million.

Montello received national attention in November 1928 when future president Herbert Hoover gave a campaign speech in the town. In 1929, the local doctor, J. D. Sherrod, was elected vice president of the American Chiropractors Association. The Montello Consolidated School Orchestra was featured on a KSL radio broadcast, out of Salt Lake City, in March 1936.

The introduction of diesel locomotives in the 1940s spelled the end of Montello's importance to the railroad as a water and fuel stop and repair facility for steam locomotives. The roundhouses and shops were removed during the 1950s, and only the huge water tower was left behind. Some improvement came to Montello in 1960 when a paved highway was completed from Oasis. Today, Montello is a quiet town with a population of about 75.

Many of the houses moved from Utah in 1904 remain today, and the original depot has been moved and converted into a house. The school, jail, and other old buildings are also standing, and the cemetery is located just north of the main street. The water tower dominates the old railroad yards, and trains continue to pass through Montello. A store, gas station, post office, and a couple of saloons still operate.

Moor

(Moors)

DIRECTIONS: *Located 8 miles east of Wells just north of I-80.*

Moor was established in 1869 by the Central Pacific Railroad as a stop and base for a wood-cutting crew, and later served as a nonagency telegraph station and siding for the Southern Pacific Railroad. Named for the foreman of the wood-cutting crew, the small camp consisted of a number of crude houses and a small store. Once the railroad was completed, the wood crew moved elsewhere.

Tragedy struck Moor early in its history. In June 1870, railroad worker

Robert Warrock was killed when a defective coupler broke, crushing him between the cars. Some minor mining activity took place near Moor during the 1870s and 1880s. The Last Chance (Jeremiah Crabb) and Emma Rencker (J. H. Wood, William O'Neil) mines had short lives and produced little. When Frederick Shearer, a traveler who mentioned Moor in his journals, visited Moor in 1884, the stop was merely a siding, and only stakes and posts were left of the buildings. The nationwide flu epidemic struck Moor in 1918. Both operators for the Southern Pacific Railroad, Alice Louise Sumwalt and W. N. McBride, died of the flu in December 1918.

Another Moor tragedy occurred in March 1941, when section foreman Sam Kawaguchi was struck and killed by Southern Pacific mail train 9. In September 1943, telegrapher LaVerne Price was killed when she accidentally stepped in front of a passenger train. She and her husband, Harold, had lived at Moor for two years. Today, all of the buildings in Moor are gone, and only wood scraps, cellars, and concrete foundations mark the site.

Noble

DIRECTIONS: *Located 2 miles southwest of Bauvard. From Nevada 233 in Montello, take a gravel road paralleling the railroad track southwest 5 miles to Noble.*

Noble was a signal station on the Southern Pacific Railroad between Ullin and Bauvard. Only a signal shed was built and nothing remains at Noble today.

Oasis

DIRECTIONS: *Located at the junction of I-80 and Nevada 233.*

Oasis was first settled in the early 1880s by E. C. Hardy, who raised horses. In 1884, the Big Springs Ranch was created by consolidating the older ranches in the area: the Oasis, Johnson, and Warm Springs ranches. Later, H. A. and H. F. Leach bought the ranch, which was purchased by the Utah Construction Company in 1917. Other owners of the Oasis ranch over the years included Russell Wilkins and Martin Wunderlich, Fred West, Oscar and Sam Rudnick, Cluster Valley Cattle Company, Big Springs Land and Cattle Company, Jack Taylor, and David Buntliff. In 1969, R. J. Beaumont bought the ranch for $1.8 million.

Oasis was also a popular stopping point for highway travelers. A gas station, small motel, and now an RV park are in operation. An interesting point of history took place at Oasis in 1947 when a suspect in the Black Dahlia murder case was arrested by the FBI. The suspect was never identified, and because the crime was never solved, apparently the suspect had an alibi. In July 1947, Sam Tooley opened the Oasis Hotel and Casino. The Big Springs Ranch still operates today as does an RV Park, gas station, and small store.

Pequop

DIRECTIONS: From Moor, take a dirt road adjacent to the railroad tracks east, then northeast for 15 miles to Pequop.

Pequop, located west of Toano, was first a sidetrack station (with two parallel tracks to allow trains to pass each other) on the Central Pacific Railroad, later the Southern Pacific Railroad. Pequop achieved notoriety on November 5, 1870, when the second train robbery in the history of Nevada occurred only twenty hours after the first train robbery in Nevada history, at Verdi.

Only a telegraph pole and railroad signal remain along the former Southern Pacific right-of-way at Pequop. (Photo by Shawn Hall)

The Reed family in front of Reed Station, 1899. (Edna Patterson collection, Northeastern Nevada Museum)

Tuscarora-Elko stage changing horses at Reed Station, 1880. (Edna Patterson collection, Northeastern Nevada Museum)

Bizarrely, the same train on the same trip was robbed twice. The train was stopped by six to eight armed men. All of the registered letters and packages were taken, along with a Wells Fargo shipment of $3,100. The messenger hid most of the money under a nearby woodpile. A group of U.S. Army deserters from Fort Halleck was suspected, and eventually three men, Daniel Taylor, Daniel Baker, and Leander Morton, were caught in Utah and sentenced to thirty years. However, none of these men were the army deserters from the fort, but one of the robbers had items obviously taken from a soldier. Nothing was ever heard from the deserters, and some people believe that the train robbers attacked and killed the soldiers before robbing the train.

This was the extent of the excitement at Pequop. The railroad built a couple of buildings to house section crews. Pequop is located high in the mountains, and snowplows were constantly needed to keep the tracks clear of snow. In February 1890, a snowplow driven by three engines derailed; the fireman was killed, and the engineer was scalded in the accident.

During the 1930s, enough people lived in Pequop to warrant the opening of a school for five students. In 1937, Mrs. M. V. Murray, wife of a railroad foreman, won a Ford V8 sedan in a contest sponsored by the American Legion and the Veterans of Foreign Wars.

The coming of diesel locomotives to the railroad in the 1940s reduced Pequop's usefulness. By the end of the 1940s, only a couple of railroad workers were left. All of the buildings are gone, and only foundations and scattered debris are left. The former right-of-way of the Central Pacific Railroad is easily visible, coming in at almost a right angle to the later Southern Pacific (now Union Pacific) tracks.

San Jacinto

DIRECTIONS: *From Contact, go north on U.S. 93 for 13 miles. Turn right on a gravel road and continue for 2½ miles. Turn right and follow the dirt road for 4 miles to San Jacinto, located on the abandoned railroad bed. San Jacinto Ranch is one more mile to the west.*

San Jacinto was one of the many ranches in the ranching empire of Governor John Sparks and Jasper Harrell. Sparks named the ranch for a town in his home state of Texas. The San Jacinto post office opened on November 17, 1898, with Eliza Hewitt serving as postmaster. A school opened in 1903 with Edith Plumb serving as teacher.

The San Jacinto ranch was sold to the Vineyard Land and Stock Company in 1908. The Utah Construction Company took over in 1914 and built houses for company officials and bunkhouses for the men. Archie Bowman, already a fourteen-year veteran of the company, was named superintendent of the company's large Elko County operation. San Jacinto was his headquarters, and Bowman and his wife, Nora, lived at the ranch until 1946.

In April 1916, the Shoshone-Hailey-Twin Falls and Wells Auto Stage began operations with a stop in San Jacinto. The stage line featured Packards, and was run by M. Silva. In 1925, the Oregon Short Line railroad was completed and just east of the ranch established a passenger and freight stop and siding, which was used extensively by the ranch for shipping cattle.

The San Jacinto post office closed on April 15, 1938. Although other postmasters served through the years, including Chandler Holmes, William Bitterridge, Moses Jones, Alex Patterson, James Parmley, and Thomas Grounsell, Archie Bowman had the longest tenure, from 1922 to 1938. During the 1920s and 1930s, a store, Bugbee's, served the area. The ranch is still operated today by the Secrist family, who formerly owned Dinner Station. Old buildings are mixed with the new. Not much is left at the location of the Oregon Short Line railroad siding, because all of the buildings were removed when the tracks were torn up in 1978.

Tecoma

DIRECTIONS: From Montello, take Nevada 233 northeast for 6 miles. Turn right, crossing the railroad tracks, for 1 mile to Tecoma.

Tecoma was born with the arrival of the Central Pacific Railroad in 1869. A town, with a small Chinatown, soon formed. A post office opened on December 1, 1871, closed on June 7, 1872, and reopened on May 2, 1873. Tecoma soon had a hotel, restaurant, cafe, and two saloons, and by 1880, a population of sixty people. A store (owned by J. C. Lee) and a school opened in the 1880s.

Tecoma became the major railhead for the mining activity in the area, particularly Buel, and for the Sparks-Harrell Cattle Company. In April 1886,

Foundation of the Tecoma railroad depot. (Photo by Shawn Hall)

Remains at the Jackson Mine, north of Tecoma. (Photo by Shawn Hall)

S. Ross Worthington, a cattleman, and John Compton, a sheepherder, became involved in an argument about Compton's dog at Mundell's Saloon. Both men fired their guns; both died of the resulting wounds.

In January 1898, Lee sold his store to Jones and Johnson of Toano, but later bought the store back and ran it until the 1910s. A railroad accident occurred in Tecoma in August 1898. Jack Rouse, the superintendent of railroad shops

Connecting the West

in Terrace, Utah, and machinist Peter Meaden were killed when a lifting tackle they were using to set up a derailed locomotive broke.

By 1900, Tecoma had a population of 124. A big boost for the town came in 1907 when the Southern Pacific Railroad built a spur from Tecoma to Buel. In addition, the Jackson mine, in the northern part of the mining district, began production at the same time. During the next five years, mines around Tecoma produced more than $40,000, but the town faded during the 1920s. The town's main business, its hotel, burned in 1918; the post office closed on August 31, 1921. Postmasters included Richard Mallett, John Brennan, William Bellinger, John Lee, Albion Bonghelthaus, Edward Jackson, Paul Merrill, William Smith, and Eva Smith.

Mining decreased around Tecoma, and Montello became the main rail station in the area. Completion of the Oregon Short Line in 1925 was another blow, because until that time, Tecoma had been the main freight shipping point for nearby Contact, a much larger town. By 1930, most of the town's residents had left and all of the businesses had closed. The railroad spur, which had not been used in years, was abandoned in January 1940.

Over the years, the remaining buildings have been dismantled for materials or moved elsewhere. Many concrete foundations and scattered debris mark the site, and a small cemetery is located nearby.

Tioga

DIRECTIONS: *Located 2 miles northeast of Cobre.*

Tioga, Iroquois for "at the forks," served as a signal station on the Southern Pacific Railroad. Few buildings were built at Tioga other than a sectionhouse, dismantled in the 1950s. Only a small foundation marks the site.

Toano

(Taono) (Toana) (Summit City)

DIRECTIONS: *From Cobre, go northwest for 1½ miles to Toano.*

Toano was established as a stop on the Central Pacific Railroad in late 1868. The new camp quickly achieved prominence when Central Pacific Railroad president Leland Stanford put together the special train at Toano, headed by the engine *Jupiter,* to attend the golden spike ceremony, commemorating completion of the first transcontinental railroad, at Promontory, Utah, in May 1869. Toano was the western terminus of the Salt Lake Division of the Central Pacific with a six-stall roundhouse.

Grave in the Toano cemetery. (Photo by Shawn Hall)

Eventually, a town formed at this site, which became the major freight and staging center in Elko County, surpassing even Elko for a time. The name Toano, Shoshone for "black topped" or "black coated," is derived from the nearby mountains, which appear to have black tops. Not only was Toano the division's western terminus, but it was also the first engine facility east of Carlin. The town quickly became the main supply point for towns as far away as Pioche and places in between such as Spruce Mountain, Cherry Creek, and Ward. Toano also served Idaho by the new Toano Road. A post office opened on August 9, 1869, with J. W. Griswold as postmaster.

By 1870, Toano had a population of 117 and businesses included the International and Railroad Hotels, L. E. Eno's Idaho Saloon, William Bellinger's saloon, Nolan and Wilcox Saloon, Toano Saloon, and blacksmith Charles Lynde. Although the post office closed on January 11, 1870, it reopened on January 10, 1872. In November 1871, Ferdinand Marx, the local Wells Fargo agent, built a twenty-five-foot-by-sixty-four-foot fireproof stone store.

In December 1871, a fatal fight took place in the Toano Saloon between W. J. Bentley and James Chamberlain. As the argument escalated, Bentley attacked Chamberlain, who was cutting tobacco. An artery in Bentley's arm was severed, and he bled to death. Chamberlain was acquitted of charges relating to Bentley's death.

During the early 1870s, a number of new stagecoach lines made Toano their base. In 1872, Billings and Ellis began running a stage to Tecoma and Buel. During 1873, Moffitt and Gossett started a twice-weekly stage to Cherry

Creek, and Woodruff and Ennor started a triweekly stage to Schell Creek. In 1874, the Toano and Idaho fast freight line began operation. Critics said the line couldn't be run because of the ever-present mud in Thousand Springs Valley, but the company had few problems. The triweekly stage went through Contact on its way to Idaho.

A school opened at Toano in August 1874 with Cecelia Hunter as the first teacher. Fires plagued Toano during its early years, and a fire on February 8, 1873, destroyed the railroad roundhouse and three locomotives. Another fire on June 17, 1874, was started by Chinese residents launching fireworks. As a result, the Railroad Hotel was destroyed, and only heroic efforts saved the freight depot from burning.

Another violent death occurred in June 1881. A. R. Smith, the railroad ticket agent, fatally shot teamster William Nelson through the heart. Smith had the bad habit of kidding around and pointing empty guns at people, but unfortunately for Nelson, a loaded gun had been left in the office that day. The court decided that the shooting was accidental, and Smith was released.

While Toano had a population of 123 in 1880, the stage and freight market was already declining. The completion of the Oregon Short Line railroad in the Snake River area in 1884 ended all of the stage traffic heading to Idaho, and the town had to rely on the dwindling stage business to and from mining camps to the south for survival.

In 1887, John Cazier took over and operated the store and hotel in Toano, as well as the post office, until 1898, when he sold his property and moved to

Foundation of Cazier's hotel in Toano. (Photo by Shawn Hall)

Trout Creek in Starr Valley. In 1888, the Oasis Ranch Company was founded nearby. E. C. Hardy was the manager of an operation that raised Norman-Percheron stallions, Spanish merino sheep, and Angus and Galloway cattle.

When the Lucin Cutoff, to the east in Utah, was completed in 1904, the town was abandoned as a terminal point, and the repair depot closed. The Southern Pacific Railroad moved some of its buildings to the new division point at Bauvard, later Montello, and other buildings were torn down. Most of the town's businesses and residents moved, and the few that were left in 1906 moved to the new town of Cobre, a mile to the southeast, on the newly completed Nevada Northern Railway.

The post office closed on March 12 and reopened in Cobre. Postmasters at Toano included James Grant, Ferdinand Marx, Albert Spencer, Albert Gobbel, John Cazier, William Probert, Henry Ferstermaker, Leon Bednark, and Cordelia Spencer. Spencer was named the last postmaster when her predecessor, Bednark, quit in August 1905 and left the mail lying in the street.

The Toano school also closed and was moved to Cobre. Teachers at the school included Ermie Robinson, Bertha Smith, Mattie Gleason, and Lucy McDermot. The town of Toano was dead by the summer of 1906. Structures that were left were razed when the Southern Pacific rebuilt the tracks away from Toano and added a second set of tracks.

Today, though no buildings remain, there is plenty of evidence of the town. Huge stone foundations of the Marx store and the hotel are surrounded by many other foundations. Broken glass from the many saloons is everywhere, and a cemetery of more than thirty graves is located on the hill above town. However, vandalism and occasional cloudbursts have left only a few graves with legible markers, all of young children.

Ullin

DIRECTIONS: *Located 8 miles southwest of Montello on Nevada 233.*

Ullin is a signal station on the former Southern Pacific Railroad (now the Union Pacific). Nothing of consequence was ever built here, and only the foundations of a water tank mark the site.

Valley Pass

DIRECTIONS: *Located 5 miles northwest of Cobre.*

Valley Pass is a signal station on the former Southern Pacific Railroad (now the Union Pacific), created when the Lucin Cutoff, to the east in Utah, was completed in 1904. The Toano depot was moved to Valley Pass, and

*Southern Pacific water
tank is the only structure
at Valley Pass. (Photo by
Shawn Hall)*

sectionhouses and a large water tower were built. Considering the amount of traffic on the passing siding, there were few accidents at Valley Pass. One fatal incident occurred in July 1939 when brakeman Harry DeYoung was decapitated after falling under an engine's tender while attempting a "flying switch." The arrival of diesel locomotives in the 1940s made Valley Pass's steam locomotive facilities obsolete, and the buildings were moved to other locations.

Today, trains still run through Valley Pass. Only the foundations of the buildings and the impressive water tank, one of the few remaining in Elko County, guard the site.

Northeastern Elko County

Southwestern Elko County

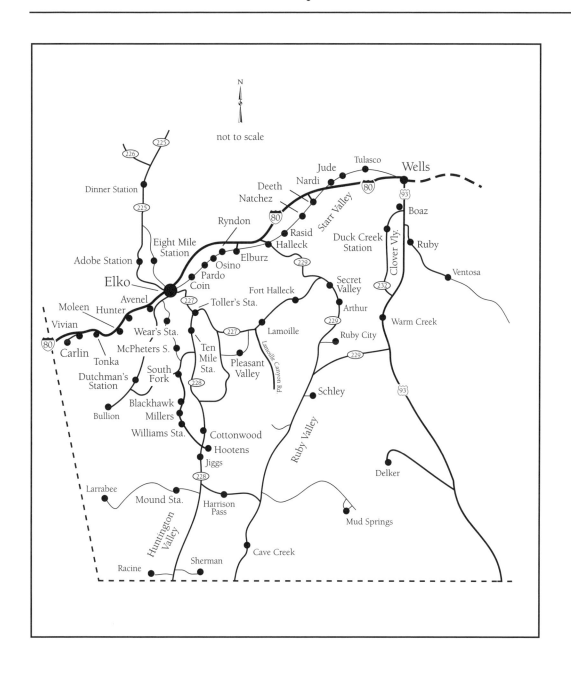

N

not to scale

225
226
Dinner Station
225
Jude
Tulasco
Nardi
Wells
Deeth
80
Natchez
93
Boaz
Ryndon
80
Eight Mile
Station
Rasid
Duck Creek
Station
Ruby
Halleck
Adobe Station
Elburz
229
Clover Vly.
Osino
Ventosa
Elko
Pardo
232
Coin
Fort Halleck
Secret
Valley
Avenel
Toller's Sta.
Moleen
Hunter
227
Arthur
Warm Creek
Vivian
227
Lamoille
229
80
Wear's Sta.
Ruby City
Carlin
McPheters S.
229
Lamoille Canyon Rd.
Tonka
Ten
Mile
Sta.
Pleasant
Valley
93
Dutchman's
Station
South
Fork
228
Schley
Blackhawk
Bullion
Millers
Williams Sta.
Cottonwood
Ruby Valley
Hootens
Jiggs
Delker
228
Larrabee
Mound Sta.
Harrison
Pass
Mud Springs
Huntington Valley
Cave Creek
Racine
Sherman

Adobe Station

DIRECTIONS: Located 7½ miles north of Elko on Nevada 225.

Adobe Station served as a stop for a number of stagecoach companies. Besides being a horse-changing stop for many years on the Elko-Tuscarora stage, Adobe was also a stop on Beachey's Elko-Idaho Toll Road beginning in 1869 until the toll road folded in 1871. With the boom at Cornucopia, a stage line and fast freight were operated from Elko by Woodruff and Ennor; unfortunately, the staging empire, once one of the largest in the West, was struggling at this time. The Elko-Cornucopia run was Woodruff and Ennor's last Nevada stagecoach line and was later sold to Smith Van Dreillan. He charged ten cents a head to feed and house horses. However, when the Cornucopia boom turned to bust, the local need for the stagecoach line ended and Van Dreillan moved on to run other stages.

Tragedy struck near Adobe in 1874. Deputy Sheriff John Ellis traveled, probably by horse, to Cornucopia to pick up a prisoner in February. However, the prisoner had escaped and Ellis headed back to Elko alone. Unfortunately, a blizzard began as he passed through Taylor Canyon. He was spotted by a stagecoach driver who encouraged Ellis to stay with him at his campfire, but Ellis was determined to get back to Elko and continued on alone. That was the last time he was seen alive. Search parties were dispatched, but his body was not found until May after the snow had melted. Ellis had apparently lost his way in the snowstorm and was found three miles west of Adobe. Various campsites Ellis had used were found, but there was no evidence of fire. Apparently Ellis's hands were too cold to use his matches to start a fire.

After Smith Van Dreillan abandoned the Elko-Cornucopia stage line, the Elko-Tuscarora Stage Company exclusively served Adobe. Fred Wilson, owner and operator of the line, built a new station after purchasing a 220-acre ranch for $2,600, which provided hay for stage horses. Adobe was the headquarters for the line, and rooms and meals were available there. However, an alternate route for the stagecoach line was established to the east through Eight Mile Station. In poor weather, this latter route was preferred, and travel through Adobe Station dropped off dramatically.

In 1886, Wilson sold the ranch to Emilio Dotta and his family, who ran the station. Dave Dotta, longtime mayor of Elko, was born here on April 1, 1887. The Dotta family sold the property in 1892 to John Paleni, who was born in Italy, who ran Adobe Ranch until 1910 when "Adobe John" Piccolo took over. By this time, the Elko-Tuscarora Stage was only a memory and the station had ceased to exist; only the ranch continued to operate. The Pattani family took over Adobe after Piccolo's death in the 1920s, and the land is still used for cattle grazing.

Not much remains of Adobe Ranch. Only crumbled buildings and scattered debris are left. It is impossible to determine which might be the ruins of the stage station.

Avenel

DIRECTIONS: Located 3 miles southwest of Elko on the Union Pacific.

Avenel, named after Avenel, New Jersey, is a nonagency siding on the former Southern Pacific Railroad (now the Union Pacific) west of Elko. Only a switching shed was constructed at Avenel. Nothing is left today.

Blackhawk

DIRECTIONS: From Elko, take the Spring Creek road southeast for 6.9 miles. Turn right and go 11 miles. Turn right and follow a gravel road west for 1 mile and then south along Huntington Creek for 4 miles to Blackhawk.

Blackhawk was a stop and horse-changing station on the Elko-White Pine Toll Road. The station, located four miles south of Shepherd's Station, was active for only a few years in the early 1870s. After that station became the main stop in the area, there was no need for Blackhawk, which was abandoned. Only a couple of rotted logs mark the site.

Boaz

DIRECTIONS: Located 5 miles south of Wells on the Union Pacific.

Boaz is a signal station on the former Western Pacific Railroad (now the Union Pacific) at the top of Clover Valley. However, when Boaz was established during Western Pacific construction in 1910, there was much more activity, Boaz having been the main shipping point for Clover Valley. Local residents gave the town a biblical name, Boaz, who was married to Ruth.

A couple of buildings were built to house a section crew and by the 1930s, a couple of families lived at Boaz. The residents at Boaz, Tobar, and Ventosa were all railroad workers, and considered each other family. They often got together for picnics; dances were held at the Tobar schoolhouse. However, the rise of truck use and improvement of the railroad reduced the need for section crews. By the late 1940s, Boaz had become just a siding. The buildings were moved or torn down, and not much remains at Boaz today.

Carlin

DIRECTIONS: Located 21 miles southwest of Elko on I-80.

Carlin, Elko County's oldest railroad town, came into existence in December of 1868 when the rails of the Central Pacific Railroad reached this point. The area had been settled in July 1868, when J. A. Palmer homesteaded in the area. Another man, S. Pierce, arrived soon after. However, no significant development occurred until the Central Pacific arrived. The town was named for Brigadier General William Passmore Carlin, a Civil War veteran, who had earlier directed the construction of Fort Weller in California.

A town formed around the railroad; a post office opened on December 4, 1868. Soon after, the Central Pacific Steam Fire Company, the first fire department in Elko County, was organized. The Carlin school district was established in July 1869 and built a $1,500 school in 1871. By 1875, a new two-story brick school replaced the original school, serving students until it was torn down in 1909.

Carlin quickly grew and became a major stagecoach hub for outlying mining towns. One of the first was George Bobier's Carlin and Idaho Toll Road, built in September 1869. An impressive stage station was built to serve the Pagne and Palmer and James Russell stagecoach lines, which ran to Mineral Hill, Bullion, Eureka, and Austin. When Cornucopia boomed in the early 1870s, the Carlin-Cornucopia stage was organized, also based at the Carlin stage station. A toll road was built up Maggie Creek to connect with the road to Tuscarora in Taylor Canyon. The road became a public thoroughfare in

1884. By the end of 1871, a variety of businesses and eight hundred people, including a Chinatown of former Central Pacific workers, called Carlin home. A library was built but burned in 1879 at a loss of $3,000.

Although Carlin had become well established by the 1870s, the growth of Elko overshadowed Carlin. During the 1870s, an intense competition developed between the two towns over the lucrative freight trade. With the emergence of Palisade, Carlin lost the Eureka trade. As the flow of wagon freight slowed down as Palisade and Elko took over, the railroad became the lifeline of the local economy. The Central Pacific had established Carlin as the eastern terminus of their Humboldt Division, and built a large roundhouse and extensive machine shops.

By 1880, Carlin's population had steadied at around five hundred and had its own jail, telegraph office, and numerous businesses that depended on travelers. The railroad was the largest employer in the town and built a new depot in 1906.

In the 1890s, a new ice-harvesting industry developed in Carlin. A number of people produced ice in local ponds, the first being W. F. Linebarger. In the first years, ice was used locally for businesses and private homes. The Western Pacific Railroad built its own ice pond and icehouse at the mouth of Maggie Creek in 1912 for use in its refrigerator cars and dining cars. However, limited water supply meant that the ice produced was reserved for Western Pacific trains. Pacific Fruit Express was organized in the 1910s and took over the Western Pacific operation. The company expanded, digging new ice ponds

Southern Pacific roundhouse at Carlin. (Leo Pacini collection, Northeastern Nevada Museum)

The Carlin railroad yards, 1920s. (Mel and Mae Steninger collection, Northeastern Nevada Museum)

on the Humboldt River, which involved extensive construction and included a mile-long loading dock, two five hundred–foot ice storage units, an office, and a two-story dormitory for the two hundred employees. The building contained bunk beds, showers, a kitchen, and dining rooms.

There were four other ice plants along the Humboldt Division, but Carlin was the only site producing natural ice. During the annual ice harvest in January and February, an additional two hundred men were hired. As much as forty-five thousand tons of ice were produced during a single harvest. The company provided much of the employment for Carlin during the Depression, but the advent of mechanical (diesel-powered) refrigeration cars meant the end of ice operations by 1950. Even during the 1940s, production greatly decreased, and the company's icehouse burned in November 1945 at a loss of $250,000. One by one, the remaining buildings were razed, and only one of the storage buildings remains to evidence the once extensive operation.

Newspapers were a short-lived but important part of Carlin's history. Although three papers were active at various times, none lasted long. The *Commonwealth* was the first, beginning publication on September 8, 1909.

The paper was founded by the Nevada Publicity Company and was a booster paper for the Democratic Party. A. B. Gray served as editor for the weekly paper, which cost $1.50 per year. Gray moved the paper to Deeth, where publication continued until 1914. The weekly *Western Home Builder* began publication on June 6, 1914, founded by W. T. McNeil, who also served as editor. The paper was suspended on November 23, 1916, when McNeil moved

Overland Hotel in Carlin, 1911. (Northeastern Nevada Museum)

Cutting ice in Carlin. (Claudia Riordan collection, Northeastern Nevada Museum)

Pacific Fruit Express ice plant at Carlin. (Ruth Nichols collection, Northeastern Nevada Museum)

the paper to Reno, where it became known as the *Nevada Home Builder* until it folded in 1921.

The last of the early papers was the *Nevada Democrat,* which began publication on February 9, 1917, with Joe Camp as owner and publisher. The paper was considered a successor to the *Western Home Builder;* McNeil was listed as an associate editor of that paper. Despite high hopes, the paper lasted only until April 6 before folding. More recently, the *Carlin Courier* began publication on May 7, 1976, run by Jan and Chuck Bunning. However, Carlin still could not support a newspaper, and it folded on August 4. In 1993, the *Carlin Express* came out with a weekly edition that is still being published.

Over the years, railroads continued to be the important part of Carlin's economy. With the phasing out of steam engines during the 1940s, the need for the roundhouse ended. It was dismantled in the 1950s except for one small part that still stands. An impressive railroad clubhouse, built in 1930 with forty-two rooms, marble counters and tables, a restaurant, and a barber shop, was nearby. The building burned in 1980 while being demolished. The locomotive turntable, originally turned manually by Chinese workers until it was electrified, was moved to Utah in 1993. Railroad operations continue today in Carlin.

A new boom now sustains Carlin. Microscopic gold was discovered along the Carlin Trend by Newmont Gold Mining Company during the 1960s. In February 1974, six men were arrested for stealing $700,000 in gold from Newmont's Carlin Gold Mine. Four of the men worked in the assay office, one was the shift boss at the refinery, and the other man was a gold dealer from California. The bullion was later recovered and new security methods put in place. Today, three of the five largest gold mines in the United States are within miles of Carlin. More than three million ounces a year are produced from Newmont and Barrick properties. Although most workers are bused from Elko, many families live in Carlin.

Today, Carlin retains much of its heritage. Most of the original town is located on the south side of the railroad tracks. Many buildings, including an old church, remain from the early years of Carlin. Sadly, a number of buildings have also fallen into disrepair. However, there are plans to restore what is left on the main street. In 1995, the Chinese Gardens Park was dedicated to commemorate the impact Chinese workers had on Carlin's early history.

Clover Valley
(Cloverdale) (Clover) (Wood)

DIRECTIONS: *From Wells, take U.S. 93 south for 5½ miles. Turn right on Clover Valley Road.*

The first homesteaders arrived in Clover Valley in 1865 when three army men from Fort Ruby (Captain Thurstin, Lieutenant Tolles, and Doctor Long) started a small homestead. They later sold their place to George Brumfield, who, at the time, also owned the Warm Creek Ranch in lower Clover Valley. After limited development, Brumfield sold to Francis Honeyman, a former lieutenant at Fort Ruby, in 1869. From 1868 to 1870, many new homesteads sprang up. Claus Schoer, John Skelton, William Gatt, John Woods, James Steele, William Smith, William Gibbs, Samuel Weeks, Mose Duval, and a number of others came to what was now called Clover Valley. A school opened in 1868 with eleven students, and by 1870, the school had thirty students. By this time, more than twenty thousand acres were being worked in the Valley. Population grew to eighty by the spring of 1870, and more than 140 by 1875.

In February of 1872, a sad event occurred in Clover Valley. A local rancher, Charles Billig, had been courting John Skelton's daughter. Billig proposed marriage but she rejected him. He later saw her riding with another man and chased after them, firing shots at the pair. The woman fainted but Billig, thinking he had killed her, stopped his horse and shot himself in the head. A letter was later found detailing his plan to murder Miss Skelton. Despite the tragedy, Clover Valley continued to grow. A post office opened on October 18, 1872, (William Smith, postmaster), but closed on September 10, 1873.

The mining boom at Spruce Mountain gave Clover Valley farmers an excellent market for their crops. Also, local residents Warren Angel and Abner and

*Clover Valley has two
extensive cemeteries
(Photo by Shawn Hall)*

Isaac Wiseman had mining interests in Spruce Mountain. Nearby Angel Lake
was named for Warren Angel. In 1872, the three men opened a store at the
Spruce Mountain camp of Jasper, and Clover Valley farmers kept miners supplied with fresh vegetables and fruits, dairy products, and beef. The Wiseman
family was a prominent family in Clover Valley. Abner was the fourth settler in
the valley, arriving in December 1867, joined soon after by his brother Isaac.
During the 1870s, Abner was a county commissioner and served on the local
school board. He died in August 1915.

Isaac Wiseman and his wife, Frances, had six children. Sarah Ann was born
in 1853 and married Robert Hamill, a telegrapher with the Central Pacific
Railroad in Wells, in 1874. She died in 1875. Hamill later married Sarah's sister Mary soon after. Hamill became a partner in the Hamill and Lassen Store
in Elko. The Hamills later moved to Wells, where Hamill opened a store with
George Meigs. Hamill also served as a Nevada state legislator from 1885 to
1893, and as a county commissioner. He died in 1894; Mary used $2,500 in
life insurance money to open the twenty-room Hamill House Hotel in Wells.

Isaac's son Abner Henry was born in 1858. He married Mary Angel, the
local schoolteacher, in 1883. Abner took over the Wiseman Ranch when Isaac
died in June of 1889. At his death, Isaac served as a legislator in the Nevada
General Assembly. Abner served six years as the justice of the peace for Clover
Valley, but died in 1907 at age forty-nine. Isaac's daughter Ruth Helen was
born in 1865 and married Warren Angel in 1885. Together they homesteaded
the Angel Creek Ranch and in 1890 built a five-room house. Angel served as
postmaster and justice of the peace in Wells.

In January 1873, the first white child, Bob Steele, was born in a log cabin on Steele Creek. His father, James, settled in Clover Valley during 1868. By 1877, the valley had a justice of the peace (H. H. Chase) and a constable (C. S. Petty), but there were no businesses in the valley. A saloon opened but was not a success among the religious residents of Clover Valley.

By 1880, Clover Valley boasted a population of 180. The Clover School, also known as the Signal School, was about one and one-half miles south of Steele Ranch. Clover Valley continued to be one of the most prosperous valleys in Elko County, but the severe winter of 1889–1890 crippled the valley, as it did most other agricultural areas of Nevada. Partners Samuel Weeks, W. B. Weeks, William Gibbs, and James Steele had put out more than five thousand head of cattle to pasture before winter, but after the spring thaw, had only 150 left. This loss forced a dissolution of the partnership. It took livestock ranchers in the valley many years to recover.

On January 7, 1896, the Clover post office opened with Charles Roland as postmaster. In March 1897, the Clover Community Hall was completed. It was a special Christmas in the valley in 1898 when Robert Steele married Katherine Honeyman, daughter of Francis Honeyman, a Fort Ruby veteran and early valley settler. In May 1901, local citizens formed the Clover Valley Building and Improving Association to build a church, library, hall, and cemetery.

The new Clover Valley Hall was the first project completed by the association and became the center of local entertainment. The Jolly Boys, a com-

Stone ruins in Clover Valley. (Photo by Shawn Hall)

edy troupe made up of local actors, was a popular attraction. In November 1901, an International Order of Good Templars lodge formed with eighteen members, Robert Steele serving as chief templar. Charles Roberts and Frank Winchell Sr. began manufacturing bricks, which were used to build many of the buildings in the valley. Another post office, named Wood, opened on the present-day Goodwin Ranch with Malinda Wood as postmaster. The office closed on December 15, 1902, and the Clover post office followed suit on March 14, 1903.

In 1905, William Gibbs, Samuel Weeks, James Steele, Horace Agee, and William Johnson formed the Clover Valley Land and Livestock Company, known locally as the Ox-Yoke outfit because of their ox-yoke brand. In 1910, the group purchased the Hardesty holdings, and became the largest operators in the valley. In 1914, some Clover Valley ranchers formed the Steptoe Company with Horace Agee as president. The company ran more than twenty thousand sheep and later merged with the Ox-Yoke Company. Agee moved to Wells, where he reorganized the Wells Bank and served as its president until 1932, when the Depression forced closure of the bank. The Depression also forced the Ox Yoke-Steptoe Company into receivership in 1933; the holdings were eventually broken up. The Western Pacific Railroad was completed through northern Clover Valley in 1908. A siding, named Clover, was constructed to feed livestock in transit. The presence of the siding made it easier for local ranchers and farmers to ship their goods.

The local ranching industry boom led to civic improvements for the residents. Although most residents were religious, a church wasn't organized until 1912 when the Wiseman, Agee, Honeyman, Weeks, and Steele families organized members of the community and built St. Luke's Episcopal Church. The church was active until the building was moved to Wells in the 1950s to serve as a sanctuary for St. Barnabas Church. Also, thanks to Samuel Weeks and the Leach Brothers, a large park was built.

A fire broke out in November 1914 on the Wiseman Ranch. Strong winds swept across the valley, devastating crops, livestock, buildings, and fences, although the valley's houses were spared. Damage was estimated at $35,000. Despite this setback, the valley rebounded and continued to be successful. The Clover Valley post office reopened on July 12, 1921, with Dessa Gibbs as postmaster until replaced by Horace Agee in 1922. The office permanently closed on October 31, 1924. The Depression caused many hardships in the valley, but did not have the dramatic impact it had elsewhere. In 1933, a Civilian Conservation Corps (ccc) camp opened in the valley.

A "geological treasure" discovered on the Weeks Ranch brought news coverage to Clover Valley during the 1930s. A number of fossils were found in the Elephant Tooth Well, a large natural hog hole on the ranch. While scraping out the hole to make a stock watering hole in 1930, the diggers found a number of white rocks. The rocks turned out to be fossilized teeth, but the well was not seriously explored until 1936 when the Nevada Department of Highways contracted with the Utah Construction Company to clean out the well to provide water for the construction of U.S. 93. During the cleaning, many more specimens were discovered and sent to Dr. Harry Wheeler at the MacKay School of Mines in Reno. Dr. Wheeler asked that work on the water hole stop so he could examine the site. In the summer of 1937, the S. Frank Hunt Foundation funded an expedition to the site by University of Nevada at Reno mining students. Hundreds of fossilized teeth from thirty different species were unearthed. One tooth was thirteen inches long and eight inches thick. The hole was examined further before most of the specimens were removed.

In May 1938, longtime resident Samuel Weeks died at age ninety-four. The Weeks family had a long legacy in Clover Valley. Weeks had come to the valley in March of 1869, and his first year was spent living in a dugout. He married Martha Ann Wood in 1874, and they had seven children. After his death, Weeks's holdings were sold to the Utah Construction Company. In 1949, due to a drop in school attendance, the Signal School consolidated with the Wells School District. Over the years, teachers at the Signal School included Mary Benson, Edna Sullivan, Kireta Portlock, Alice Van Leer, Nellie Anderson, and Jessie Ware.

In the early 1950s, local resident Ula Van Diver organized the Wells Chapter of the Nevada Association for the United Nations. News of her activities reached Washington, D.C. In October 1954, she received a personal letter on United Nations Day from President Eisenhower praising her efforts in "strongly advancing the cause of world peace."[1]

Clover Valley continues as a prosperous agricultural area. A number of pre-1900 homes and buildings still stand, and two cemeteries are located in the valley. The Wiseman Cemetery contains more than seventy graves. More than twenty graves are of infants, including six from the Duval family. The Clover Valley-Lampman Cemetery also has more than seventy graves. Clover Valley is one of the most beautiful areas in Elko County, nestled at the base of the East Humboldt Range mountains.

Coin

DIRECTIONS: *Located 3 miles northeast of Elko just south of I-80.*

Coin has served as a side track and signal station for the Western Pacific and Southern Pacific Railroads for many years. Coin's only claim to fame is that a small temporary camp formed here during the construction of the Central Pacific Railroad in 1869. However, nothing permanent was constructed because the construction camp moved with the advancement of the rails and nothing is left at Coin today.

Cottonwood

DIRECTIONS: Located 4 miles north of Jiggs on Nevada 228.

Located where Cottonwood Creek crossed Nevada 228, Cottonwood once had a post office, which was located on Cottonwood ranch, established by Billy Clendenning in 1869. The post office opened on December 14, 1869. The ranch also served as a stage stop on the Shepherd and Hill Beachey roads, which were active during the Hamilton and White Pine booms. The post office, with Mason Dexter as postmaster, lasted until July 12, 1870. Once the stage and freight lines to White Pine stopped running, Cottonwood returned to being a ranch. Owners of the ranch have included William Bellinger, James Riordan, Harold Arnold, J. J. Hylton, H. V. Hansel, Frank Rogers, Taylor Lawrence, and Lee Wilson.

Deeth

DIRECTIONS: From Wells, go west on I-80 for 18 miles. At the Deeth exit, go south for 1 mile. Turn left and continue for ½ mile to Deeth.

Before the town of Deeth was settled, the area was used as a seasonal Shoshone camp. Beginning in the 1840s, emigrants began passing the future Deeth townsite on the California Trail. There are two stories about the origins of the name Deeth. One is that an enterprising man named Deeth

Overview of Deeth, 1910. (Courtesy of Pauline Quinn)

Connecting the West

opened a small store and trading post on the banks of the Humboldt River about two miles from Deeth. Another is that early emigrants came up with a variation of the name Deeth, having called the site "Death" because if travelers didn't stock up with water at the Humbolt River, it meant death later on in the desert to the west. Journals from the 1840s refer to a place called Death to the west of Humboldt Wells (Wells). Because of the transient nature of travel on the emigrant trail before the coming of railroads, a settlement at Deeth did not develop at this time, although thousands of emigrants passed through.

Deeth formed in 1869 when the Central Pacific (CP) Railroad was built. As construction continued east to Promontory, Utah, the railroad built a siding station complete with a telegraph line. Only a couple of railroad employees lived at Deeth at first, and then slowly a town began to form. A post office, which was located in a boxcar that doubled as the railroad depot, opened on November 2, 1875, with John Donne as postmaster.

That same year, Tom Atkinson opened the first business in Deeth, a saloon. In 1877, James Porter built a two-story building that served as a store and hotel, and his brother, John, opened a livery business. Atkinson sold his saloon in 1879 to Ed Seitz, who was one of the first settlers in Pleasant Valley, and also served as an Elko County sheriff. Seitz immediately built a hotel addition to his saloon.

Deeth's population rose to thirty-one by 1880. The CP built a warehouse and water tank, and added a section crew. Deeth became the supply center and shipping point for Starr and Ruby Valleys, and a stagecoach to Mardis (Charleston) ran three times a week. In 1887, C. C. Truett built another hotel in Deeth, which was later purchased by William Mayer, who would eventually run the Mayer Hotel in Elko.

The Bradley cattle company was a boost to Deeth's economy and in particular, J. R. Bradley, who opened a store in Deeth, and later another at Mardis. His company competed directly with Porter; Bradley's newspaper ads listed Porter's prices and Bradley's lower prices. This spirited competition had Deeth residents smiling because the price wars led to prices as low as those in nearby Elko. In 1899, Porter gave up the battle with Bradley, and sold his store, eight-room hotel, house, corrals, and stables to A. C. Dorsey.

The Reverend Merchant Riddle organized the *Deeth Tidings* in January 1896. Riddle used the paper to promote the Free Silver Party platform. The newspaper was an eight-page weekly, with a subscription rate of $2 per year, edited by members of the local Good Templars lodge. Residents of Deeth relished their local paper, but there were too few subscriptions to make the paper viable. In September, Riddle moved his newspaper plant to Elko, and started the *Nevada Silver Tidings,* published until July 1899.

A school was also built in 1899; Isora Stevens taught thirty students during the first year. By 1902, the Dorsey Store and Hotel was run by William Mayer and Oliver McCall. In September 1903, Seitz's former hotel, then owned by Charles Standley, was set on fire by a cook smoking opium in his room. The hotel was destroyed.

By 1910, Deeth was approaching its peak, with new gold strikes at Jarbidge leading to a great revival of the stage and freighting business. Local businessmen and ranchers, along with financial backing from the Southern Pacific Railroad, raised $10,000 to construct a stage road to Jarbidge in an attempt to lure business away from Jarbidge's other source of supplies, Twin Falls, Idaho. The effort paid off and, except for when snow closed the road, Deeth enjoyed a lucrative trade. The fare to Jarbidge was $10; ten-horse teams left daily for Jarbidge.

In 1910, construction was completed on the Western Pacific Railroad through Deeth and a large depot. The town was surveyed by C. M. Haws in December 1910 and the township of Deeth was established. The town suffered a flood in 1910 when an ice jam piled up against the Western Pacific bridge east of town. This caused the Humboldt River to overrun its banks and flow through town. Luckily, damage was slight.

New businesses continued to open, including the Deeth Mercantile Company (Forbes and Hobson), housed in a four thousand–square-foot building, and the Deeth Creamery, built by A. B. Gray and E. C. Riddell in May 1912. The creamery produced two hundred pounds of butter per week, but closed within a year. The creamery building was later moved to Trout Creek at Welcome, and was used as a fish hatchery until abandoned when the Ruby Marsh hatchery opened. Gray brought other interests in Deeth, including his *Commonwealth* newspaper, which moved from Carlin to Deeth in February 1912. The paper was a Democratic weekly, published until October 1914 when Gray moved to Carson City, purchasing the *Carson Weekly*.

In 1912, Oliver McCall, part owner of a local store and hotel, won the mail contract to Jarbidge. He set up stations at Pole Canyon and Hank Creek. McCall developed a strong reputation, maintaining his twice-weekly delivery schedule even during tough winters. During the early 1910s, Deeth's population peaked at 250. There were two stores, two hotels, a dance hall, the Bradley Opera House (Lew Bradley), five saloons (Truett, Stanley, Mahoney Brothers, Nichols, and Parker), a slaughterhouse (Frank Orr), a red-light district, the Cannon Pool Hall, and twenty-five houses.

In July 1913, the Mahoney Brothers and Nichols Saloons burned at a loss of $10,000. This was the first in a series of devastating fires in Deeth. A huge fire, which started in the Mayer Hotel, struck Deeth in October of 1915. Before it had burned out, two-thirds of the business district was destroyed. Businesses burned included the Nicely Store, the Truett Saloon, the post office, and the rebuilt Mahoney Saloon. Although the exact cause of the fire was never established, inspectors labeled it suspicious, possibly to collect insurance money. This fire effectively ended Deeth's prosperous times.

The Southern Pacific and Western Pacific Railroads both had large depots in town, but the opera house was the pride of the town. Many touring troupes as well as the Deeth Orchestra performed there. Although religious services were occasionally held by Elko preachers in Deeth, no church was ever built in Deeth.

In January 1915, John Seabury started a new weekly newspaper, the *Deeth Divide*. However, no further mention is ever made of the paper, which apparently folded shortly after it began.

The arrival of the automobile lessened the importance of Deeth's remaining businesses. Many buildings and houses were later moved to Wells, Elko, and other locations. Another fire in the 1930s claimed the Bradley Opera House, since converted to a hotel, and the old Smiley store, home of the post office.

The Deeth school closed in 1957 after it consolidated with the Wells School District. The Western Pacific depot was moved to Crested Acres in the 1950s, where it is still used as a restaurant and bar. Deeth has a population of about twenty, but only a handful of original buildings survive. The Deeth post office remains open in a cinder-block building.

Through its years, Deeth had a number of prominent citizens. Two Nevada governors, Bradley and Russell, came from Deeth. State legislators included James Riddell, Ebenezar Riddell, David Johnston, Joseph Johnston, Jim Russell, Edward Murphy, Morley Murphy, and Hugh McMullen. Stanford Weathers was a West Point graduate, and Arthur St. Clair a Rhodes Scholar.

Duck Creek Station

DIRECTIONS: *Located on Wiseman Creek in northern Clover Valley, 2½ miles south of the junction of Clover Valley Road and U.S. 93.*

Duck Creek Station, located on Wiseman Creek in Clover Valley, was a stage stop on the Wells-Hamilton road beginning in the late 1860s. Martin Rush initially ran the station, but he left in 1879 after the Hamilton boom had ended and there was no further need for the station. A stone foundation marks the site.

Dutchman's Station

DIRECTIONS: *Located 6 miles northeast of Bullion on Bullion Road.*

Dutchman's Station was a horse-changing stop on the Bullion road, serving both George Shepherd's stagecoach line and J. F. Ray's Railroad Canyon Toll Road in the early 1870s. The station was abandoned by 1875 and not used again. Nothing remains of the station today.

Eight Mile Station
(The Barrels) (Pudjeau's)

DIRECTIONS: *From Elko, go north on Eight Mile Creek road for 8 miles to Eight Mile Station.*

Although not an official railroad stop, Eight Mile Station served an important purpose. The station was originally run by a Frenchman named Pudjeau, later mayor of Carson City, who collected tolls from travelers. Later, it was incorporated into the Smith Van Dreillan stagecoach line to Tuscarora. It was not a regular stop, but rather an emergency horse-changing station used primarily during winter when the alternate route over Adobe Summit was snowed in. Originally, three fifty-gallon whiskey barrels were sunk in the ground at the springs to provide water for horses and travelers. Only the springs remain today.

Elburz

(Peko)

DIRECTIONS: *From Elko, go east on I-80 for 15 miles to Devil's Gate interchange. Exit and follow a gravel road southeast for 3 miles to Elburz.*

Peko was the original name of Elburz station on the Central Pacific Railroad, completed through the area in 1869. It was named for a Chinese tea, in honor of the many Chinese workers employed during the railroad's construction. Long before the railroad was built, many emigrants passed through this area. The California Emigrant Trail, also known as the Humboldt Trail, came through the Peko site. During the 1840s and 1850s, approximately two hundred and fifty thousand emigrants passed through Nevada on their way to California. Although faint, the trail is still recognizable and has been marked by the Oregon-California Trails Association.

Matthias Glaser and partner Oliver McDonald purchased land at Peko in 1869 for $4 per acre. Glaser first camped at Peko in 1852 while on his way to California and remembered the place, eventually making it his home. Glaser built a large house, part of which was made from adobe bricks made at the ranch. He married Mary Peterson in October 1872, although she died in January 1880. Glaser then concentrated on expanding his ranch. The ranch's proximity to the railroad made it easy for Glaser to market his cattle herd. He married Anna Christine Brown in September 1888, and their first child was born the next year, when Glaser was sixty-two years old. During the next ten

Katherine, Walter, George, and Matthias Glaser. (Norman and Nelda Glaser collection, Northeastern Nevada Museum)

years, the couple had four more children at the ranch. The Glasers established a number of other ranches in the Halleck area, a few miles to the east. Two of these Halleck ranches are still in the Glaser family.

In 1899, Glaser bought out his partner's holdings. The next year, one of the coldest temperatures in Nevada history—60 degrees Farenheit—was recorded at Glaser's ranch. In 1903, a school opened with Stella Mayhugh teaching the Glaser children and others from the area. Glaser purchased the first mowing machine used in the area. The Buckeye mower cost $225 and although it was successful, its high cost limited its appeal. Telephone lines were strung to the ranch in 1905.

Glaser, who had struggled with a kidney disease for a several years, died of it in October 1907. An obituary in the *Elko Independent* showed the community's view of Glaser: "Matthias Glaser was one of the best citizens of this county. He was industrious, honest, and thrifty. His word in a business transaction was as good as minted gold. There was no evasion of trickery in his makeup. He dealt with his fellow men as he would like to be dealt with. In short, Matthias Glaser measured up to the true standard of American manhood."[2] Similarly, the *Elko Daily Free Press* reported: "He was very neat, everything had a place. The ranch was always spic-and-span and the building well-painted. He was kind and generous; never borrowed for himself, but lent money freely to worthy people without interest. He was honest, sincere, and friendly; respected and liked by his neighbors. He was a man typical of the Old West, his character possessing all the attributes which distinguished the old-time ranchers."[3]

After Glaser's death, his wife took over running the ranch until the children were old enough to do so. In 1916, the Glasers brought the first automobile to Elburz, a seven-passenger Studebaker, in which most of the Glaser children learned to drive. In 1922, the ranch holdings were divided among the children, each receiving their own ranch. In 1923, a $10,000 dairy plant was built at the main ranch, providing milk for Elko County for ten years before closing. Christine Glaser enjoyed her final years as a grandmother. She died of a thyroid condition in August 1935. Matthias and Christine Glaser's legacy lives on in their descendants who still live at Elburz.

Peko was renamed Elburz during the construction of the Western Pacific Railroad in 1908. Several railroad mishaps occurred at Elburz. In May 1877, the Central Pacific Railroad sectionhouse burned, killing one man and burning another. Another time, a train stalled in the snow between Elburz and Ryndon. Christine Glaser cooked meals for the crew and passengers for two weeks until the train was freed. In October 1913, H. H. Wright and some other friends were attacked by a drunken section crew, managing to escape only when a train came by. Disappointed, the section crew burned the water

Haying on the Glaser Ranch in Elburz, 1890s. (Norman and Nelda Glaser collection, Northeastern Nevada Museum)

tank. Two Western Pacific Railroad trains collided at Elburz in June 1928. A cook was hurt, and locomotive engines sustained $8,000 in damage.

Today, a number of ranches still operate at Elburz. Many original buildings, including Matthias Glaser's house, survive. In addition, railroad building foundations and other railroad equipment remain between the tracks.

Elko

DIRECTIONS: *Located on I-80, 289 miles east of Reno.*

THE EARLY YEARS

Long before a town was established here, thousands of emigrants passed by the California Emigrant Trail, or Humboldt Trail, during the 1840s–1860s. Many stopped at the Hot Hole, located just west of the future townsite. Elko, the heartbeat of Elko County, came into existence in December 1868 when the Central Pacific Railroad arrived. The central location of the town to mining camps and ranches ensured its permanence. Officials of the railroad began laying out lots on December 29. A number of stories explain the naming of Elko. However, the most commonly accepted version is that Charles Crocker, one of the Central Pacific's owners, having a strong fondness for animal names for railroad stops and engines, simply added an *O* to *Elk*. However, this notion seems incorrect since a number of other towns in the eastern states are named Elko and predate Elko's establishment.

On January 1, 1869, there were four canvas tents on the townsite selected by Len Wines and Frank Denver. Within another month, a tent town had sprung up and quickly became the center of an immense stage and freight system. A post office opened on January 29. Booms at Tuscarora and Hamilton (White Pine County) used Elko as the nearest and most easily accessible railhead. D. H. Haskell, Central Pacific land agent, began selling lots in Elko on January 15, 1869. The lots measured twenty-five feet by one hundred feet. The lots were $300 for inside and $500 for corner lots.

Within the first six weeks of 1869, six stage lines had been organized to run to the White Pine district, using the Denver-Shepherd Toll Road and the Gilson Turnpike, both running through Huntington Valley. By March 8, eight were active: Len Wines' Pacific Union Express, Hill Beachey, Woodruff and Ennor, Wells Fargo, Hughes and Middleton (former employees of Hill Beachey who ran numerous stage lines in Elko County and throughout Nevada), Thomas and Hall, Leander Swasey, and Payne and Palmer, who ran a stage line from Boise to Hamilton and used Elko as its hub. Beachey also had stage lines running to the north via the Elko-and-Idaho and Idaho Central Toll Roads.

Competition for freight and passengers to Hamilton was intense. At first, it cost a passenger $40 for the twenty-four-hour trip, but competition cut the

price quickly to $5, and travel time was down to seventeen hours. The intense competition forced many of the lines out of business. The Pacific Union line was sold to Wells Fargo, which didn't really want the line. However, the Pacific Union was controlled by the Central Pacific, which told Wells Fargo the railroad wouldn't carry their goods unless they purchased the Pacific Union. Len Wines, in turn, bought out the Thomas and Hall stage line.

In September, Wells Fargo left the stage business, selling their holdings to Hill Beachey. Soon after, Beachey and Wines merged their holdings. This was an interesting merger because the two, the most prominent stage operators in Elko County, had been bitter rivals. The Elko and Idaho toll road had been completed in July. In November, Beachey and Wines took over the Morgan and Enright Express and set up nine stations between Elko and the booming Cope District (later Mountain City). By the end of 1869, Beachey and Wines as well as Woodruff and Ennor were the only principal stage operators left in the county.

The bridge over the Owyhee River was completed in May 1870 and allowed Beachey and Wines to run mail, Wells, Fargo and Company shipments, passengers, and freight to Silver City, Idaho. The pair bought out Woodruff and Ennor's stage line during the summer, but it was too much for Beachey and Wines. Wines sold out to his partner, but Beachey was starting to have troubles. His vast empire began to fall apart and was losing mail contracts.

A new line, the Northwestern Stage Company, running from Elko to Boise, Idaho, made the situation worse. Competition between the two lines and failing mines in the Cope and Hamilton districts led both companies to suspend

operations at the end of 1871. The Elko-Boise route was later sold at the sheriff's auction for $115. Beachey, once the king of western stage lines, died broke in San Francisco of a stroke on May 23, 1875. However, stage lines continued to be a large part of Elko's economy. The emergence of Tuscarora and new mining discoveries in the northern part of the county kept stages and freight wagons running full, heading out on new stage lines.

Elko continued to grow and a new county, Elko, was formed by the Nevada legislature on March 5, 1869. Until that time, all of Elko County had been part of Lander County. By June 1869, Elko had twenty-two stores, ten blacksmiths, seventeen restaurants, eight doctors, eight attorneys, two hotels, and two banks. Elko also had five hundred tents and shanties, and a population of two thousand. Lot prices rose to $1,500 to $2,000. The *Elko Independent,* today the oldest continuously published newspaper in Nevada, began publication on June 19, 1869. A Western Union telegraph line was completed on July 7. W. P. Monroe began construction of a $17,444 brick courthouse.

The Central Pacific Railroad built a train depot, a hotel, and three large freight depots to accommodate the goods heading out on the freight lines. The Cosmopolitan Hotel also served as the ticket office for a number of the stage companies. The Cosmopolitan was renamed the Chamberlain, and later the Depot Hotel. The eighty-room hotel, one of the finest along the railroad, served passengers until it was torn down in 1904. One of the first businesses in Elko was the Reinhart Store, which continued to operate for more than ninety years.

By the end of 1870, Elko's population had settled down to a little more than one thousand. More than 120 businesses were in operation. The courthouse, at a final cost of $25,000, had been completed, as had a brick schoolhouse which accommodated one hundred students. In addition, the Presbyterian church was finished.

In October 1871, fire swept through Elko after starting in the Elko Hotel. High winds fanned the flames which burned everything from Third to Sixth Streets and wiped out Elko's Chinatown. Only four buildings were left after the fire, which caused $75,000 in damage. However, the fire did little to slow Elko's growth. The town continued to be the important shipping center for huge numbers of cattle. Extensive stockyards were constructed near today's site of Franklin Building Supply, near the junction of Idaho Street and the Mountain City Highway. Although mining booms came and went, the cattle industry was a mainstay of Elko's economy. Ranchers, with their consistent businesses, have helped many Elko companies survive when otherwise they might not.

In 1871, plans were made for the building of the Eastern Nevada Railroad. The line was planned to run along the old Elko-White Pine toll road, going from Elko to Eureka, then Hamilton, and finally, Pioche. The Eastern Nevada Railroad Company was incorporated on January 21. Incorporators were Volney Spaulding, John Mott, William Hendrie, Herman Sadler, Frank Wheeler, D. J. Elmore, John Treat, M. P. Freeman, L. Wilsey, N. Wescott, J. B. Fitch, and M. Lake. Treat was owner of the Cosmopolitan Hotel, Freeman was an Elko banker, Wilsey was owner of Elko Lumber Company, and Fitch was an Elko County Sheriff.

To facilitate the railroad's construction, the railroad company issued $150,000 in bonds in 1871. The company, however, made a big mistake. A petition signed by two-thirds of the taxpayers was needed to pass an ordinance authorizing the issuance of bonds, but hundreds of people had left Elko since the 1870 census. It became apparent that even if everyone voted, two-thirds still wouldn't be achieved. A reevaluation of the lists, however, allowed passage of the ordinance. In addition, White Pine County passed a similar ordinance for $200,000. Grading for the railroad started in Elko in August with Judge J. S. Mayhugh as superintendent of construction.

Unfortunately, the steam went out of the project, especially when a new railroad was planned from Palisade to Eureka and then Pioche. In January 1873, Salisbury and Gilmer of Salt Lake City revived the Eastern Nevada Railroad plans and organized the Elko and Hamilton Narrow Gauge Railroad Company. In February, the company reportedly bought 1,100 tons of rails, and a ball was held at the Cosmopolitan Hotel in April for the railroad executives. However, the plans were just a smoke screen for construction of another Gilmer and Salisbury railroad, the Salt Lake, Sevier Valley, and Pioche Railroad.

Local residents were outraged when the scam was revealed. Then, to make

Hot Springs Hotel in Elko, 1908. (Flora Billeci collection, Northeastern Nevada Museum)

matters worse, beginning in late 1873 Gilmer and Salisbury were instrumental in building the Eureka and Palisade Railroad. The Eastern Nevada Railroad was dead. After the floods of 1910 severely damaged the Eureka and Palisade Railroad and facilities at Palisade, there were hopes that the Eastern Nevada Railroad bed, already graded down to Eureka, would finally be utilized, but that never became a reality.

The Elko Hot Hole, near the White Sulphur Springs, was an early social center for Elkoans. The Hot Hole was discovered by the Frémont expedition of 1845. Although it was visited by early emigrants, the Hot Hole wasn't developed until 1869 when two men, Groepper and Laumeister, built the Humboldt Hot Springs Spa, which included a hotel, barn, and an enclosure around the springs. In 1870, Laumeister was replaced in the partnership by C. R. Van Aelstyn. In 1871, Van Aelstyn became sole owner.

The Elko Mining and Soap Deposit Company bought the property in 1879 and leased the bathing department to J. J. Garrecht. Garrecht died in 1880 but his wife, Gertrude, with the help of her father and four children, ran the business and eventually bought the property. Under her ownership, the hot springs became a popular resort. Four times a day, carriages brought people from the Humboldt House in Elko, one and one-half miles away. In June 1882, fire destroyed all of the buildings, but Garrecht soon rebuilt them with the aid of the townspeople of Elko. Fire again destroyed the hotel in June 1899 and Garrecht rebuilt again, this time with bricks.

An interesting phenomenon occurred during April 1916. The hot springs were violently disturbed by a distant earthquake. The water turned milky, rose a couple feet, and the temperature rose dramatically. Within a few months, the springs had returned to normal, but they were now much hotter, so much so that bathing in them was uncomfortable. Needless to say, this led to a drastic drop in business for Garrecht. She continued to operate the hotel until it was sold in October 1919 to Elko County for use as a county poorhouse, later a rest home, and finally a home for the mentally retarded. Gertrude Garrecht died in November 1933 at age eighty-nine, after being a resident of Elko for sixty-four years.

The hotel continued to serve the county for many years, but time took its toll on the facility. In 1989, it was closed because of structural weaknesses. A number of attempts were made to save the building but there was insufficient financial backing. The hotel was demolished in January 1992, and an important part of Elko County's history was lost forever. The Hot Hole, still too hot to swim in, is fenced off. Over the years, some people have perished in the waters. The bottom of the springs has never been found, and some of the victims' bodies were never recovered.

ELKO NEWSPAPERS

Newspapers have always played an important role in Elko's history. The *Elko Independent* came into existence after Edward Davison Kelley bought the plant of the *Humboldt Register and Workingman's Advocate* of Unionville and brought it to Elko. The first issue appeared on June 19, 1869. The paper was four pages long; a subscription cost $8 per year. The paper was published on Wednesday and Saturday. Kelley's greeting to the town was published in the first issue:

> In modern times, no young town or city can hope to become great or prosperous in the land without a newspaper to herald abroad its rising glories and to convince the outside world that it has a local habitation and a name.
>
> In assuming to become the medium through which the public voice of Elko shall be made to reach and vibrate on the living, throbbing nerves of the commercial system throughout the civilized world, we propose to map out roughly the aims and purposes which will govern our course.
>
> Of political literature the country has had a surfeit, and now demands nothing so much as to be let severely alone; and while this is the case generally throughout the country, it is more especially so in all new communities, where the chief business of the people is to subdue the wilderness, coerce the treasure-ribbed mountains to yield up their virgin stores, and to mold and direct the channels of commerce in obedience to their will.
>
> Amid the perils which environ the pioneer at every step amid the doubts which lower over and shroud in the mists of uncertainty his every enterprise, whether in mining, commercial, or agricultural pursuits, he has but little spare time to waste in giving ear to the partisan shrieks of the political vultures who would climb to power over their country's ruin, did it but promise to them a selfish reward. Knowing that the people are weary of political discussion and long for a season of tranquil repose, we have

resolved to sound a truce to distracting contentions upon the philosophy of human government, and will therefore carry no bunting aloft inscribed with partisan devices.

We believe we rightly comprehend and appreciate the true wants of our fair young village, and to meet and supply these wants will be the burden of our thoughts and the aim of our labors. Already has our town suffered great detriment abroad from the malice of willful defamers, and the envy of ambitious rivals. To correct false impressions that may go abroad, and to present in truthful colors the manifold advantages which this locality possess[es] over all others on the line of the Continental Railway from Sacramento to Omaha as a commercial emporium and depot of supplies for a vast area of rich mineral country, will be our constant aim.

We will endeavor to make the *Independent* a true and faithful expositor of the material interests and resources of Elko County, and a faithful medium for conveying to the outside world a complete record of everything transpiring in our midst from day to day worthy of note. We will start a semi-weekly, to be followed by a daily as soon as the general news dispatches can be had at this place over the wires, which will be in the course of a month, or as soon as the new line of telegraph, now being pushed from both ends of the road, can be completed. At present no dispatches can be had over the company's wire, as it is too much occupied with company business to accommodate the public.[4]

First advertisers in the paper included the Humboldt Brewery (L. Bischoff), P. M. Eden and Company, bankers (Commercial and 4th), Oppenheimer and Company dry goods (Commercial St.), Goldstein Brothers store (Commercial St.), Morris Badt and Gabriel Cohn dry goods, Elko Hotel (Henly and Fisher), Elko Lumber Yard (L. Wilsey & Co.), P. Quinn dry goods (Commercial St.), California Restaurant (Liebes Brothers), Tuolumne Saloon (Haag and Daverly), Lager Beer Bakery and Brewery (L. Kraus), Brilliant Restaurant (William Evans), St. Charles Hotel (Frank Drake and A. Skillman), Railroad House (Parkell and Nolan), Ocean Spray Saloon (Brady and Mulick), Miners' Restaurant (Henry Bramley), Central Pacific Hotel (Marcel, Towne, & Co.), Elko Chop House (Alfred Mendessol), San Francisco Bakery (Jacob Hiersen), and Smith and Douglas, druggists.

Kelley, however, quickly became disillusioned with Elko and sold out in July to Judge George Berry and Charles Perkins. Kelley left Elko and later became Nevada surveyor general. In 1870, Perkins was elected state printer and moved to Carson City, where he purchased the *Nevada Appeal*.

C. S. Wright and S. S. Sears bought the *Elko Independent* on January 4, 1873. A daily edition ran from August 17, 1875, to January of 1919, when it was reduced to a tri-weekly, and then a weekly. Sears ran the *Independent* until selling it to C. W. Grover on December 31, 1886. W. W. Booher took over in

1892 and ran the *Independent* until he retired in September 1914. A number of other owners ran the paper for short periods until Harold Hale purchased it in September 1920. Hale's tenure continued until his death in January 1931. Warren "Snowy" Monroe bought the *Independent* on March 1, 1937. His tenure was the longest, lasting until 1975, when longtime employee Max Wignall took over. He sold the paper in January 1994 to the Sam McMullen family.

The *Elko Chronicle* was first published on January 5, 1870, and was organized primarily to promote Republican candidates in the 1870 election. This, of course, put it in direct competition with the staunchly Democratic *Independent.* The paper was run by the Chronicle Publishing Company and was edited by T. J. Butler. After the election, the paper was sold to William Taylor. However, the owner of the *Independent,* Charles Perkins, had left to serve as state printer. He offered the running of the *Independent* to Taylor, who accepted. Taylor closed down the *Chronicle* after two issues. The paper's equipment was moved to Pioche and used to publish the *Pioche Review* and later the *Pioche Record.*

The *Elko Leader* is a mystery. The first issue appeared on January 1, 1873, but it apparently folded soon after. No copies of the paper have ever been located and additional information as to ownership is unknown.

The *Elko Post* came into being on September 11, 1875, and was owned by C. C. Powning and E. A. Littlefield. Littlefield became sole owner on October 7, 1876, but his biggest claim to fame was that he established the *Times,* a forerunner of the *Tuscarora Times-Review,* in Tuscarora in March of 1877. The weekly *Post* continued to April 30, 1881. Littlefield then moved the presses to Ogden, Utah, to start up the *Ogden Pilot.*

The *Elko Free Press* came into being on January 5, 1883. Charles Sproule, who had been running the *Lander Free Press* at Battle Mountain, moved his press to Elko and organized the *Free Press* as a Republican weekly, with a subscription rate of $5 per year. For more than one hundred years now, the Republican *Free Press* and Democratic *Independent* have carried on a lively banter and friendly competition. During election years, Sproule would increase the paper's publication to a daily to help spread the Republican word. He fell ill in September 1904 and had to retire after twenty-one years.

The paper was purchased by a group of Elko businessmen who formed the Free Press Publishing Company and began producing a daily edition in addition to the weekly. On November 14, 1910, E. M. Steninger bought the Free Press Publishing Company, and began a Steninger tradition that continues today. The weekly edition ended in February 1917. Chris Sheerin, a prominent Elko resident, joined the *Free Press* as editor in 1941. E. M. Steninger retired in 1945 and sold the paper to his son, Eber, and Chris Sheerin. After their retirement in 1969, Mel Steninger and Earl Frantzen took over the publishing of the paper. Both have since retired, but the Steninger family still owns the paper.

Other newspapers served Elko but were short-lived and had relatively little impact: *Nevada Silver Tidings* (September 1, 1896–July 15, 1899), *Daily Argonaut* (September 1897–February 6, 1899), *The Telegram* (May–June 1909), *Elko Enterprise* (December 1, 1916–February 9, 1917), and *Nevada Farmer and Stockman* (published by the Free Press Publishing Company in 1921 and 1922).

EDUCATION

Education also played an important role in Elko's development. The first school was built after School District #1 was organized in 1869. A $3,000 brick schoolhouse was opened on January 3, 1870, with 70 students. This building still stands at 421 Court Street. Only six months later, 140 students attended school. This necessitated the construction of a new two-story brick school in 1877. It wasn't until 1895 that the Elko County High School opened. This was the first county high school in Nevada. Boardinghouses were built nearby to house students who came from all over Elko County to live and attend school.

The pinnacle of local education was the establishment of the University of Nevada in Elko during 1874. The process began in February 1872 with a meeting to submit a bid before a March 1 deadline. A great advantage for Elko was that the governor at the time was Elko County businessman Lewis Rice "Broadhorns" Bradley. Other towns bidding for the university were Genoa, Carson City, Washoe City, Washoe Valley, and Reno. Elko's bid of $28,000 far surpassed that of the next nearest city, Reno, which tendered a bid of $10,000.

On March 7, 1873, Governor Bradley signed the bill establishing the university at Elko. The University Executive Committee was made up of Chairman Merrill Freeman (county commissioner and banker), Simon Reinhart (merchant), Gabriel Cohn (merchant), Samuel Mooser (merchant), John Mayhugh (local U.S. land registrar), J. H. Lucas (lawyer and district attorney), G. B. Kittridge (water company official), Levi Wilsey (owner of Elko Lumber Company), Thomas Biglin (liquor store owner), Thomas Henley (superintendent of schools), and Deputy Sheriff J. J. Ellis. Clinton Day was selected as the architect and local contractors J. B. Fitch and James McBurney were paid $5,000 to provide stone and brick.

The main building was thirty feet by fifty feet with two wings of twenty feet by twenty feet each. The building ended up costing $15,000. The school was completed in January 1874, one month ahead of schedule. David Sessions was appointed principal on July 18 and classes began on October 12. Although the school had a capacity of one hundred, only seven students attended the

D. R. Sessions, first principal of the University of Nevada in Elko. (Northeastern Nevada Museum)

The main University of Nevada building in Elko, built in 1873, which later served as the Elko County Hospital. (Elko County Library collection, Northeastern Nevada Museum)

first semester: Margaret Yeates Keyser, Jessie Yeates Hesson, Frank Rodgers, Allen Penrod, James Gallagher, Sarah Gillan Muller, and Charles Rood.

Opposition to the school being placed in Elko came from all parts of the state, and only softened after the regents visited the university at the end of the school year. When school started in the fall of 1875, there were sixteen students. In January 1876, a dormitory was completed at a cost of $7,000. By March 1877, the university fielded its first athletic team, a baseball squad captained by James Gallagher. The first game was played against the Elko Royal Exclusives, which the students won, thirty-one to twenty-two.

Problems were increasing for the university. Enrollment continued to be low and most of the students were local. This prompted other towns, particularly Carson City and Reno, to label the school a failure. In January 1880, Charles Stevenson of Storey County was reappointed as regent. He was an outspoken critic of the Elko site and constantly worked to move the school to western Nevada. The *Reno Gazette* reported, "The State University reopened in Elko today. As the pupil is not due until next week, the faculty will not have anything to do until he arrives."[5] However, in 1882 the school had its highest enrollment yet of thirty-three.

The legislature continued to be extremely stingy with funds for the school. In 1883, the principal's salary was cut from $5,000 to less than $2,000. The 1884–1885 school year was the last in Elko. Although some newspapers in western Nevada supported keeping the school where it was, Elko's population had dropped below one thousand while Reno's had risen to more than four thousand. The university in Elko closed on July 10, 1885, and moved to Reno. The university building was converted into a county hospital until it was demolished in March 1920 to make room for the Elko High School gymnasium. The building was torn down by George Bowers of Lamoille. He paid $300 for the structure and used the wood to build a barn on his property in Lamoille.

In 1967, a group of Elkoans, including Bob Burns Jr., Mark Chilton, Hugh Collett, Fred Harris, Al Huber, Mike Marfisi, Les Moren, Paul Sawyer, Carl Shuck, and Bill Wunderlich, spearheaded the drive to form the Elko Community College. This was the first community college in the state. The group raised $46,000 and in September the school opened.

When the Nevada State Legislature refused to provide funds for Elko Community College in 1968, an unlikely benefactor, Howard Hughes, saved the school by donating $125,000 for operating costs. In 1969, the state began providing funds for the school and later made it the cornerstone of the Nevada community college system. For six years, the college was run in Elko High School and Grammar School #1, later called the Kate St. Clair Elementary School. The school's name was changed to Northern Nevada Community College. It was moved to its present campus in 1973 and continues to grow and expand with a new name, Great Basin College. There are plans to make it a four-year institution.

Another important educational facility for Elko began to be organized in 1919. The Elko County Library was formed by women members of the Twentieth Century Club. The first official library was opened on the second floor of the old Elko County High School building. The first librarian was Rae Caine. Disaster struck the library in April 1942 when fire completely burned out the second floor, which housed the library. Some books were saved, but most were lost.

The library was temporarily housed in the Knights of Pythias Hall until the first floor of the original building was refurbished. Ruthe Gedney Gallagher was extremely dedicated to the library and, beginning in 1941, served more than forty years on its board of directors. Thanks to the Max Fleischmann Foundation and other donors, a new library, built at a cost of more than $550,000, was dedicated in April 1974. Under the guidance of recently retired library director Hailie Gunn, who served for twenty-five years, the Elko County Library has continued to be a progressive organization, providing the best for both students and residents.

ELKO MATURES

The town of Elko was incorporated by a special act of the Nevada legislature. In May 1917, a city council was formed and John Alexander McBride was selected the first mayor. McBride and his wife, Emily Bonnifield, moved to Elko in 1886. He managed the W. T. Smith Company, served as Elko

1907 Elko High School girls' basketball team, the first to compete with other schools. (Alberta Keppler collection, Northeastern Nevada Museum)

County treasurer, and in 1915, he and his son, Allen, bought the Elko Lumber Company. Before becoming mayor, he was instrumental in the passage of the legislation that established the Elko County High School.

David Dotta was another prominent Elko mayor. He served from 1929 to 1955. Dotta was born at the Adobe Ranch, north of Elko, on April 1, 1887. His family ran the station on the Elko-Tuscarora stage road. He helped his father, Emilio, develop real estate. While in high school, Dotta played on the first Elko High School football team in 1903. His first political office was on the city council in 1921. During his long tenure as mayor, he purchased a large volume of property for the city, thereby allowing for future growth. David Dotta died in 1975.

ELKO ENTERTAINMENT

Entertainment had always been a big part of Elko's history. The first opera house operated out of a tent owned by Bob McGinley in 1869. Grotto Hall was the first permanent entertainment structure in Elko, built during the summer of 1869. Due to demand for a stylish performance center, banker Merrill Freeman built the adobe brick Freeman Opera House on Railroad Street. Later, the Bradley Opera House, located where the Commercial Hotel parking lot is today, served the community from the turn of the century until its demolition in the 1960s, a host to travelling troupes, stage plays, graduations, dances, and athletic events. The opera house was the cultural center of Elko for many years.

Sometimes entertainment came in the form of celebrity visits. In July 1928, Charles Lindbergh radioed Elko from his airplane that he was running low on fuel. By the time he landed at the airport, a crowd had gathered to watch him refuel. Sports have also provided local entertainment. High school sporting events have always drawn enthusiastic crowds. For many years, Elko had a semipro team in the Humboldt Valley Baseball League, active from the 1910s to the 1930s. In addition, Red Ellis, owner of the Commercial Hotel, also sponsored a semipro team in the 1940s. During the Depression, with the Henderson Bank failing, local entertainment became a necessity to help ease the pain of the era.

Elko, long before Las Vegas achieved prominence, was the first home of big-name entertainment and gambling in Nevada. The prime mover was Newton Crumley Jr., owner and operator of the Commercial Hotel. When the show lounge in the Commercial Hotel was completed in April 1941, the first entertainer was Ted Lewis and his world-famous orchestra. He was paid $12,000 per week. The local population could not believe that Lewis was actually coming to Elko. Rumors flew that perhaps Lewis's orchestra would be there, but surely Lewis would not. The rumors were wrong, Lewis appeared

Looking down Railroad Street in Elko from the Depot Hotel, 1876. (Tony and Ellen Primeaux, Northeastern Nevada Museum)

Elko's Humbolt Valley Baseball League semipro team, 1897. (Jack Smales collection, Northeastern Nevada Museum)

with his orchestra, and soon a parade of stars followed. Casino owners found that having big-name entertainment raised gambling revenues by a substantial amount. In fact, Lewis spent all he earned and more at the Commercial tables and had to sign an IOU promising a return engagement.

Over the next few years, huge crowds showed up at the Commercial Hotel to see entertainers such as Sophie Tucker, Paul Whiteman, Ray Noble, Chico Marx, Ted Fio Rito, Gertrude Miesen, and Donald Novis. In every contract signed, there was a clause which required each performer to give a free performance to the children of Elko. The children's shows were held in the Hunter Theater. Crumley also brought the shows to the Wendover Army Air Base during World War II. The Stockmen's Hotel also got into the act when its Round-up Room opened. The opening act in August 1946 was Hi Davis, Ann Triola, and the Andrini Brothers. Other stars such as Burl Ives, Margaret Whiting, Rex Allen, and Tennessee Ernie Ford followed.

With the Crumleys and Red Ellis in competition, Elko residents were treated to only the best entertainment. Upon completion of the Ranchinn, which had a large showroom, more entertainers made the trek to Elko. The

Ranchinn's grand-opening celebration in the late 1940s featured Tex Ritter and Henry Busse. Other stars such as Bing Crosby, Spike Jones, Nelson Eddie and Jeanette McDonald, Rudy Vallee, Tommy Dorsey, the Sons of the Pioneers, Vikki Carr, and Wayne Newton (then twelve years old) also performed in Elko. At the peak of Elko's entertainment boom during the 1950s and 1960s, the Commercial Hotel had a budget for entertainment of $600,000. However, the emergence of Las Vegas and Reno, with their fabulous facilities and higher wages, brought an end to big-name entertainment in Elko. However, the Stockmen's, Commercial, and Red Lion Hotels continue to bring live shows to Elko, which will always be remembered as the first home of Nevada's entertainment industry.

ELKO HOTELS AND CASINOS

Hotels played a major role in Elko. Among the early facilities were the Humboldt Lodging House and Depot Hotel, both built in the early 1870s. The Humboldt Lodging House evolved into the Commercial Hotel, while the Depot Hotel closed in 1904 and was razed by the Southern Pacific Railroad. Charles Mayer, the Depot Hotel's last manager, built the Mayer Hotel on the site of the old Gem Hotel. Years later, the hotel was remodeled and renamed the Stockmen's. Other post–turn-of-the-century hotels included the Star Hotel (built by Pete and Matilda Jauregui in 1910), the Overland Hotel (built in 1908 by Domingo Sabala and Eulalie Onandia), the Clifton (1915), the Pioneer (1913), and the impressive Ranchinn (1946).

The Stockmen's Hotel opened on July 24, 1944, after William Mayer, son of Charles, sold the old Mayer Hotel to Red Ellis and A. C. Bigham. The two men opened the Roundup Room, which hosted some of the biggest names in show business at that time. Red Ellis sold the hotel in 1952 to Dan Bilbao Sr., J. B. Dollard, and V. J. McGee, and then temporarily retired. In 1955, he bought the Commercial Hotel and Ranchinn for more than $1 million. The Stockmen's Hotel burned in a spectacular fire in March 1957. Local people wept as they watched the flames destroy the hotel and its centerpiece, a $5,000 stuffed Kodiak bear. The building was rebuilt quickly and had a grand reopening in October 1958. A million-dollar expansion was completed in 1968.

The Commercial Hotel grew from the Humboldt Lodging House. It was built by John Krattinger in 1871 and was purchased in 1873 by J. J. Garrecht. Joseph Lang entered into a partnership with him in 1877. Lang took over sole ownership in 1879 and ran the lodging house until he sold out and retired in June 1893. J. B. Abel remodeled, added livery and feed stables, and renamed it the Commercial Hotel. Newton Crumley Sr. bought the Commercial from William Doyle in October 1925 for $70,000. His son, Newton Crumley Jr., began to work with his father in improving the hotel, including the addition of The Lounge, which brought in top name entertainers for the first time to Nevada.

Newton Crumley Jr. took over operation of the Commercial when he returned from serving as a pilot in World War II. He immediately built the Ranchinn Motor Hotel, the first state-of-the-art casino resort built after the war, which had its grand opening on December 21, 1946. In 1949, *Life* magazine ran a story on Elko County and named Crumley Elko's number one businessman-impresario, with links to Hollywood and Broadway. Crumley sold the Commercial and Ranchinn in June 1955. He then bought the Holiday Hotel in Reno. Crumley died in a plane crash in Monitor Valley (Nye County) in February 1962. The military flying ace lost control of his plane after it iced up heavily and then plunged to the ground. Also killed was E. J. Questa, president of the First National Bank of Nevada.

Red Ellis and Dick Warren bought the Commercial in October 1955. They added a new lounge and purchased Lee McCarty's famous Gunfighter Collection of paintings. The trademark Kodiak bear, White King, was installed above a new entrance in 1970. Ellis continued to run the Commercial until his death in 1991. He also developed a number of shopping centers and the Red Lion and Holiday Inn properties. Ellis was also one of the founders of the Silver State Stampede and sponsored a semipro baseball team in Elko, which was affiliated with the Boston Red Sox. The Commercial Hotel and Casino, which underwent a complete renovation in 1994, and the Stockmen's have been owned since 1995 by Marcie and Jack Simon and Pete Lusich.

The Pioneer Hotel has Elko roots back to 1868 when the Pioneer Saloon opened in a tent on the present site of the hotel. The impressive three-story brick hotel was completed in March 1913. The Pioneer Saloon was incorporated into the new building. The saloon's original mirrored back bar is still at the Pioneer Hotel today. The hotel, originally owned by Frank Robinson and George Ouderkirk, cost $50,000 and was one of the town's first fireproof structures, and the first building in Elko to be electrically lighted. The hotel had thirty-four rooms. Kenneth Scott, who purchased the hotel at a county auction in August 1945, obtained a gaming license, and for the first time, legal gambling took place at the Pioneer Hotel.

In 1950, Scott added a penthouse as living quarters for himself and his wife, Jeanette. The bar also had an odd attraction, a stuffed two-headed calf. The calf was born on the W. W. Kane and Sons ranch in South Fork and lived only a short time. The calf served as a strange conversation piece for many years. Scott sold the hotel to the Chilton and Trounday families in April 1981. It was the first time the saloon had closed in 112 years.

Over the years, the Pioneer Hotel building had greatly deteriorated and had to be completely gutted. After $2 million was spent, the hotel re-opened in September 1983 but closed in December when backing from a Florida partnership ended. However, the building, after years of being empty, was reopened in 1992 to serve as the Western Folklife Center, sponsor of the world-famous annual Cowboy Poetry Gathering. The old back bar has been restored, and the main floor houses exhibits, a gift shop, and a performance auditorium. Upper floors are now used as offices.

BING CROSBY AND ELKO

Bing Crosby was the most popular entertainer in Elko and the town became his adopted home. Crosby ended up buying seven ranches during the 1940s in Elko County: the PX, Spring Creek, Bellinger, Evans, Wright, Truett, and Johnson-Laing. He bought the PX ranch from Newton Crumley Jr., for $221,000, and the two men were close friends until Crumley's death in 1962. Crosby, his wife, Dixie, and their four sons all lived in Elko County during the summers. Crosby loved life in Elko. It was an escape from the pressures of Hollywood and a chance for seclusion and privacy. The people of Elko made him feel comfortable, and he said, "If I'm known at all, it is simply as that fellow from California with a pretty nice cattle-cow-and-calf outfit up near Wildhorse." He greatly appreciated Elkoans' neighborliness and their respect for his privacy.

Bing Crosby was named Honorary Mayor of Elko in 1948. February 7 was proclaimed Bing Crosby Day, and Elko mayor David Dotta presented Crosby with the key to the city. His first act was to donate $5,000 for the construction of a new swimming pool. He then pledged to close down all of Elko's saloons, once everyone was inside. A photograph that appeared throughout the country showed David Dotta teaching Crosby how to properly sweep the

Blue Serge Day in Elko in honor of Bing Crosby, June 30, 1951. From left to right: *Lee Frankovich, Mayor Dave Dotta, Honorary Elko Mayor Bing Crosby, and Dick Warren (Dave Dotta family collection, Northeastern Nevada Museum)*

streets with a broom. In 1950, Crosby was adopted into the Western Shoshone Paiute tribe at Owyhee. A big celebration was held, and he was given the Indian name *Sond-Hoo-Vi-A-Gund*, "Man of Many Songs."

Bing dressed casually when away from Hollywood, favoring jeans and a straw hat. In 1951, a hotel clerk in Vancouver, British Columbia, refused to allow Crosby to register because he looked like a bum. Hearing this, members of the Elko Silver State Stampede made arrangements with Levi Strauss to make a pair of Levi Tuxedos. Blue Serge Day was held on June 30, 1951, and the tuxedos were presented to Bing and Dotta. The label on the inside, signed by Levi-Strauss president D. J. O'Brien, read: "Notice to Hotel Men Everywhere. This label entitles the wearer to be duly received and registered with cordial hospitality at any time and under any conditions. Presented to Bing Crosby, on Elko Blue Serge Day, Silver State Stampede, June 30, 1951."

Because of Bing's appreciation of the Elko residents, he hosted a number of benefits for local causes. In July 1951, Elko was the scene of a world premiere of the Bing Crosby movie *Here Comes the Groom*. Money raised during the three-day celebration went to the Elko County Hospital Building Fund. Celebrities from all over the country were in Elko that day: Utah governor J. Bracken Lee, Nevada governor Charles Russell, Nevada congressman Walter Baring, Alexis Smith, Dorothy Lamour, the Cass County Boys, Ray Evans, Jay Livingston, and Ted Husing. CBS hosted a live radio coast-to-coast broadcast. Nearly $10,000 was raised for the hospital building fund. Bing later helped raise funds for a new city swimming pool, even bringing his friend Roy Rogers to attend a fund-raising box social hosted by the Tuscarora Homemakers Club.

Crosby also wrote a song titled "Comin' to Elko," as a tribute to the friends he made while living here:

> Well, we moved to Elko County about a dozen years ago.
> We bought a ranch on the river when the river was nice and low.
> But when things started melting, the river it began to swell.
> And all the cattle went swimming and the haystacks went to hell.
> Oh, this was pretty badda but we wouldn't leave Nevada, oh, no.
> While the buckaroos went boating and the privy went a floating, we
>   refused to go.
> We even stood for old Bill Moffat when he spit in our beer.
> So no matter how you pushed us, we stayed right here.
> We thought we would try and find a little higher piece of soil.
> We thought we found just what we wanted when we ran into old
>   Howard Doyle.
> A place he owned in partners with the Democratic leader Flynn.
> It seems they're gonna be subpoenaed so they thought they'd get us in.
> So sure and begora, we took off for Tuscarora where it's nice and dry.

Part of Robert "Doby Doc" Caudill's collection from Elko County, which also contained buildings, wagons, and other valuable artifacts. Caudill moved the collection to Frontier Village in Las Vegas, and later sold it off. (Ruth and Roy Roseberry collection, Northeastern Nevada Museum)

Where we'd drink with Suer and Jacker and sing with Willis Packer
   when he's feeling high.
But when those out of state hunters came and started banging away
   (with Keppler and Berger furnishing the crossfire).
We didn't have a flack suit so we just couldn't stay.
And now comes the time when we were really put upon the block.
We met a high class operator, a fella named Doby Doc.
He told us of some ranches belonging to the Crumley clan.
He said we'd get them for nothing, or at least that was his plan.
But when our kids are ten and twenty, we will still be paying plenty.
I'll be singing sweet little Annie while Newt's sitting on his fanny
   counting up my dough.
But when next fair time rolls around, Doby Doc and I are fixing a race,
   we're going to run Stymie in a beard.
And as long as I'm the Mayor, I like this place.
I'll get my jack back if I must deal crooked blackjack.
Elko, Nevada.
I'll stay right here.

Eventually, when Crosby realized that none of his sons was going to take over his ranches, he sold them and never returned to Elko, although he did keep in touch with the many friends he made in Elko County. Crosby was still the honorary mayor of Elko when he died while golfing in Spain in 1977.

G. S. GARCIA

Although many businesses have flourished during Elko's history, a few stand out because of their uniqueness. The G. S. Garcia Harness and Saddlery opened in Elko during early 1894. G. S. Garcia was born in October 1864 in Mexico. He grew up in California where he married his wife, Saturnia. He was attracted to Elko because it had long been a major center for ranching and cowboy supplies. He first rented the Mayhugh building, but with business booming,he moved to the larger Litton and Hunter building in 1896.

Despite his growing business, the bits and spurs that would later bring Garcia fame were purchased from outside sources and resold. In November, Garcia hired his first silver artisan to begin producing the trademark bits and spurs. By 1899, the company issued its first mail-order catalog. A blacksmith shop was added and twelve people were employed. Cowboys all over the West sought Garcia's bits, spurs, and saddles because of the fine workmanship, quality, and durability: "Not only did cowboys dream of owning a pair of Garcia silver inlaid spurs and guiding their horses with a Garcia silver in-

Looking north up 5th Street in Elko, 1896. (Mrs. Brown collection, Northeastern Nevada Museum)

laid bit, but owning a Garcia saddle really separated the ordinary cowpoke from the high ridin' roughneck."[6]

One of Garcia's crowning achievements took place in 1904, when he and his workers made an ornate saddle that won the gold medal at the St. Louis Exposition in St. Louis. The production of this saddle was a major undertaking. Garcia hired eight more workers just for this saddle, including one woman. He was ahead of his time because he hired for ability and didn't worry about gender. The saddle was dyed black and ornately decorated with carved roses. In addition, gold and silver were used all over the saddle, including $20 gold pieces with the portraits of President Theodore Roosevelt and Nevada Governors William Nye and John Sparks. When other saddle makers arrived at the exposition and saw Garcia's saddle, they turned around and left, knowing there was no way they could compete with Garcia's saddle. Following the exposition, the saddle made numerous tours across the United States and was used by a host of famous people, including Roosevelt. The saddle is now part of the Nevada State Museum collection. Garcia repeated the award in 1905 at the Lewis and Clark Exposition in Portland, Oregon. He is the only saddle maker ever to achieve this.

In 1912, Garcia started his own rodeo, which soon became one of the most popular and famous rodeos in the West. Garcia owned a ranch in Diamond Valley where he brought purchased rodeo stock and raised his own stock. His horses had the reputation of being some of the meanest ever seen. Garcia took great pride in his rodeo because it was a chance to proudly promote his hometown of Elko and also showcased the talents of the cowboys and ranchers who had been so important in the development and economy of northeastern Nevada. However, during the 1920s, Garcia's health began to fail and he had to spend an increasing amount of time in California in hopes of improving his health.

In 1924, a former Garcia employee, Joe Capriola, opened the J. M. Capriola Company, a saddle and leather. Like Garcia's business, Capriola's shop boomed. In 1929, he moved his shop to an adobe building, one of the town's oldest structures, at 500 Commercial Street. Although competition developed between Garcia and Capriola, it was friendly. Garcia's health continued to deteriorate. In 1932, he and his wife moved permanently to California and left his shop in the hands of his sons, Leslie and Henry. G. S. Garcia died in 1932. His sons ran the store until 1938 when the shop was relocated to Salinas, California. The shop remained open there until 1957. Leslie maintained the Garcia Bit and Spur Company name with a new shop in Reno.

Meanwhile, the J. M. Capriola Company became the main saddle supplier in northern Nevada. Capriola continued to run the store until the 1950s when he sold it to Frank Jayo. When Jayo died in 1958, Capriola, at the age of seventy-four, had to take the store back. In July 1958, Capriola sold the store to Paul and Betty Bear. Fire struck in October and, although much of the mer-

chandise was saved, the building was a total loss. The fire department was trapped on the other side of the railroad tracks from the building while a train passed. The Bears built a new shop on the same site within six months. The Bears' sons, Bob and Bill, and daughter, Paula, took over the business in 1972. In 1978, the owners brought the Garcia Bit and Spur Company back home to Elko by buying the name and store from Les Garcia. Capriola's continues to be an important source for the best in saddles, bits, and spurs.

ELKO'S ICE INDUSTRY

With Elko's quick and early growth in 1869 and the 1870s, the demand for ice to keep perishable goods from spoiling rose dramatically. Elko, for many years, had a thriving ice industry. The earliest ice business opened in 1869 and was run by Fred Wilson. For many years, the ice companies in Elko provided ice not only for local residents but also for the many trains passing through town. During the 1900s, two large ice companies, the Eshleman Ice Company and the Artificial Ice Company, ran a spirited competition. Chris Eshleman made ice the old-fashioned way by cutting it from his ice ponds, located just east of the 12th Street bridge. His ponds also served as a major recreational facility for Elko residents, who used them for ice skating during winter.

Eshleman Ice Company advertising claimed that "Natural ice is considered safer for human consumption than artificial ice."[7] The Artificial Ice Company, which made ice in large refrigerator units, rejected that notion, and claims and counterclaims ensued, backed by alleged scientific proof. By the 1930s, however, the combination of the Great Depression and the arrival of convenient electric refrigerators and refrigerated railroad cars doomed the ice business. The era of deliveries of ice blocks to local homes was over, and the once prominent ice companies folded and faded into memory. Remnants of Eshleman's operation are still visible, including the concrete retaining dam and ponds, now split by railroad tracks. Only a small part of the sawhouse remains to mark the once large complex of buildings built by the company.

ELKO ROLLER MILL

The Elko Roller Mill was built in 1876 with the financial backing of John Ainley and George Bobier and was located at the corner of Seventh and Commercial Streets. Costs were kept low because there was plenty of locally raised grain, so expensive grain didn't need to be imported from California and Utah. The mill ran twenty-four hours a day during the fall and winter. Once all the grain was processed, the mill would be idle until the next year. In 1879, James Davis bought the mill. He made many improvements which made the mill extremely successful. In 1886, Davis sold the mill back to Ainley. Various owners ran the mill during the following few years.

While W. T. Smith owned the mill, beginning in 1889, the mill's flour won the Silver Medal at the 1898 Omaha Exposition. Smith began using a new label, Silver Medal, for his flour. Smith also installed a gas engine in the mill, which generated the first electricity in Elko. The power plant was bought by the Elko–Lamoille Power Company in 1913.

During the 1910s, local boys used to sneak into the mill, take bags of grain, go into the office, and sell them back to the company. It worked for awhile until the company caught on to the scam.

By the 1910s, the utility of the roller mill was fading. A combination of smaller local harvests and the inability to produce the new style of white, bleached flour forced the mill to close in the 1920s. In 1923, J. J. Hylton, who had bought the bankrupt mill, removed all of the remaining machinery and sold it to a mining company at Tenabo. The facility was torn down in September 1934.

CATLIN SHALE

The Catlin Shale Products Company, while not as financially successful as the roller mill, made dramatic improvements in technology that continue to be used in the oil and gas industry. Robert Catlin developed the shale oil deposit one mile south of Elko, beginning in 1890. He left Elko in 1895 but returned in 1912 and set up a laboratory on Seventh Street. After a few years of testing and development, he dug a shaft on the deposit in 1916 and built a processing plant.

The plant began operations in April 1917, funded entirely by private citizens. The start of World War I helped the Elko facility. There was a tremen-

dous shortage of fuel and many new sources, including shale, were explored. The Standard Oil Company built a shale plant next to the Lamoille Highway. The Southern Pacific Railroad financed the construction, and the Bureau of Mines ran the facility.

Only the Catlin plant was a successful venture. In 1919, a larger retort was installed and fifteen thousand gallons of oil were produced. Thirty-five men were employed at the plant by 1920. In 1921, Catlin bought the equipment from the Bureau of Mines plant and moved it to its own facility. Although oil had been produced on an experimental basis during the previous few years, commercial production, the first of its kind in the United States, didn't begin until 1922. After an investment of $500,000, the plant began producing ninety-six barrels of oil a day. Cans of Catlin "Hi-Power" oil went on sale in Elko. Unfortunately, the motor oil for automobiles, while of high quality, tended to gum up the engine during cold weather.

The plant was remodeled in 1923. More than twenty-six gallons of oil per week were now being produced and fifty men were employed. The mine had more than four miles of workings. However, shale oil was quite expensive to produce. Paraffin was the main production by-product and was the ingredient that caused the problems for the oil in winter. The plant had evolved into its own little town with about ten small houses, a dining hall, and a boardinghouse.

Catlin oil received national attention when its oil was tested at the Indianapolis 500 in 1924 by the Durant Motor Company. Back in Elko, a three-day party called the Catlin Oil Celebration was held in September. Two thousand people attended a special performance of the Garcia Rodeo, a circus, street dance, parade, and boxing matches. A barbecue held at the Hunter Ranch drew four thousand people, more than twice Elko's population. The company handed out Catlin paraffin chewing gum to the local youngsters.

Much to Elko's shock, the Catlin plant closed down during the following month, never to reopen. Robert Catlin returned to Elko in 1925 and stressed that the plant was never more than an experiment; he said the closure occurred because it was costing more to produce the oil than the company could charge. Over the years, Catlin had used more than $1 million of his own money on the project. Catlin is still recognized as the founder of shale oil research. Today, all that remains of the Catlin plant are concrete foundations and scattered mining debris.

ELKO MEDICAL SERVICES

Elko's medical services have always been extremely important not only to local residents but also to people living throughout northeastern Nevada. The first hospital was built in 1869 on the corner of Third and Railroad Streets. The county hospital was moved to Sixth and Court Streets in 1875. After the University of Nevada moved to Reno, the county hospital was moved to the abandoned university building in 1886.

The original Elko General Hospital shortly after completion. (Butch and Sue Smales collection, Northeastern Nevada Museum)

In 1919, thanks in part to the efforts of Dr. A. J. Hood, the Nevada Legislature passed legislation that allowed Elko to create the Elko General Hospital. The thirty-four-bed, $130,000 building was completed in 1920. A $1.1 million addition built in 1957–58 increased it to seventy-four beds and led to the hospital's accreditation. Another addition was constructed in 1974. The original hospital building was used for storage for a while and was later demolished.

Another important part of Elko's medical history was the organization of the Elko Clinic in 1948 by Doctors George Collett, R. P. Roantree, A. J. Hood, Leslie Moren, Dale Hadfield, and Charles Secor. Dr. John Read joined the clinic's staff the following year, and A. J. Hood's son, Thomas, in 1954. Many doctors have served over the years and all have contributed to building the positive reputation the clinic now enjoys. The present Elko Clinic facility was built in 1967 and continues to provide top-level care for Elko's growing population.

CRIME AND PUNISHMENT

Potts Case

Elko has been the scene of a number of sensational murder trials, the most famous of which was the Potts case. Josiah and Elizabeth Potts lived in Carlin until they moved to Rock Springs, Wyoming, in September 1888. On January 1, Carlin resident Miles Faucett disappeared after being invited to the Potts home for New Year's. That was the last anyone saw of him. Faucett, Elizabeth's ex-husband, and the Pottses were old acquaintances from England. Elizabeth Potts did Faucett's wash and cooked for him while in Carlin. At the end of 1888, the Brewer family moved into the house where the Pottses formerly resided and made a gruesome discovery. In January 1889, Brewer found in his basement a dismembered body that was missing its head. Attempts had been made to burn the pieces, but a knife found was recognized as belonging to Faucett.

Elko County Sheriffs L. R. Barnard and Constable Triplett traveled to Rock Springs and arrested Josiah and Elizabeth Potts. On the trip back, Josiah claimed that Faucett had committed suicide, and, fearing that he would be under suspicion for murder, Potts had cut up and buried the body. The Pottses were indicted on February 15, 1889, and the trial was filled with wild accusations and countercharges. The Pottses claimed that Faucett had tried to rape their daughter. The prosecution pointed out that when Faucett had disappeared, Potts claimed that Faucett had left on the train and sold all his belongings to Potts. Potts claimed he confronted Faucett about the attempted rape. Faucett then pulled a gun, put it to his head, said, "You folks will be blamed for this," and pulled the trigger.

The trial, which started on March 12, ended on March 15 with a conviction for first-degree murder. On March 22, the Pottses were sentenced to be hanged on May 17. The decision was appealed, but in November 1889, the Nevada Supreme Court reaffirmed the judgement. On April 25, 1890, the Pottses were resentenced to die, this time on June 20. However, there was considerable sentiment against the hanging of a woman. To make matters worse, Elizabeth was a large woman and people feared she would be decapitated when hanged. Elko County residents filed a petition asking the court to commute her sentence to life. This request, and another from the presiding judge, were both rejected.

A double gallows, originally built in Placerville, California, was assembled in the jail yard. Official black-bordered invitations were sent by Sheriff Barnard. The day before the hanging, Elizabeth slashed her wrists but a doctor was able to stop the bleeding. Fifty-two men attended the hanging; women were not allowed. The day of the hanging, the Pottses both continued to plead their innocence. The trapdoors were sprung at 10:44, and the crowd was horrified because Elizabeth's head was almost severed and blood covered her white dress.

The Pottses were buried in the Elko Cemetery. When the cemetery was moved to its present location, the Pottses were exhumed and reinterred in a common grave, which, ironically, is believed to also be the final resting place of Sheriff Barnard. Elizabeth Potts was the first and last woman legally executed in Nevada. The hanging of the couple was also the last legal execution in Elko County.

Bob White Case

The murder of Louis Lavell by Bob White in 1928 was another sensational criminal case. White was a large man who ran a taxi service, drove a school bus, and was considered a good man. Louis Lavell was a good friend of White's. White had a dark side that few knew about and associated with local gamblers and bootleggers. Lavell, White, and another man, Mike Connis, set up a gambling scheme with marked card decks to illegally win at the Commercial Hotel. The three then split their winnings.

On the night of May 6, 1928, Lavell said good-bye to Connis and left the Commercial with more than $1,000. He met White outside the hotel and was never seen again. After an extensive search the next day, Connis was unable to find Lavell. He confronted White, who denied seeing Lavell, even though Connis had seen the two together. Suspiciously, on the night of May 7, the cabin White had been renting in Secret Pass burned to the ground.

At the same time, three men discovered a hat with a bullet hole in it and a pool of blood near the Hesson Powder House, just south of Elko. Connis confirmed that the hat belonged to Lavell. Sheriff Harris rechecked the burned cabin and found evidence, including a monogrammed "Louis" belt buckle.

A murder warrant was issued for White. A nationwide manhunt took place and a week later, White was arrested at a farmhouse near Arlington, Illinois. White was returned to Elko, and his trial began on October 8.

The evidence was compelling enough that the jury convicted White of first-degree murder on October 18. White was sentenced to die in the gas chamber. Sixteen months of appeals ensued. White was executed on June 2, 1930, in the Nevada State Prison's gas chamber. When asked if he had any last words, White replied, "Yes, would you please bring me a gas mask?"

Luther Jones Case

The Luther Jones murder case shocked Elko residents because of the gruesome nature of the crime. Three men, Manuel Arrascada, Walter Godecke, and Otto Heitman, disappeared after last being seen at the Southern Pacific stockyards on October 16, 1936. A day later, Luther Jones was arrested in Carlin for resisting arrest after a gun fell out of his pocket at the Sperlich Saloon. At the time, Elko authorities were looking for Jones because he had been seen with the three missing men. Although Jones had cashed a bogus check in Elko, he had much more money with him when he was arrested subsequently than the amount of the check cashed.

When brought back to Elko, Jones confessed. Apparently, Jones had gone to the stockyards to rob Godecke and Heitman. Arrascada showed up and was also robbed by Jones. The total taken was only $40. He forced the three men into a nearby shack owned by Johnny Elias. Including Elias, four men were now imprisoned in the cabin. Jones forced Elias to tie up the others. When Elias tried to disarm Jones, Jones shot and killed him. Jones then fatally shot the other three men. Once the bodies were discovered, a large crowd of angry people gathered at the courthouse. Fears of a lynch mob grew, but friends and relatives of the victims were able to calm the crowd.

Jones later withdrew his confession and blamed a friend, Bert Wilson, for the murders. However, an investigation proved that Jones acted alone. Jones then changed his plea to not guilty by reason of insanity. Jones himself was the only defense witness. It took the jury only thirty-five minutes to find him guilty on November 18. He was executed on January 26, 1937, in the gas chamber. Jones hated the Elko law officers to the end. His last words were, "I would like to take the sheriff with me."[8]

U.S. AIRMAIL AND THE ELKO AIRPORT

The Elko Airport provides a vital transportation link for Elko, with Skywest scheduled flights and charter flights for the Red Lion Casino. The airport's early beginnings provide another facet of Elko's unique history of firsts in the country. The airport, initially called Rickenbacker Field, was constructed in 1919; the first plane landed on May 8. The airport came about

U.S. Air Mail hangar at Elko Airport. Elko was part of the first airmail system in the United States. (Dean and Sharon Rhoads collection, Northeastern Nevada Museum)

to accommodate the first transcontinental airmail route that was being organized by the government. The field was enlarged in 1920 to prepare for the initiation of service.

The first mail plane, a twelve-cylinder de Havilland DH-4, also known as the Flying Coffin, landed on September 9. For two years, the planes and equipment were housed in large canvas tents. A new hangar, still used by El Aero, was completed in December 1922. In 1926, Elko Airport was the scene of another national first, the initial commercial airmail flight. The new airline was run by Walter Varney. The route ran from Pasco, Washington, to Elko, where it connected with the main cross-country Columbia route. On April 6, 1926, pilot Leon Cuddeback arrived in Elko on time with the first sixty-four pounds of mail carried on a commercial air flight. A great welcoming committee greeted him, including most of the population of Elko. Varney moved his base of operations to Salt Lake City in 1926, but Elko remained on the main line. During the years, many prominent pilots flew through Elko, including Eddie Rickenbacker, Richard Byrd, Charles Lindbergh, Amelia Earhart, and Wiley Post.

In addition to the many minor crashes during the 1920s, the airport was once the scene of a major tragedy. On September 5, 1946, a Trans-Lux airliner carrying twenty-two people crashed about two and one-half miles west of Elko.

There was a dense fog, and the pilot apparently mistook a light beacon as the airport runway and crashed into the hillside. When the first rescuers reached the site, they were confronted with a gruesome sight. Bodies were strewn all over the area, and it appeared that everyone was dead. Then Robley Burns, a local mortician, heard a baby crying. A two-year-old child, Peter Link, had been thrown from the plane and was lying in the sagebrush. Another person, Irene Baralus, was still alive when removed from the wreckage but died soon after. Link was the lone survivor. His parents and infant sister died in the crash.

United Airlines served Elko for many years, but ended flights to and from Elko in 1981. However, the airport remains busy today and besides the jet flights, Elko is a popular stop for many small planes.

OPERATION LIFESAVER

Throughout Elko's history, the railroads played an important role. However, because the railroads passed through town, they were also a source of numerous tragedies. Many deaths and injuries occurred because of pedestrians and automobiles being hit on the tracks. There were twenty downtown crossings.

The Federal Highway Act of 1973 included the Rail-Highway Demonstration Project, which provided federal funding for railroad track relocation. In Elko, this provided the opportunity to move the tracks to the south, away from the busy part of town. "Operation Lifesaver" was born. It wasn't until 1976 that Elko's plan was approved by the federal government. Construction began in September 1978.

The operation was an immense undertaking because not only did the tracks have to be moved, but also the switchyards had to be moved from west of Elko to the east side. After five years of work and $43.5 million, the relocation was completed. On November 12, 1983, Elko had a "Last Train Through Town" celebration. Although the celebration went off without a hitch, it was a little premature. The Southern Pacific Railroad main track wasn't completed, and trains continued to come through town until early December, when the last freight train, #8374, actually went through the town.

While a number of other towns around the country also applied for relocation programs, Elko was the only project funded and completed. The mainline relocation not only increased the safety of downtown, but also proved to be a boon for downtown businesses because a business corridor between Railroad and Commercial Streets was created, providing a large area for parking, something that had always been in short supply.

MILITARY

When the call to arms has come, Elko residents have always responded. Many local soldiers have given the ultimate sacrifice in the country's wars. As a response to European tension with the start of World War I, some residents of Elko formed the Elko Home Guard in 1915. G. C. Jensen was elected captain of the group, which had 107 members. The group was instrumental in organizing support for Liberty Loan drives to help the war effort. The home guard also trained as a band and performed in parades and benefit functions. Once World War I ended, the home guard was disbanded, its honorable work completed.

Many Elko residents again volunteered, or were drafted, during World War II, including participants in D-day and Pearl Harbor. The town received a special honor when a new victory ship, the *Elko Victory,* was launched on December 8, 1944. Marilyn Patterson christened the ship, which was named for Elko thanks to the efforts of Nevada Senator Patrick McCarran. More than one hundred Elko residents attended the christening at the Kaiser Permanente Metal Corporation Shipyard in Richmond, Virginia. The ship served both the military and the Maritime Administration until it was mothballed on Christmas Eve 1971.

Contrary to some written accounts, the *Elko Victory* was not scrapped but still floats with a mothball fleet in Virginia. Brigadier General David Henley visited the ship in the late 1980s and was able to obtain the original wood nameplate, which he donated to the Northeastern Nevada Museum in Elko. While 10 of the 531 victory ships carried Nevada-related names, the *Elko Victory* is the only surviving vessel.

ELKO TODAY

Throughout Elko's history, its varied ethnic groups have always had a profound influence on the city. The first people to live in the area were the Native Americans. When the Central Pacific Railroad was completed in 1869, many Chinese and Irish railroad workers settled in and around Elko. Later, the Basques immigrated to the area and heavily impacted the local ranching industry and opened many successful businesses, including restaurants that are a must stop for visitors and residents. Today, while the Chinese and Irish influence has greatly decreased over the years, the Native American and Basque communities still have a vibrant impact on Elko.

Elko's population has ebbed and flowed throughout its history. With the emergence of microscopic gold along the Carlin Trend in the late 1960s, Elko has undergone the biggest boom in its long history. Barrick, Newmont, Independence, and Dee, among others, have paved the way for this new gold rush. Three of the five largest gold mines in the world are located near Elko and produce more than three million ounces of gold a year. Most of the employees live in Elko and are bused to work.

The influx of mining money has been a boon for businesses in Elko. The mining companies have assisted schools and nonprofit groups with donations that have made impossible dreams realities. For example, Barrick donated $10,000 to the museum in Elko during 1993 to initiate an oral history program. In addition, the companies have lent their support to the Northern Nevada Community College. The population of Elko, as a result of the influx of miners and their families, has climbed to about thirty thousand. Many new businesses have opened, and services have greatly improved.

This history has provided an overview of Elko's past, but it is impossible to present a complete history of the town in a few pages of text. More information is available from the museum's archives. The museum, founded in 1968, is a national award-winning facility that has complete newspaper records, a manuscript collection, oral histories, and research and photograph files. The museum is also worth a visit to see the extensive displays that give a complete history of Elko County and northeastern Nevada.

Elko remains the supply and social center for ranches scattered over thirty thousand square miles. It also serves as a transportation hub, tourist stop, and hunters' paradise. Elko's citizens take great pride in their town that still manages to preserve the flavor of the old West. This makes it an enjoyable place to live. Elko was recently selected the "Best Small Town in America," in Norman Crampton's book, *The 100 Best Small Towns in America,* based on government statistics and surveys. The town is also known as the City of Festivals. Annual events include the National Basque Festival (held every 4th of July weekend), Silver State Stampede, Cowboy Poetry Gathering, Elko County Fair, Indian powwows, Mining Expo, and many others. A historic walking tour of the town is available at the Northeastern Nevada Museum.

IMPORTANT DATES IN ELKO'S HISTORY

1868   December 29, Elko founded by the Central Pacific Railroad. Townsite laid out.

1869   March 5, Elko County formed by Nevada legislature and Elko named county seat. Courthouse built at Sixth and Idaho Streets. Humboldt Lodging House constructed. Pioneer Saloon began business on the northeast corner of Fifth and Railroad. Elko's first newspaper, the *Elko Independent,* began publication. A resort, White Sulphur Springs, was built near the Hot Hole off Bullion Road. Elko's forty-five saloons outnumbered other businesses in town.

1870   Presbyterian church built at Sixth and Pine Streets. First school opened at 421 Court Street. Population estimated at forty-five hundred.

1871   Fire destroyed most of the business district. Elko cattleman Lewis "Broadhorns" Bradley elected second governor of Nevada (1871–1878).

1872   Ben Fitch started a brickyard and turned out twenty-eight thousand to thirty-five thousand bricks daily.

1873   Cosmopolitan Hotel renamed the Chamberlain Hotel.

1874   Elko became the first site of the University of Nevada. Population estimated at five thousand.

1875   Elko Flour Mill began operations and provided the first water system for the town. Central Pacific Railroad erected 62,500-gallon water tank next to tracks in downtown area. University of Nevada dormitory built on Ninth Street.

1877 Two-story brick school building opened on Court Street between Eighth and Nine Streets.

1881 Estimated population is six hundred.

1882 White Sulphur Hot Springs resort burned down on June 6, rebuilt.

1883 *Elko Free Press* began publication on January 5.

1885 University of Nevada moved to Reno. Population estimated at one thousand.

1890 Elko Flour Mill generated first electricity for the town by supplying power for several streetlights. Josiah and Elizabeth Potts hanged behind the courthouse on June 20.

1892 December 11, Episcopal Church dedicated at Fifth and Idaho Streets.

1896 Elko County High School, first county school in the state, opened on Court Street at Sixth. County library was moved to second floor in 1926 where it remained until the upper level burned in 1942.

1899 Hot Springs hotel burned down again and rebuilt. The Southern Pacific Railroad began serving meals on trains and local hotel business dropped.

1904 Depot Hotel was demolished. Population was about eight hundred. Mayer Hotel constructed.

1907 Elko Chamber of Commerce formed.

Laying the Western Pacific Railroad tracks through Elko, 1908. (Northeastern Nevada Museum)

Western Pacific passenger and freight depot in Elko, 1910. (Northeastern Nevada Museum)

1908 Western Pacific Railroad build tracks through town and builds depot.

1909 Gambling banned by Nevada legislature.

1910 New courthouse built on previous courthouse site, cost $150,000.

1912 First Garcia Rodeo held on Panorama Drive; site used until 1927 for county fair; annual Garcia Rodeo held until around 1932.

1913 Elko-Lamoille Power Company began operations, providing DC electricity to Elko. Nevada Industrial School opened four miles east of town, now the Nevada Youth Training Center. Pioneer Hotel is completed.

1915 Elko-Lamoille Power Company switched to AC.

1916 Catlin Shale Products Company opened an experimental oil extraction plant. Population estimated at twenty-five hundred.

1917 Elko incorporated as a city. J. A. McBride was first mayor. Elko municipal waterworks established.

1918 Grammar school on Court Street burns down on Christmas Day. New Elko County High School constructed for $106,000 on College Avenue.

1919 New elementary school, Number One, built between Eighth and Ninth on Court Street. Renamed Kate St. Claire school in 1973; demolished in 1974.

1920 Elko designated as an airmail station on the first transcontinental route. First county fair was held on the Garcia Rodeo grounds with exhibits in the old high school building.

1921 Elko General Hospital built at the corner of College Avenue and Thirteenth Street.

1925 Catlin Shale Products Company closes its extraction plant.

1926 Elko became terminus of the first commercial airmail flight in the nation when Varney Airlines (later part of United Airlines) completed flight from Pasco, Washington. County library moved from courthouse to the second floor of the old high school building.

1927 County fairgrounds built on part of old China Ranch where Chinese residents once raised vegetables for sale in town.

1929 New gymnasium built at the high school; older gym built in 1918 was converted to an auditorium. Henderson Bank Building, tallest in town, opened.

1930 Elko Flour Mill torn down. First Elko High School band formed.

1932 Gambling legalized by the Nevada legislature. Henderson Bank failed.

1933 Present post office building opened.

1934 Elko attorney Morley Griswold became the sixteenth governor of Nevada when Fred Balazar dies in office. First street-paving program began.

1934–36 The Ranchinn opened on December 18 with sixty-eight rooms. Trans-Lux airliner crashed west of town, twenty-one dead, lone survivor is two-year-old boy, Peter Link.

1939 Elko attorney Edward Carville became the eighteenth governor of Nevada (1939–1945), later appointed U.S. senator (1945–1947). J. Harvey Sewell organized the Nevada Bank of Commerce, which later became Nevada National Bank.

1941 Big-name entertainment began in Nevada in the Lounge of the Commercial Hotel with Ted Lewis and his orchestra.

Southern Pacific depot at Elko, 1910. (Northeastern Nevada Museum)

1944 Mayer Hotel turned into the Stockmen's Hotel. On December 8, Marilyn Patterson christened the military ship SS *Elko Victory*.

1947 DeLuxe Cleaners building at 511 Railroad Street collapsed, killing three people.

1948 City Hall at 723 Railroad opened. Elko's first radio station, KELK, began broadcasting.

1951 Former Elkoan Charles B. Russell became twentieth governor of Nevada (1951–1958). World premiere of *Here Comes the Groom*, starring Bing Crosby, held at the Hunter Theater.

1957 Stockmen's Hotel burned; new larger hotel and casino built on the same site.

1959 Elko attorney Grant Sawyer became Nevada's twenty-first governor (1959–1966).

1960 Elko High School dormitory torn down.

1966 New high school gymnasium built.

1967 Elko citizens formed first community college in Nevada. The college was originally housed in the Kate St. Claire school until its new campus was started on Elm Street. First called Elko Community College, it was later renamed Northern Nevada Community College.

1968 Northeastern Nevada Museum opened; expanded in 1982.

1972 New city hall built at 1751 College Avenue.

1979 Elko Convention Center completed.

1983 Operation Lifesaver completed, moving railroad tracks out of downtown.

1985 First Cowboy Poetry Gathering held.

1992 Elko named "Best Small Town in America."

1995 Elko High School band performed in Rose Bowl Parade.[9]

Halleck

DIRECTIONS: *From Elko, go east on I-80 for 19 miles to the Halleck exit. Go south for ½ mile to Halleck.*

Halleck came into existence in 1869 when the Central Pacific Railroad was completed through the future townsite, which immediately became the shipping point for supplies heading to Fort Halleck. During 1869, two hotels, the Bell and Griffin, were built and Frank Hughes constructed the first house, made of adobe.

By 1870, Halleck had a population of thirty-five. During the early 1870s, Halleck underwent a building boom of sorts when F. T. Greenberg opened a brewery and Hamilton McCain built a saloon, which catered to the soldiers and officers of Fort Halleck.

In 1873, Bell, also the Halleck depot operator, expanded his Halleck Hotel to two stories, complete with a second-story porch, but horses tied to the support columns loosened the supports so much that the porch collapsed. Sam Moser opened a store, and a school was built in 1874. The Halleck School District, also sometimes referred to as the Peko School District (although a school by the same name existed in Elburz), remained open until the 1950s. A post office opened on April 24, 1873, with Henry Hoganson as postmaster. Hamilton McCain built a two-story hotel of his own, adjoining his popular saloon.

Halleck developed into the busiest livestock shipping point on the Central Pacific. In the mid-1870s, Bell sold the Halleck Hotel to John Deering although Bell stayed in Halleck, where he served as postmaster and constable. By 1875, Halleck's permanent population had grown to fifty although there always were more people than that in town.

A tragic event occurred in Halleck on April 9, 1877, when Sam Mills, a one-eyed man who had been fired by Mrs. Deering for poor work at the Halleck Hotel, reacted angrily, and another man knocked him down to protect Mrs. Deering. Mills pulled a knife but left and went to the Griffin Saloon where he got a gun. A friend of Mills, James Finnerty, felt he could talk to him, but as soon as he opened the door, Mills shot him dead. Mills fled and was later captured in a haystack near Lamoille. He was found guilty of first-degree murder, which Mills vigorously objected to because he never intended to kill his best friend, and he condemned the jury for their verdict. On December 22, Mills was hanged in Elko, the first legal execution in Elko County.

During the ensuing years, Halleck's population gradually grew, and by 1880, it was ninety-seven, and by 1900, had risen to 126. At its peak, twenty-six buildings were built and numerous businesses flourished, but the abandonment of Fort Halleck in 1886 ended Halleck's glory years, and the town had to depend on local ranchers for survival.

Ranching has been and still is important in the Halleck area. One of the most famous ranchers was Dan Murphy, who, with his father, four brothers, and four sisters, was part of the Stevens-Murphy-Townsend Party, the first emigrant wagon train to California in 1844. Murphy was also the first settler to see Lake Tahoe. Although the bulk of Murphy's cattle empire in Elko County was in the North Fork area, his base of operations was in the Griffin Hotel, and in 1877, he built a home of his own in Halleck. When Murphy died in 1882, he owned four million acres of land, making him one of the largest landowners in the world.

Samuel McIntyre also was a prominent local cattleman. Phillip Witcher had established the ranch in 1880. McIntyre purchased it in 1888 and ran fifteen thousand head of Black Galloway cattle imported from Scotland. Because this type of cattle was unique in the area, McIntyre did not have to brand his cattle. McIntyre was also interested in mining and discovered the Mammoth mine in Utah. In 1898, he added the Brennen and Dorsey Ranches to his holdings. Surprisingly, much of his holdings are still intact and are owned by Frank and Phyliss Hooper, who use the original McIntyre Ranch as their headquarters.

The 71 Ranch, established by Joe Scott in 1877, is one of the largest ranches

One of the remaining buildings in Halleck. (Photo by Shawn Hall)

Connecting the West

in the area. Caleb Hank joined with Scott in partnership during 1879, and in 1889, the two formed the Halleck Cattle Company. The ranch prospered until the property was sold at public auction in 1911 for $170,000 to William and Grace Large, who formed the 71 Ranch Corporation in 1913. The Union Land and Cattle Company took over the corporation in 1917, but folded in 1921 when cattle prices fell. John Marble bought the ranch and three generations later, the 71 Ranch was still in the Marble family, until it was sold to the Ellison Ranching Corporation in 1995.

During the 1890s, the Halleck baseball team provided local entertainment. But the town was slowly dying, and many of the buildings were moved or torn down. The Halleck Hotel was the only substantial building left by 1900. Stanley Wines ran the hotel and store, and also had the mail contract between Halleck and Ruby Valley. He sold the hotel in 1913 to Samuel McIntyre but by the time the Halleck Hotel burned in 1915, there were only a couple of buildings left. McIntyre vowed to rebuild the hotel but later decided it was not worth the investment.

The Halleck post office continues to operate from one of the two remaining buildings and serves the many local ranches. Over the years, postmasters have included Albert Hatch, Henry Deacon, William Better, Frank Ambler, William Haseltine, William Hawk, Louis Hardy, Stanley Wines, Elizabeth Rathfon (who served for thirty-four years), Earl Conrad, Nelda Glaser, and Marianne Glaser.

For many years, the post office had a mascot named "Little Dog." The dog had lived in the backroom of the post office when Earl Conrad was postmaster. Conrad died in 1966 but the dog stayed, being taken care of by Nelda Glaser and post office patrons. In 1972, the small dog was attacked by a pack of other dogs and was severely injured. Dr. A. A. Cuthbertson, of Elko, operated on the dog and noted it was the longest surgery he had ever done, three hours. While the dog recovered, patrons of the post office brought extra food and scraps to help out. Many contributed towards the dog's veterinarian bill, including a former resident of Halleck living in Nampa, Idaho, who had heard about the attack. "Little Dog" remained a fixture at the Halleck post office until she died a few years later. Only a couple buildings are left at Halleck as evidence of the once important railroad town.

Hootens
(Mound Valley)

DIRECTIONS: *Located 1 mile north of Jiggs on Nevada 228.*

Hootens was a stage station, located just north of present-day Jiggs, on the Elko-Hamilton toll road. David Hooten, a former Virginia City miner, built a ten-room log hotel in 1869, which also had a restaurant and saloon. During those early years, Mound Valley tended to be a lawless place, and Hootens tended to be the center of this activity. A post office, named Mound Valley, opened on March 26, 1879, with Hooten as postmaster, but didn't last long and closed on March 17, 1881.

By this time, travel to Hamilton had ceased, and the stages had stopped running. Hooten turned to ranching and remained until his death in November 1889. Years later, when the saloon was torn down, there was an unsubstantiated rumor that two bodies were found, perpetuating Mound Valley's earlier reputation. Zane Grey, the famous western author, having heard stories about the area's wild days, made Mound Valley the headquarters for his character King Fisher. Although the original buildings are long gone, the site is still an active ranch.

Hunter

DIRECTIONS: *Located 8.8 miles west of Elko via I-80.*

Hunter has been a ranch since the 1870s when Thomas and William Hunter built a large ranching empire so immense it controlled twenty-six different branding irons, the first of which was registered in 1873. The Hunters had lived in Elko, where William had erected the first frame house in that town. However, Hunter's history began long before the 1870s. The area was where the California Emigrant Trail was joined by the infamous Hastings

George Banks in front of the Hunter & Banks barn. (Opal Banks collection, Northeastern Nevada Museum)

Connecting the West

Cutoff taken by the Donner Party. During the 1840s and 1850s, more than two hundred thousand emigrants travelled these two emigrant trails, and the wagon ruts are still visible around the Hunter area.

By the dreaded winter of 1889–90, the Hunters controlled a huge area with range as far north as Lone Mountain and were running three thousand head of cattle. The harsh winter, which devastated the cattle industry throughout Elko County, took all but nine hundred head. The brothers bought huge amounts of hay to try to save the herd, and because of the hay bills, the Hunters were forced to sell the remaining cattle. They then began the slow process of re-building their herd, and in 1910, George Hunter, son of Thomas, and George Banks, raised by William Hunter, formed the Hunter-Banks partnership and took over the Hunter Ranch.

In 1908, the Western Pacific Railroad was constructed and the Hunter siding established, which provided an easy shipping point for their cattle. The Hunter family built a legacy in Elko County. Thomas, who died in 1930, served as a state senator. William's son, John, ran the Hunter Store, and later the Home Bakery in Elko where he also built three theaters: the Hunter (1926), the Elvada (1937), and the Rainbo (1943).

George Hunter died in 1917 and Banks maintained the home ranch during the next eight years, but most of the other holdings were sold off. Despite his efforts, Banks went bankrupt in 1925. The ranch has seen many owners over the years, and continues to operate today. The most recognizable building at the ranch is the old Hunter & Banks barn. There is a concrete marker com-memorating the emigrant trail located at the Hunter exit off of Interstate 80. The Oregon–California Trails Association has marked the trail in the area and erected an informative kiosk.

Huntington Valley

(Huntington) (Robinson Station) (Taft Station)
(Hardy Station) (Sadler Ranch) (Dutchman's)

DIRECTIONS: *Huntington Valley stretches southward along Nevada 228 from Jiggs to the Elko County line.*

Huntington Valley was first settled during the 1860s. The origin of the name is a source of dispute, with two possibilities offered. One is that the valley was named by explorer J. S. Simpson for Lott Huntington, an over-land mail agent stationed near here, who discovered a spring in the area in 1859. The other version is that it was named in honor of Oliver and Clark Huntington, guides for the E. J. Steptoe Party, which came through the val-ley in 1854. The Hastings Cutoff traversed the valley, and the Donner Party passed through in 1846 on the way to their fate in the Sierra Nevada.

*Remains of the Brown
homestead in Huntington
Valley. (Photo by
Shawn Hall)*

With the establishment of the Hill Beachey and George Shepherd stage roads to Hamilton, a number of stations were set up in the valley. Robinson Station was the break-off point for a branch of the stagecoach line that went to Eureka via Red Rock Pass. Taft Station, also known as Hardy Station, was a diversion point for Beachey's line to Eureka which went through Railroad Canyon.

The Sadler Ranch, named for Nevada governor Reinhold Sadler and later run by his son Herman, was the junction for both the Beachey and Shepherd roads. One of the early settlers included Charles Hale, part owner of the Hale and Norcross Mine in Virginia City, who established the Twin Creek Ranch. Other early arrivals included Joe Dahms, Edward Hudson (Frost Canyon), and Judson Dakin (Warner Mitchell Ranch).

By 1873, enough people had homesteaded in the valley to warrant the establishment of a post office. On March 17, George Taft, owner of Taft Station, opened the office at his ranch. In 1877, Thomas and Henry Porch settled in the valley. Henry Porch established the ranch later known as the E. L. Cord Ranch (Cord bought the ranch after 1900), and Thomas purchased the Hudson Ranch in Frost Canyon. Thomas and his wife, Martha, built a fifty-by-thirty-foot home constructed of stockades; a well, springhouse, and reservoir were dug to provide water. In addition, they built a smokehouse and twenty-horse barn. During the 1870s and 1880s, the Porch Ranch was a popular stop on the road to Eureka and Hamilton, and it was common for twenty people to dine there. Porch sold most of his dairy products in Eureka.

The 1880 census listed the valley's population at 101, which included seven Porch children: Owen, Oren, Mary Jane, Augustus, Sarah, William, and Larna. When Oren died on February 7, 1883, the family started a small cemetery at the ranch. Most of the children, and other relatives, had their weddings at the ranch. Thomas Porch died in 1893 but Martha continued to run the station and dairy business until 1910. She was well known as a generous hostess and was often taken advantage of.

In 1884, a small log building with a dirt roof and one small window was

Ranch headquarters and stage stop at the Sadler Ranch in Huntington Valley. (Photo by Shawn Hall)

built to serve as the valley school, located at the Ed Hudson Ranch. Amenities included a wood heater and plank table. The teacher, Pearl Lindsay, had the only chair. Another school, the Liberty School, opened at the Porch Ranch and was in operation until around the turn of the century.

A new school, the Huntington School, was built by Charlie Mitchell in 1925 near the Brown Ranch. The school was later moved to the Sestanovich Ranch in Frost Canyon. It closed in 1932, moved to Lee, and was later torn down. Teachers in the three schools included Aloysia O'Leary, Hattie Finegan, Pansay Stuart, Lou Craighead, Marion Stone, Annie Grant, Georgia Pollard, Belle Lindsay, Emma Scherff, Annie Toyn, Pearl Lindsay, Clara Mather, Flora Wittenberg, Jennie Gleason, Ella Crosson, Belle Butler, Alice Decker, Lizzie Wilkerson, Edna Mills, and Elsidora Brinck.

The post office closed on July 15, 1904. Postmasters from 1873 to 1904 included Joe Crawford, David Lindsay, Augustine Brown (also served as Huntington justice of the peace), John Fitzmaurice, and Seraphine Lani. The office reopened from December 7, 1923, to January 31, 1931, and Ruby Hinton, Tex Smith, and Edna Howard served as postmasters.

Many ranches are still active in Huntington Valley, and most include pre-1900 buildings. The quarried stone building built at the Sadler Ranch remains. Although the Porch homestead is long gone, foundations are left, as is the small family cemetery containing a few graves. The old stage roads and wagon ruts of the Hastings Cutoff trail are also visible.

Jude

DIRECTIONS: *Located 10 miles west of Wells on the Union Pacific.*

Jude was a signal station located between Deeth and Wells and served the Southern Pacific Railroad. Only a small sectionhouse was built at Jude, and only scattered wood scraps are left.

McPheters Station

(McPeters' Station)

DIRECTIONS: *From Elko, go southeast on the Spring Creek road for 6.9 miles. Turn right and go south for 5 miles. Turn right and follow gravel road for 4 miles to McPheters Station.*

McPheters Station was a stop on the old White Pine Road, located on Frank McPheters ranch. McPheters and his wife, Emma, established the ranch and station in 1869 where the old telegraph road crossed the South

Fork of the Humboldt River, between the Crane and Griswold Ranches. A fire destroyed the property in September 1870 while everyone was out threshing in the fields. The fire was believed to be a coverup for a robbery because $600 in gold coins was missing and never found.

McPheters never rebuilt the station and it faded into history. He and his wife moved to Osino where she drowned in the Humboldt River in August 1876. McPheters ranched for many years in Elko County and became a highly respected member of the community. He died in May 1918. Nothing at all remains of McPheters Station.

Millers

DIRECTIONS: From Elko, take the Spring Creek road southeast for 6.9 miles. Turn right and go for 11 miles. Turn right and follow a gravel road west for 1 mile and then south along Huntington Creek for 6 miles to Millers.

Millers was a stop on the Elko-Hamilton road. Used primarily as a horse-changing stop during the late 1860s and early 1870s, Millers was abandoned once use of the road to Hamilton diminished. Only a depression marks the site, located on a private ranch. Millers was also the name of a stop on the short-lived Railroad Canyon toll road run by J. F. Ray. The road opened in 1870 but was abandoned a couple of years later. Only a cabin and small corrals were built, and nothing is left at that site.

Moleen

DIRECTIONS: Located 2½ miles southwest of Hunter, 11½ miles southwest of Elko. Located on the south side of railroad tracks, adjacent to I-80.

Moleen was first a sidetrack and signal station on the Central Pacific Railroad and now on the Southern Pacific Railroad. The into and eight blankets and $22 were stolen. In 1900, S first historic mention of Moleen was on May 20, 1874, when the sectionhouse was broken. G. Weston, prominent mining man at Lone Mountain, worked some claims in Moleen Canyon. He sold them for $5,000 but soon after had to take the mine back. After a few years, he gave up and concentrated on his holdings at Lone Mountain.

In April 1901, the Moleen sectionhouse was destroyed by a fire that was started by a spark from a passing locomotive. A boxcar was brought up from Carlin to serve as a replacement until the building was rebuilt. The telegraph station burned in June 1907 when the operator fell asleep and kicked over a lamp. In March 1916, Weston's old mine was relocated by Ike Cowling, Bert Hammer, and Frank Smith. Small amounts of silver and copper were removed during the next few years before the trio gave up. All of the buildings at Moleen have long since disappeared and only concrete foundations are left.

Mound Station

DIRECTIONS: *From Jiggs, go south on Nevada 228 for 6½ miles. Turn right and follow for 4 miles to Mound Station.*

Mound Station, not to be confused with the station at the present town of Jiggs, was a stop and horse-changing station on Denver and Shepherd's Elko–White Pine Road in the late 1860s and early 1870s. The station, which consisted of a log cabin and corrals, was located two miles south of Robinson Station. Nothing remains at the site today.

Nardi

DIRECTIONS: *Located 4 miles east of Deeth on the Union Pacific.*

Nardi served as a signal station on both the Southern Pacific and Western Pacific Railroads (now both part of the Union Pacific). The only mention of Nardi in historical records occurred in June 1946 when Omer Sheppard, a Western Pacific Railroad assistant foreman, was killed by a passing train when the suction pulled him in. Sheppard had just been released from a chain gang. Only a signal shack was built at Nardi and nothing remains.

Natchez

DIRECTIONS: *Located 4 miles southwest of Deeth on the Union Pacific.*

Natchez served as a signal station on the Southern Pacific Railroad. The station was named for the son of Winnemucca, a chief of the Paiutes. There were a couple of tragedies that took place here early in the century. In August 1907, twenty-one-year-old signalman James Urton was struck and killed by a passing train. Another twenty-one year old, Alfonso D'Olivo, a section worker, was killed by a train in October 1915. Only concrete foundations are left at Natchez.

Osino

DIRECTIONS: From Elko, go northeast on I-80 for 8.7 miles to Osino.

Osino came into being as a sidetrack station for the Central Pacific Railroad in 1869 and later served as a stop and signal station for the Southern Pacific Railroad. A train accident on January 4, 1879, created excitement in Elko. A passenger train and freight train collided in heavy fog and although the locomotives were smashed and several cars were destroyed, no one was injured. A tragedy took place in October 1881 when brakeman Elmer Jones was killed by a railroad car that jumped the switch and crushed him.

During the 1880s, a small settlement developed, mainly due to the formation of the Arthur Lowe and Company cattle partnership. Lowe, from Derbyshire, England, was a partner with Judge Bigelow; the two men had one of the largest cattle companies in the county. The company was listed in the first brand book issued by the Nevada Livestock Association in 1884. Lowe died at age thirty-nine, but his wife and daughter continued to run the operation until it was sold to Charles Clubine. William Moffatt also later owned the property.

As with many of the railroad stops in Elko County, tragedy struck with a death on the tracks. In August 1899, David Tobin of Butte City was found mangled on the tracks. Apparently he had been knocked from the train when it started, fell onto the tracks, and was killed by an oncoming train. In November 1901, the few residents left were modernized when a telephone line to Osino was completed from Elko. The original ranch house, built in 1882, still stands at Osino. Almost all of the other buildings in the area are new, part of the expansion of the Elko boom.

Pardo

DIRECTIONS: Located 10 miles west of Elburz near Ryndon on the Union Pacific.

Pardo has served the former Western Pacific Railroad as a siding and the former Southern Pacific Railroad (now both Union Pacific) as a signal station. The only structure built at Pardo was a sectionhouse and that disappeared long ago.

Pleasant Valley

(Blaine)

DIRECTIONS: From Elko, go south on Nevada 227 for 17 miles. Turn right and continue for 4 miles to Blaine, which is in the middle of Pleasant Valley.

The first settlers of Pleasant Valley, Frank Williams and George and Edward Seitz, arrived in 1868. The valley was named by George and Edward. A list of early settlers reads like a "Who's Who" of Elko County: George Ogilvie, Henry Butterfield, Joseph Hennen, H. A. Young, John Ainley, Evan Jones, N. F. Peterson, George Williamson, George Taylor, J. P. Hough, James Mitchell, Bob Skaggs, and Amos Roach.

There was excitement in the valley in 1870 when robbers of the Central Pacific Railroad hid out at the Young Ranch while the owner was away. Soldiers from Fort Halleck finally located the thieves, and they were arrested without incident.

A school opened in 1873 with Lizzie Hough, daughter of J. P. Hough, as the first schoolteacher. A new school was built in 1875 and had twelve students. By 1881, Pleasant Valley had a population of eighty-eight, which included fifty-nine registered voters. Besides the many ranches in operation, Evan Jones ran a large dairy. Milk sold for fifty cents a gallon, and Jones supplied a large area, including Tuscarora. A variety of other produce was raised in the valley and sold at markets in Austin, Eureka, Hamilton, Tuscarora, and Elko.

Blaine post office opened at the Brennen Ranch on May 26, 1884, with Frank Hough as postmaster. The office was named for James Blaine, Republican candidate for president. Evan Jones became postmaster in 1887, and his son, Thomas, took over in 1899. Thomas Brennen ran the office from 1900 until it closed on December 31, 1914.

Even though Pleasant Valley is a relatively small valley, a number of ranches were based there, and many stayed in the same families for generations. For example, Hennen Ranch was in the family from 1873 to 1959. Thomas Brennen moved to Blaine in 1896 and combined the Grant, Peterson, and Ainley Ranches.

Realizing the need for a new and roomier schoolhouse, Brennen donated a building on his ranch for use as a school. It was used until the Pleasant Valley School District was abolished in 1918. Teachers who taught at this school included May Foley, Effie Madson, and Sadie Wright (her sister, Maggie, taught at Lamoille).

Around the turn of the century, a new school was established at Rabbit Creek on the Skaggs Ranch. Although it has been reported that the Pleasant Valley School was moved there, this is now known to be wrong because

Former Blaine post office in Pleasant Valley. (Photo by Shawn Hall)

a separate building was constructed at the Skaggs Ranch. Until 1918, two schools operated in the valley. Kate St. Clair, prominent educator and later Nevada deputy superintendent of public instruction, taught at Rabbit Creek in 1912.

In the early 1900s, dry farming became popular in Elko County. Dry farms created communities at Tobar, Afton, Metropolis, and Decoy. In 1909, Frank Winters, an Elko assemblyman, introduced a bill to establish an experimental dry farm in northeastern Nevada. The bill passed and Frank Winters, E. C. Riddell, and Frank Fernald were named to the Dry Farm Commission. After visiting possible sites near Wells and at Clover Valley, Pleasant Valley was selected. Elko County purchased the John Thompson Ranch (also known as the Squires Ranch) for $2,000 in August. Title was transferred to the director of the State Agricultural Experiment Station, and the Nevada Department of Agriculture and Animal Husbandry took over management of the Elko County Dry Farm in June of 1910.

Gordon True, professor of agriculture at the University of Nevada, and Walfried Sohlman ran the dry farm. The property was in terrible condition and required a lot of hard work to make it operational. Charles Knight replaced True, but most of the work was actually done by Sohlman.

The dry farm got off to a rocky start. During 1911, limited rainfall and a combination of jackrabbits, ground squirrels, and birds left crops in poor shape. From 1912 to 1914, conditions improved and crop production increased. In 1914, the farm began a program of seed distribution and more than one-half ton of wheat seed was sold to Elko County dry farmers.

Although 1915 proved to be the dry farm's best year, attempts were already being made in Carson City to close the farm. A bill for closure passed the Senate but was defeated by the assembly, and $8,000 was appropriated for operations in 1915 and 1916. However, Governor Emmet Boyle surprised everyone by vetoing the appropriation, which caused outrage in Elko County.

Sohlman tried to get Boyle to reconsider the closure, but the governor stated that the farm would be closed at the end of the 1915 farming season. Sohlman, not wanting to see all of his hard work go down the drain, defied the closure order. He harvested a fall grain crop and planted a new crop. The Dry Farm Commission was reactivated by Governor Boyle because it was the only authority that could dismiss Sohlman. He was formerly discharged in March of 1916 and given one month to vacate the farm.

The farm was officially abolished by the legislature in 1917, and records, equipment, and property were returned to Elko County. Although dry farming was still done elsewhere in Elko County for a couple of years, its days were over in Pleasant Valley. The farm was sold at public auction in July of 1920 to F. J. Brennen for $600 and was incorporated into the Brennen Ranch.

Thomas Brennen died in July 1932. Not only had he been an influential Pleasant Valley rancher, but he had also been active in county and state politics. He served three terms as a member of the first Elko City Council and three terms as an assemblyman in the Nevada legislature. Brennen was born in 1855 in London and married Mary Killeen of Virginia City in 1890. They had eight children, most of whom stayed in the Pleasant Valley area.

Over the years, most of the small, separate ranches in the valley have been consolidated. Today, most of the smaller ranches are operated by the larger ranches. Some ranch land has become part of the Spring Creek housing development. A number of old buildings remain in the valley and the Blaine post office and Pleasant Valley School still stand on the Brennen Ranch.

Rasid

DIRECTIONS: *From the Halleck interchange on I-80, go southeast for 2 miles. Turn left onto the road paralleling the railroad tracks. Continue for 4 miles to Rasid.*

Rasid served the former Western Pacific and Southern Pacific Railroads (now both Union Pacific) as a signal station. For a time, there was a sectionhouse at Rasid, but it was removed in the 1950s. Only the foundation of the sectionhouse remains.

Ruby

DIRECTIONS: *Located at the north end of Clover Valley, adjacent to U.S. 93.*

Ruby is a siding on the former Western Pacific Railroad (now the Union Pacific) located at the north end of Clover Valley. At times since the railroad was built in 1910, the siding has been used to ship cattle and other perishable goods from Clover Valley. The corrals built at the siding are now gone.

Ruby Valley

DIRECTIONS: *From Elko, go east on I-80 for 19 miles to the Halleck exit. Go south on Nevada 229 for 22 miles to Arthur, located at the head of Ruby Valley. The valley stretches south for more than 50 miles, across the White Pine County line.*

Much of Ruby Valley's history has been mentioned in histories of specific towns and sites in *Old Heart of Nevada: Ghost Towns and Mining Camps of Elko County.* However, in this section the history of other areas not mentioned in the first volume will be covered.

The first nonnative to traverse the valley was Jedediah Smith in 1827. Later, the Hastings Cutoff from the California Trail, which was the path of the ill-

Residents of Ruby Valley in front of the stone school, 1901. (Skosh Bell collection, Northeastern Nevada Museum)

fated Donner Party in 1846, came through the valley. Lieutenant E. G. Beckwith named Franklin Lake in honor of President Franklin Pierce when he passed through the area in 1854.

The first settler in Ruby Valley was William "Uncle Billy" Rogers, employed by the United States Indian Agency to find a reservation site. He chose the future Overland Farm. Although the site was rejected for a reservation, Rogers decided to settle there. The establishment of Fort Ruby, just over the county line in White Pine County, in 1862 led to the settlement of the valley although some had come the year before.

The first white child born in the valley was Tom Williams, son of Archy Williams, in 1861. The initial settlement was the Overland Ranch, which was organized by the Overland Mail Company because of the exorbitant prices being charged for grain by the Mormons. Chester Griswold, L. H. Head, and Samuel Woodward set about managing the ranch. Indian labor was used for clearing and preparing the large fields for planting. Because of their success and the high cost of transporting the grain, the trio built a gristmill at the ranch. It was the first such mill in what was then Lander County. Demand was high and the flour sold as soon as it was processed.

Ever the businessmen, Head and Woodward built a distillery at the ranch and produced products called Old Daybrook Whiskey and Early Dawn Whiskey. The Kingsbury Saloon was established to provide a proper venue for the sale of the product.

During the 1860s, many new homesteaders took up land in Ruby Valley,

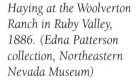

Haying at the Woolverton Ranch in Ruby Valley, 1886. (Edna Patterson collection, Northeastern Nevada Museum)

The Ira D. Wines family in front of their home at the Overland Ranch in Ruby Valley. (Blaine Sharp collection, Northeastern Nevada Museum)

most of them soldiers from Fort Ruby who received land as part of their severance pay. By 1870, there were 53 people living in the valley. The next year, the number had increased to more than 150. The settlement of the valley began to spread northward, with ranches and small communities springing up. Ranchers such as Arthur Gedney, Ira and Len Wines, Joe Smith, Oren Vaughn, Jeremiah Moore, Tom Harrison, William Gardner, Willard Griswold, William and James Myers, John Helth, Mickey Flynn, John Thompson, Andrew Dibble, A. G. Dawley, and Thomas Short settled in Ruby Valley. Many descendants of the early settlers still live in the valley today.

Thomas Short, the only person in Ruby Valley with any medical knowledge, served as the valley doctor. Moore had been the commander at Fort Ruby from 1863 to 1865 and in 1869 was elected the first Elko County state senator. Willard Griswold was the first in a long line of Griswolds in Ruby Valley. He married Margaret Woolverton and they had ten children, one every two years. Their first child, Oscar, grew up to be a three-star general who received many accolades during his service, particularly during World War II.

Ira D. Wines had served as a relief rider for the Pony Express when he was only fifteen. He married Margaret Tayer in 1865 and later took over the Over-

land Ranch when the original partnership broke up in the early 1870s. By this time, in addition to the gristmill and distillery, there was a three-room log community center, a store, and a post office, which had opened on April 30, 1862. His brothers, Len and Norman, also were early Ruby Valley settlers. Ira and Margaret had twelve children but five died while very young.

Although early Ruby Valley accommodations were crude, brick buildings began to appear in 1871 and 1872. A two-story brick hotel, which still stands and is used as a residence, was built by Chester Griswold at the Overland Farm. Ruby Valley quickly became a major center for both agriculture and cattle raising. In January 1873, a killing took place at Chester Griswold's saloon at Overland. James Armstrong was stabbed by a blacksmith named Pike. He was cut on the arm, and at first the wound didn't appear serious; he bled so profusely, however, that he died before the doctor from Sprucemont could arrive.

By 1880, Ruby Valley's population, scattered over a huge area, had grown to more than 250. During the 1880s, new arrivals included John and Jube Wright. John married Jan Gedney and Jube married Jessie Gedney. Jube built a ten-room house on his ranch which John helped manage.

A school, the first of many, opened in 1883 with thirteen students. At one point, there were six schools in the valley in operation at the same time: Secret, North Ruby, Arthur, Central Ruby, South Ruby, and Cave Creek. The original school, made out of rocks, was located next to a more recently built schoolhouse, also made of rocks, that still stands in central Ruby Valley.

Schools have played a major role in Ruby Valley's history, and some of the larger families were able to fill a school by themselves. For example, in 1901, the Ruby Valley School had fourteen students and all were from the Vaughan, Hankins, and Short families. The large Griswold family kept the Arthur School full for many years. Some of the teachers that served these many schools included Ella Hill, Agnes Griswold, Maggie O'Hare, Beth Vaughn, Blanche Harrie, Lourinda Wines, and Minnie Mau. A number of the old schools still stand throughout the valley, but only one is still active. Most students now attend school in Elko.

During 1892, a promoter began development of the town of Meadowville, located on the east side of Franklin Lake. It was planned to be a resort town, and an artesian well was dug by the Wright brothers. By April, a hotel, the Betsy (owned by Ross Wright), three saloons, one store, and a church had been built. One major drawback was that nobody came to the resort. By the end of summer, the brothers realized their mistake, sold or dismantled everything, and left Ruby Valley.

Although mining in Ruby Valley is discussed in other sections on Battle Creek, Harrison Pass, and Valley View in *Old Heart of Nevada: Ghost Towns and Mining Camps of Elko County,* other unique mining took place above the Gardner Ranch, where mica was discovered in the 1870s. The Great Republic Mining Company was formed in September 1877 by Simon Peake, Felix Herbert, H. M. Grant, and J. L. Tonkins. It was a unique discovery because there were very few mica mines outside of Vermont and New Hampshire.

Although the mine was abandoned in the 1880s, it was revived by the

Old rock school in Ruby Valley. (Photo by Shawn Hall)

Mutual Mica Company in 1924. The company was incorporated in February, and the mine was purchased from Fred Bender. A Hardinge conical pebble mill used to crush ore and company offices were built at the mine. Two of the owners were H. A. DeVaux, a prominent businessman from Contact, and Roy Rigsby. For the next two years, the company shipped five hundred pounds a day, but by the summer of 1927, the best deposits were gone. The mine was sold at a forced sale to C. W. Kennedy in October for $2,900. Kennedy's offices were located at Tobar, but only limited production took place until 1931, when the mine was abandoned for good.

Electricity finally came to Ruby Valley in 1916 but it wasn't until 1960, when the Wells Rural Electric Company installed lines, that everyone had easy access to power. Sports provided entertainment for the valley residents. A baseball field was laid out near the store next to the Wines Ranch, and a team was fielded for many years. Games made for popular valley outings. While the valley had a strong Mormon influence, an official church wasn't completed until 1954; the school between the Wines and Sharp Ranches was converted to an Episcopal church in July 1936.

The last old business in the valley, the Rock House Bar, has now closed. The post office, which has operated at many locations throughout the valley during its one hundred and thirty years, is still in operation at a ranch in the northern part of the valley. Postmasters who have served include Wellington Griswold, Chester Griswold, Lou Wines, Ira Wines, Len Wines, Sam Wines, Stanley Wines, Lourinda Wines, William Myers, John Garrecht, Myra Coolley, Leonard Hopkins, Emma Wilson, Alice Gardner, and Marion Saxton.

Central Ruby School.
(Photo by Shawn Hall)

Connecting the West

During the 1960s, Ruby Valley had some celebrity ranch owners. Actors Joel McCrea and "Wild" Bill Elliott bought ranches in the valley. Elliott, who starred in ninety westerns, bought the Lutts and Smith Ranches for more than $500,000, and commented that "it's so neat and compact in a setting under the Ruby Mountains. It's just plain beautiful."[10] Elliott hired George Smiraldo as his ranch foreman. Elliott greatly enjoyed the companionship of his neighbors (Roger Smith, Blaine Sharp, and Lourinda Wines), saying, "These wonderful people have made me, a stranger, feel right at home. They have been a guiding hand to me from the first day I came on my ranch."[11]

Ranching is still the lifeblood of Ruby Valley, and the fertile and beautiful valley continues to be a prosperous area. Ruby Valley is a spectacular place to visit, not only for the history but for the scenery as well. Old buildings of stone, brick, and wood abound throughout the valley. One building of particular interest is an old rock structure at the Wines Ranch that served as the ranch refrigerator. The building had a stream running through it to keep its contents cold.

The old stone schoolhouse stands near the ranch. The Wines ranch house is built of brick, and there are a number of other beautiful brick ranch houses in the valley. There are at least five cemeteries in the valley, at Cave Creek, Gardner Ranch, Wright Ranch, upper Ruby Valley, and at the Mormon church. Other family plots exist on some of the older ranches. For more information on Ruby Valley, please see other sections in *Old Heart of Nevada: Ghost Towns and Mining Camps of Elko County:* Arthur, Secret, Battle Creek, Cave Creek, Harrison Pass, and Valley View.

Ryndon

DIRECTIONS: *From Elko, go east on I-80 for 12.8 miles to Ryndon.*

Ryndon first served as a grading camp during the construction of the Central Pacific Railroad in 1869. Later, a siding was added by the Southern Pacific Railroad. In 1902, the Southern Pacific established Ryndon as a construction camp during the digging of the Ryndon tunnel. The camp was established by Erickson and Peterson, and, in addition to the many boardinghouses, a powerhouse and telegraph station were built. The camp was a wild and dangerous place that quickly earned a reputation as one of the most lawless towns in Nevada, where shootings and knifings were commonplace.

A post office opened at Ryndon on January 22, 1903, with Louis Orstad as postmaster. The Ryndon tunnel was completed in 1903 but a terrible price had been paid. During construction, five men were killed by premature explosions in separate incidents. Once the tunnel was completed, the camp was

disbanded, although Ryndon was still home to a section crew, and the post office closed on March 31, 1904.

As with most railroad towns, Ryndon had its share of accidents. In January 1911, one occurred in the tunnel when a boxcar broke an axle, which then smashed some of the supports, causing a cave-in. Repairs cost the Southern Pacific more than $100,000. Another deadly accident took place in September 1926 when Hiram Wood was killed by a mail train in the tunnel. He had been the tunnel tender for seven years. Workers yelled at Wood, trying to warn him, but another passing train drowned them out. He left a wife and seven children.

A school opened at Ryndon in 1918 with Elvira Blevins teaching. The school remained opened for more than ten years. Former teacher Flo Reed remembered that the building was only thirty feet from the railroad tracks, which caused many distractions. The school was twelve feet by sixteen feet, had ten desks, and averaged an enrollment of about fifteen students.

In 1923, Guy Aguirre was hired as foreman for Ryndon. It was the beginning of a long tenure that lasted for forty-five years. During those years, Aguirre and his wife raised seven children at Ryndon. When Aguirre retired in 1967, the railroad part of Ryndon closed for good. Although nothing is left of the Ryndon camp, many new homes in the area were built during the recent Elko boom.

Schley

(Schly)

DIRECTIONS: *From Wells, go south on U.S. 93 for 28 miles. Turn right on Nevada 229 and go 14 miles. Turn left and go 3½ miles. Turn left onto a poor road and continue for 2 miles to Schley. Located 4 miles south of the Ruby Valley maintenance station.*

Schley was a post office on the Tom Short Ranch in north Ruby Valley from September 26, 1898, to July 15, 1903. Tom Short served as postmaster during the entire time the office was active. The office was named in honor of Admiral Winfield Scott Schley, commander of the American fleet who defeated the Spanish navy at Santiago de Cuba on July 3, 1898.

The creation of the post office was the result of a dispute between Short and Ira D. Wines, who brought the mail from Halleck to the Ruby Valley post office at the Overland Ranch. Despite repeated requests, Wines refused to drop off Short's mail on his way. Short filed for his own post office and named it not only for Admiral Schley, but also because his name was pronounced "sly." Short was a Civil War veteran who had served with General William T. Sherman. He and his wife, Mary Ann, came to Ruby Valley in the 1870s, originally settling at Cave Creek, and then moving to the old R. B. Thompson Ranch in 1875.

More information on the Short family is found in the Ruby Valley section of this book. However, one item bears mention here. In May 1900, due to problems with his son, Tom Short was forced to place the following classified ad: "I hereby warn all persons not to trust my son, Emmet Short, in my name for any purpose."[12] Short had problems with his sons until he died in 1918. However, he was the cause of some of these disagreements. The ranch stayed in the Short family, under Bill Short's ownership, until his death in 1941. The ranch is now owned by Jack and Brenda Gardner. The old two-story brick house and rock barn still stand at the ranch.

Secret Valley

DIRECTIONS: *From Arthur, go north on Nevada 229 for 3 miles to the middle of Secret Valley.*

Secret Pass was so named because it was a hard-to-find short cut through the Ruby Mountains. Peter Skene Ogden was the first nonnative through the pass, in December 1828. In 1841, the Barleson-Bidwell Party used the pass, as did the Murphy-Stevens-Townsend Party in 1844.

The first actual settlers didn't arrive in Secret Valley until 1874. Besides new ranching ventures, a short-lived attempt was made at mining. During

1878, J. A. Stone and A. J. Shorey worked some placer claims along Cotton-wood Creek. Two lode mines, Adeline Nelson and Maggie Mitchell, were also worked. However, the pair abandoned their mines by the fall of 1879.

In 1880, a public road was built through the pass. A school opened in Secret Valley in 1883 with thirteen students, mostly from the Gardner and Wright families who had ranches in the valley.

In 1904, A. S. Coleman discovered a mineral spring alongside Secret Creek and formed the Ruby Mineral Springs Company. The spring provided seventy-five thousand gallons of water a day, bottled as Ruby Mineral Spring Water. Coleman planned to build a health resort and sanitarium at the spring, but the plan didn't come to anything, and the company folded in a couple of years.

In March 1900, Ed Murphy Sr. and his wife, Emma Gardner, bought the Lemon Creek Ranch from William Gardner. Murphy purchased more of Gardner's property in 1903. He also bought the Anderson Ranch, which had originally been owned by Charles Grover, in 1907. Murphy was the first person in the area to own a threshing machine.

In 1914, the United States Forest Service built a new road through Secret Pass that cost $10,000. This road was paved in 1957 and is still used today. A post office opened at the Murphy Ranch on October 27, 1916, but remained in operation until October 15, 1918. Pollie Murphy served as postmaster for those two years. In 1918, James Ryan purchased a small ranch in Secret Pass, later leased to Bob White. In 1928, White killed Louis Lavell in Elko and brought Lavell's body to the ranch, burning the house with the body inside to destroy the evidence. For a complete account of the White murder, see the Elko section of this book.

In 1935, Eddie Murphy Jr. bought the ranch from his father. Murphy had married Ellen O'Rourke in 1929, and the Murphys hired teachers, including Blawnie Mae Fairchild and Fay Guldager, to educate their children. The Secret School finally closed in 1951, and the only student, Morlene Murphy, then attended the Pole Canyon School, located a couple of miles to the east. Murphy finally retired and sold the ranch to Loyd and Von Sorenson in 1958. The Sorensons still own the ranch today. Two other ranches, the Sharp and Wright, also are active in the valley.

The William Crane Ranch in South Fork, 1886. (Reginald Heard collection, Northeastern Nevada Museum)

South Fork

(Shepherd's Station) (Coral Hill)

DIRECTIONS: From Elko, go south on Nevada 227 for 7 miles. Then go south on Nevada 228 for 11 miles to South Fork.

The South Fork area was first settled in 1867 by George Crane, John Richardson, William Tucker, Thomas Chandler, and Robert Toller. Two trips a year were made to Austin, Texas, to stock up on supplies. George Shepherd organized the Denver-Shepherd toll road, also known as the Elko-Hamilton road, which ran to Hamilton, in the fall of 1868. This was the first toll road in eastern Nevada. At the time, it was the only road heading south from Elko to White Pine County, but the Gilson Turnpike was completed the next spring on the east side of the valley, ending Shepherd's monopoly.

Until Elko formed in 1869, the Taylor and Morton stage used Shepherd's Station as its terminus. Taylor was well known for his skill with a shotgun and was so feared that his stages were never harassed. Shepherd occasionally rode shotgun for Wells Fargo on its stages. Shepherd settled at South Fork, and his station was the first overnight stop south of Elko. In 1869, Shepherd built a larger stage station and a hotel, which contained a bar, dining room, and large wine cellar featuring French wines. A post office, named Coral Hill, opened on March 25, 1870, but closed on July 19, 1871.

Shepherd's toll road fell victim to the vicious stagecoach wars that occurred during the 1870s. When Hill Beachey took over the Gilson road, his lower prices and faster route hurt Shepherd. In 1870, when the Woodruff and Ennor line was changed to run on the Gilson road, Shepherd's route was virtually abandoned. Not one to give up, Shepherd opened a new toll road from Elko to Bullion in 1870. On February 24, 1874, the post office reopened, named South Fork although the name was changed back to Coral Hill on May 1, and remained in operation until March 14, 1877. Shepherd was postmaster the entire time.

Shepherd eventually quit the stage business and returned to ranching, but his hotel remained open and was the "in" place for Elkoans to go for dances, parties, holiday gatherings, and weddings. He always promised that "the table would be full and the bar stocked."[13] Elko County bought Shepherd's old toll road in 1882 and made it into a public road. Shepherd later served as Elko County treasurer, followed by two terms as state senator.

In 1875, Shepherd founded the Mineral Soap mine. The soap was marketed by the Elko Mineral Soap Company and was shipped to a soap factory in Oakland, California. The Shoshone word "San-Too-Gah-Choi," meaning good soap, was printed on the wrapper. Sheperd's soap won an award at the World's Fair at Chicago in 1894 because it was the only natural soap product displayed. The soap was marketed until 1900.

In April 1885, Elko County mourned when George Shepherd died. Over the years, memories of Shepherd's Station have faded, but the area continues to be the home of many ranches. With the completion of the South Fork Dam, the area is now a popular recreation area. Not much remains at Shepherd's Station except some foundations and scattered debris.

Starr Valley

DIRECTIONS: *Located generally south and east of Deeth. Nevada 230 from Deeth to Welcome is in Starr Valley.*

Starr Valley was named in honor of Lieutenant Augustus Washington Starr, who first settled in the valley in 1868 and was one of the original establishers of Fort Halleck. While Starr left the valley in 1870 after being discharged from the fort, many other settlers had come into the area in the meantime and the population of the valley stood at sixty-nine in 1870.

Early settlers included George and John Ackler, Sam Davis, Samuel Mc-Mullen, Lee St. Clair, Joseph Scott, John Crosson, David Johnston, Archy Wil-

The Johnston home in Starr Valley. The building was built out of adobe bricks made on the property in 1875. (Pauline Quinn collection, Northeastern Nevada Museum)

liams, William and Guy Weathers, Malcolm Hall, Ben Armstrong, and Charles Gerboth. St. Clair was an old Confederate soldier whose home had been destroyed by General William T. Sherman, and he remained extremely bitter about it. To make local matters worse, a nearby settler, John Crosson, had marched with Sherman. When the two men were in the same vicinity, words flew, although the men never actually fought. David Johnston served in the state legislature and officiated at local funerals.

By 1875, the valley population had risen to ninety-five. An old saloon was converted into a school by Mrs. Malcolm Hall. In 1876, valley residents raised $1,250 to build a new school. The school, which initially had sixteen students, still stands and is used as the chapel at the cemetery. In 1877, a justice of the peace (D. V. Johnson) and a constable (Levi Cox) were appointed for the valley. The proximity of Deeth with its railroad connection made it easy for the ranchers and farmers to ship their goods.

One of the biggest ranches to develop in Starr Valley was the 71 Ranch, located at the southern edge of the valley. The ranch was established in 1877 by Joseph Scott who brought the first purebred Herefords to the United States from England. In 1889, Scott and Caleb Hank organized the Halleck Cattle Company, which survived the hard winter of 1889–1890. The ranch was sold in 1913 to William and Grace Lange. In 1917, the Union Land and Cattle Company acquired the 71 Ranch, and when that company folded, Peter Emerson Marble bought the ranch. His son took over the ranch in the 1960s. The Marble family owned the 71 Ranch for sixty-nine years before it was sold to the Ellison Ranching Company in 1995.

During the 1880s and 1890s, Starr Valley continued to grow. A population of 169 resided in the valley in 1880 and by 1890 had increased to 230. In 1888, the Starr Valley Lodge of the International Order of Good Templars was organized with William Weathers elected leader. A new hall was completed in January 1892. During the 1890s, Frank Jeanney had the largest orchard in Starr Valley. In 1897, Charles Black purchased the first threshing machine and was kept busy harvesting the valley's grain.

In 1898, John Cazier purchased the old Woodruff and Ennor Ranch on Trout Creek. The future of this ranch and the Caziers had a great impact on Elko County's history. In 1915, the John H. Cazier and Sons Company was organized. Later, Cazier's son Harry took over the company and in 1927 built the first fully automatic hydroelectric plant in Nevada. The Starr Valley power distribution system, serving twenty-seven customers, was the first rural electrification system in the state. It was later organized as the Wells Power Company and sold to the Wells Rural Electric Company. The power plant supplied electricity for Wells, Deeth, and Starr Valley until 1959.

Also, in 1928, Cazier built the first Elko County Fish Hatchery on Trout Creek, which was used until a new hatchery was built in southern Ruby Valley. Cazier had many other interests. Besides the ranch and power company, which he ran with his wife, Ellen Nevada Dewar, he also served as president of the Nevada Monarch Mining Company at Spruce Mountain for twenty years. He was one of the founders in 1934 of the Elko County Cattle Association, which later became the Nevada Cattlemen's Association. He also served

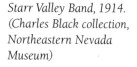

Starr Valley Band, 1914. (Charles Black collection, Northeastern Nevada Museum)

The Starr Valley School, built in 1872. It now serves as the chapel for the Starr Valley cemetery. (Pauline Quinn collection, Northeastern Nevada Museum)

on the Elko County School Board and was director of the Wells Chamber of Commerce. Cazier died in 1963; Ellen died in 1966.

By 1900, 410 people lived in Starr Valley. The school was overcrowded: teacher Nevada Hardesty Griswold had to cope with more than seventy students. In 1903, another school, North Starr, or Hook, opened in the northern part of the valley between the Black and Smiley Ranches. At the same time, the Starr Valley Hall was built and the Starr Valley Band organized. The Starr Valley Progressive Club was organized in 1913 and is the oldest club in Elko County. Hannah Smiley was elected the first president. The club, which took over the empty Good Templars Hall, became popular for hosting many plays.

In 1912, the first substantial school was built on Boulder Creek. At that time, three other schools were in operation: Starr, Hook, and Mountain Home. The Boulder Creek School, built on land donated by the Weathers family, was the largest, with two classrooms, a gymnasium, full basement, inside toilets, and a large bell tower. Many dances and plays sponsored by the Starr Valley Progressive Club were held at the school. During the 1920s, the

Boating on the pond at the Mountain View resort in Starr Valley. (Tony and Ellen Primeaux collection, Northeastern Nevada Museum)

Starr Valley basketball team, made up of local residents, had a reputation as one of the best in the state. Some of the standouts were Fritz Smiley, Paul and Blaine Jeanney, Mark Scott, Morley and Leslie Murphy, Tom Griswold, Bill Goodale, and Aaron Hylton.

In 1919, a new North Starr school was built to replace the old school, which had been built out of railroad ties. The building also served as the Odd Fellows and Rebekah Lodge halls. Once the old school closed, it was used by Bob Black to house his Starr Inn and Tavern. All of the remaining schools closed in 1957, when they were consolidated with the Wells School District. The Boulder School was sold to local residents for $10. They planned to use it as a community center. However, plans never turned to action, and the building was torn down in 1968. The North Starr School was purchased by the Odd Fellows and Rebekah Lodges, where meetings are still held. Some of the teachers for the valley schools included Nevada Hardesty Griswold, Mary Fuller, Connie Keith, Emily Sparks, Anna McMullen, Flo Reed, Helen Boyea, Erina Holmes, Ruth English, and Ethel St. Clair.

Mountain View, at the north end of the valley, had been settled by Samuel Davis in 1880. Large ponds were built, and a successful ranch was organized. In 1923, Davis and his family made big changes at the ranch. A large dance hall was built on the shore of one of the ponds. In addition, a restaurant and cabins for automobile tourists were constructed. The resort featured fishing, swimming, boating, and trails for horseback riding. Every week, a boxing match was held in the dance hall. However, when the highway was moved in 1930, the resort closed down. Sam Davis, still the owner, died in 1939. During the 1960s, the Gerber family began using the facility as the base for their Starr Valley Outfitters, which is still in operation today.

A tragic murder occurred in Starr Valley in March 1925 when Deputy Sheriff Charlie Lewis, also a local resident, was killed by Guadaloupe Acosta, a Mexican prisoner. Lewis laid in state at the Starr Valley Chapel and was buried in the cemetery. Acosta was sentenced to death, but was declared insane in 1926 and never executed.

Many ranches still operate throughout Starr Valley. While many are a consolidation of the smaller original ranches, there are many old ranch buildings left, including a beautiful brick house built by Joseph Johnston just after the turn of the century. Johnston was born in the valley in 1873 and served as president of the Starr Valley Farm Bureau. Johnston married Maud Crosson in 1902, and they were a popular couple, traveling all over the county playing violin and piano. The first Elko County Fair was held at the Johnston Ranch in 1920.

The old school, now a chapel, guards the extensive Starr Valley Cemetery. The cemetery is on land donated by pioneer Julia Ann Armstrong. The cemetery and chapel are well cared for by valley residents and are two of the most interesting in the county. Besides these sights, there are a number of beautiful old homes located in the valley. The scenery and sights of Starr Valley warrant a long visit.

The Boulder Creek School in Starr Valley. (Edna Patterson collection, Northeastern Nevada Museum)

Ten Mile Station

(Beachey Station) (Clayton Station)

DIRECTIONS: *From Elko, go east on Nevada 227 for 6.9 miles. Go south on Nevada 228 for 3 miles to Ten Mile Station.*

Ten Mile Station was established as a stop on the Elko-Hamilton road, or Gilson Turnpike, in 1869. The station was located on the south bank of Ten Mile Creek and was run by George Clayton. During the 1890s, John Yowell took over the ranch and station.

A school opened at the ranch in 1903 and was in operation off and on until the early 1920s. By this time, the stages had long since stopped running. During the 1920s, the old Ten Mile Station was used as a speakeasy, run by Evelyn "Little Eva" Mason. Federal agents closed the operation in 1929. A ranch is still in operation at the station site today, and a couple old stone buildings remain.

Toller's Station

DIRECTIONS: *Located near the junction of Nevada 227 and Nevada 228.*

Toller's Station was the first stop south of Elko on the Gilson Turnpike, a toll road established in 1869. The station was the entrance to the toll road. Fees were collected by proprietor George Toller. Once the toll road became a public road, the need for the station ended, and it was abandoned by the mid-1870s. Nothing is left at the site today.

Tonka

DIRECTIONS: *Located 5 miles east of Carlin on the Union Pacific, just south of I-80.*

Tonka now serves as a signal station for the Union Pacific (on the former Western Pacific and Southern Pacific main lines), located where the two railroads join just east of Carlin. Tonka was named for the seed of the cucimana plant, which was used to flavor snuff and came into being during the construction of Tunnel 1 on the Southern Pacific, completed in February 1903, between here and Vivian. In addition to serving as a siding, sectionhouses and cattle pens were built.

In February 1939, local rancher Manuel Machado was killed at Tonka while he was herding cattle to be loaded on the train. An automobile skidded

The siding at Tonka shortly before the buildings were removed. (James and Larry Monroe collection, Northeastern Nevada Museum)

into him after the driver tried to avoid the cattle. Machado, sixty-eight, had ranched in the area since 1912.

Today, Tonka is only a signal station. The sectionhouses and cattle pens were removed years ago.

Vivian

DIRECTIONS: *Located 3 miles east of Carlin on the Union Pacific, just south of I-80.*

Vivian is a siding on the former Southern Pacific Railroad (now the Union Pacific), three miles east of Carlin. In 1903, Tunnel 1 between Vivian and Tonka was completed. From 1919 to 1922, the Trip-O-Lite Products Company ran a diatomaceous earth mine at Vivian, and a twelve-ton-per-day mill was built in 1919. Foundations and part of the mill mark the site of Vivian.

Wear's Station
(Four Mile Station)

DIRECTIONS: *Located 4 miles south of Elko on the old White Pine road.*

Wear's Station was a station on the old White Pine road. The toll station, run by R. G. Wear, was the beginning of the Denver-Shepherd Toll Road and George Shepherd's toll road to Bullion, built in 1870.

The station was abandoned when the Gilson Turnpike, on the east side of the valley, became the major thoroughfare to White Pine County. Shepherd's Bullion road became a public road, and the need for the toll station was eliminated. Nothing remains at the station site.

Williams Station

DIRECTIONS: *Located 4 miles northwest of Jiggs on the Twin Bridges road.*

Williams Station, located near where Smith Creek joins Huntington Creek, was a stop on the Denver-Shepherd White Pine Toll Road beginning in 1869. The station was run by Warren Williams, but was abandoned once the Gilson road on the east side of the valley became the preferred route to White Pine. Williams continued to ranch in the area for a number of years before leaving. Nothing remains of the stage station today.

Southeastern Elko County

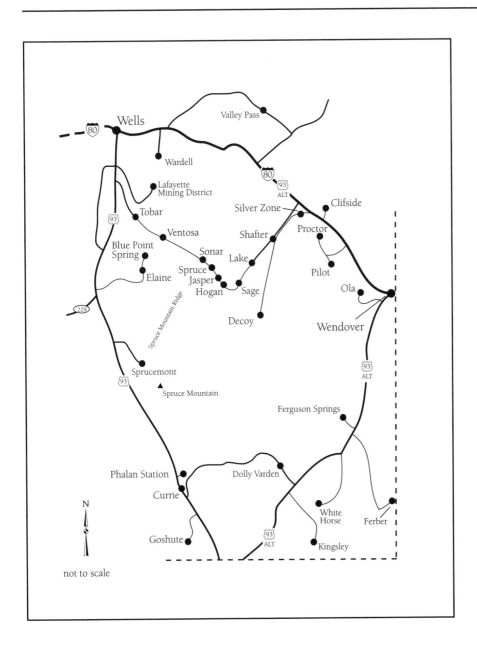

Wells

Valley Pass

80

Wardell

80

93 ALT

Lafayette Mining District

Silver Zone

Clifside

Tobar

93

Shafter

Proctor

Ventosa

Blue Point Spring

Sonar

Lake

Spruce Jasper

Hogan

Pilot

Elaine

Sage

Ola

Decoy

Wendover

229

Spruce Mountain Ridge

Sprucemont

93

▲ Spruce Mountain

93 ALT

Ferguson Springs

Phalan Station

Dolly Varden

Currie

N

White Horse

Ferber

Goshute

93 ALT

Kingsley

not to scale

Blue Point Spring

DIRECTIONS: From Tobar, take a gravel road southeast for 4 miles to Elaine. Located 2 miles north of Elaine.

Blue Point Spring was originally a small ranch incorporated into the Wells-Spruce Mountain stagecoach stop. The stop was located two miles north of Elaine, and was used as a horse-changing point with limited overnight accommodations and meals available. Once the boom at Spruce Mountain faded in the late 1870s, the stagecoach line folded, and Blue Point Spring returned to ranching. The ranch was abandoned in the 1890s. Today only a couple of log buildings struggle against the elements to remain standing.

Clifside

(Cliffside)

DIRECTIONS: Located 3 miles east of Silver Zone Pass, just north of I-80.

Clifside, as it is listed today, started as a small station on the main line of the Western Pacific Railroad (now the Union Pacific Railroad), but saw very little use and was soon demoted to signal-station status. The small platform and house that served as the station were dismantled in the 1920s.

Currie

(Bellinger's Spring)

DIRECTIONS: Located 62 miles south of Wells, on U.S. 93.

The springs at Currie were used as a stop on the Toano and Cherry Creek roads long before the town existed. The town of Currie formed in 1906 when the Nevada Northern Railway was constructed. Tracks were built to Currie on May 18. The first passenger train arrived on May 22, although the railroad was not completed to Ely until September 1906. Triweekly service began on June 2. The Nevada Northern built a depot that served passengers, shipped freight and livestock, and was the home of the railway agent.

The town was named for Joseph Currie, who had been owner of a ranch on nearby Nelson Creek since the 1880s. The first substantial building constructed was the two-story Currie Hotel, owned by Currie. A post office, housed in the hotel, opened on August 8 with Currie as postmaster. Another hotel, the Steptoe, was soon built by Henry Phalan, a local rancher.

Currie developed into the transportation and livestock center for southeastern Elko County with a consistent population of twenty. However, a diphtheria epidemic in July 1907 caused the entire station to be quarantined, but luckily, prompt action prevented any deaths. In 1908, Earl and Leona Reynolds moved to Currie to open a new telegraph office and railroad agency station. They also opened a store with Jim Byron. A one-room schoolhouse was built in 1908 near the Phalan Ranch. Two years later, due to increased demand, two more rooms were added to the school, one of which was used by Monroe, the teacher, for her home. The school also served as the Currie civic center, and was the scene of the local dances.

By 1910, Currie was in its heyday. Besides the depot, hotels, and school, a store and saloon also opened. In addition, the railroad constructed a sectionhouse and turntable. Many jackrabbits lived in the Currie area, and the Nevada Northern ran special Sunday trains from Ely for rabbit and rattlesnake hunting. Joseph Currie died in October of 1912 and was buried in Cherry Creek.

The Reynolds soon bought out Byron and quit working for the railroad to build a new store. The post office was moved to the store, with Leona Reynolds as assistant postmaster to her husband. The Steptoe Hotel was taken down in the 1910s, and the Currie Merchandise Store, which housed the post office, was built on the site. Currie continued to serve the railroad, and when the road from Wells to Ely was paved, a gas station and store were built. In 1941, the Nevada Northern Railway discontinued passenger and mail service at Currie, due to slow business and the departure from Currie of the depot agent, Jerry Cormer. The limited business did not justify finding a replacement agent.

Freight and ore trains continued to rumble through Currie until the 1980s, and the post office remained open until May 28, 1971. In sixty-five years of operation, postmasters included Earl Reynolds, Alice Fappiano, Samuel Hagans, Manuel Edo, and Louise Lear. Edo had the longest tenure, from 1926 to 1961. The original Currie depot still stands, as does the Currie Hotel. Other buildings from Currie's early years also survive. A gas station and store are in operation, and Currie has a highway maintenance station. The town has a current population of about twenty.

Decoy

DIRECTIONS: From the Shafter interchange on I-80, 28 miles northwest of Wendover, head southwest along the railroad for 6 miles to Shafter. At Shafter, head south on a rough road along Nevada Northern Railway line for 12 miles to Decoy.

Decoy came into being with the construction of the Nevada Northern Railway in 1906, first as a siding until the Decoy Mining District was organized and began producing manganese ore from mines located eight miles east. At that time, loading platforms were built for loading the ore.

Before mining, the area around Decoy was used for dry farming, a farming method that was popular during the 1910s. By 1915, as many as twenty dry farms were located around Decoy, but a combination of drought and an excess of rabbits caused the failure of 70 percent of the crops. Although more established dry-farming communities like Metropolis and Tobar kept going, the relatively new farms at Decoy had a high failure rate. The year 1916 was even more devastating, and of the seven farms left, five failed completely. By 1917, all dry farming around Decoy had ended.

In 1917, the Darky (Black Rock) mine, owned by Holmquist and Johnson, began producing manganese, shipping 4,500 tons of ore in 1917 and 1918 through the Decoy siding. However, this was the only significant production from the district. Duval International (now known as Battle Mountain Gold Company) did some exploratory drilling in the 1980s, and a microscopic gold deposit was outlined but has not been mined yet.

Ruins of the loading ramps and sectionhouse mark the Decoy siding. A number of old farming homesteads dot the area west of the railroad tracks. At the Darky mine, collapsed shafts, an open pit, and mine dumps remain.

Elaine

DIRECTIONS: From Ventosa, take a gravel road southwest for 3 miles to Elaine.

Elaine was a stop on the Wells-Sprucemont stagecoach line during the 1870s and 1880s. Located on a small ranch on the east side of Snow Water Lake, the station was used as a horse-changing stop and for meals for stage passengers. A short-lived post office operated at Elaine from May 10 to December 9, 1880, with Frank Heattman and William Scott as postmasters. When Sprucemont died in the early 1880s, the stage stopped running, and the small ranch was unable to keep operating. More than one hundred years after abandonment, only some scattered debris remains at the Elaine site.

Goshute

(Gosiute) (Goshiute)

DIRECTIONS: *From Currie, go south on U.S. 93 for 6 miles. Turn right and continue for 2 miles to Goshute.*

Named for a local Indian tribe, Goshute was a stop and siding on the Nevada Northern Railway. During the railroad's construction in 1906, a small stationhouse and boardinghouse were built. Nearby Goshute Lake was named by E. G. Beckwith during the surveying of a Pacific railroad route in 1855. A post office, spelled Gosiute, opened on January 22, 1907, with Charles Harlow as postmaster. The office closed on September 30 of the same year. Only a couple of foundations are left today.

Hogan

DIRECTIONS: *From Wells, take U.S. 93 south 14 miles to the Tobar turnoff. Turn left and go 4 miles to Tobar. At the Tobar site, take the road parallel to the tracks southeast for 17 miles to Hogan.*

Hogan is a siding on the former Western Pacific Railroad (now the Union Pacific) southeast of Ventosa and southwest of Shafter. Nothing substantial was ever built at the site and only the concrete footings of a water tower remain.

Jasper

DIRECTIONS: *Located 2 miles northwest of Hogan (see above).*

Jasper was established in 1910 as a signal station on the Western Pacific Railroad (now the Union Pacific), serving for many years as a shipping point for Spruce Mountain ore. It was named for Jasper Harrell, a mining man at Spruce Mountain. Mail for Spruce Mountain was shipped through Jasper. In April 1926, due to increased demand from a revival at the Spruce Mountain mines, the Western Pacific built a telegraph office, an express and freight warehouse, and a couple of small houses for railroad employees.

In January 1932, eight cars from a trail derailed inside the Jasper Tunnel, and Western Pacific trains had to be detoured on the Southern Pacific tracks via Cobre until repairs were made. A tragedy occurred in the tunnel in September 1936 when a young boy, John Stocks of Moab, Utah, was thrown off a train and killed. He was buried in potter's field in Elko, and his identity took several months to establish because he had been traveling alone.

When the Spruce Mountain revival faded in the late 1930s, the Western

Pacific closed the telegraph office and warehouse, and all of the buildings were dismantled. When the Western Pacific rebuilt its rails in the 1970s, Jasper siding was eliminated. Only concrete foundations mark the site.

Lake

(Luke)

DIRECTIONS: *Located 4 miles southwest of Shafter on the Union Pacific.*

Lake, listed as Luke on some maps, was a former siding between Shafter and Hogan on the Western Pacific Railroad (now the Union Pacific). In March 1902, helper engine 2618's boiler exploded while moving cars on the siding, killing William Wilton, the engineer, Leroy Munsee, the fireman, and William Myers, a soldier. Another tragedy occurred in February 1951 when a section worker, Regino Tabarez, was found frozen to death between Lake and Shafter. He was stationed at Lake, and had hiked to the store in Shafter but was caught in a snowstorm on his way back and died.

Lake siding was eliminated when the Union Pacific rebuilt their line during the 1980s. Only the concrete foundations of the water tank and sectionhouse mark the site.

Ola

DIRECTIONS: *Located 5 miles west of Wendover on the Union Pacific.*

Ola is a signal station and siding on the former Western Pacific Railroad (now the Union Pacific). Ola was established in 1910, and is still used today. The original signal shack still stands at the site.

Phalan Station

DIRECTIONS: *From Currie, go north on U.S. 93 for 4 miles. Turn right and continue for 1 mile to Phalan Station.*

Phalan Station was a stop on the Cherry Creek road beginning in the 1880s. The station was established by John Phalan, a former miner at Cherry Creek, who bought the ranch from Eddie Lichlyter. The Wells-Cherry Creek stagecoach line ran for many years and was extended to Ely in the 1890s.

During the 1890s, Phalan ran covered coaches on the line. At the same time, his ranch grew, and at its peak he had more than 1,400 head of cattle on his range. However, once interest in Cherry Creek and Ely faded, Phalan sold the ranch and moved away. The Phalan Creek Ranch is still in operation today, although not much remains from the early days. Some books and maps incorrectly list the name of the ranch and creek as Phalen.

Pilot
(Pilot Peak) (Pilot Peak Mining District)

DIRECTIONS: Pilot Peak is 18 miles north of Wendover east of Pilot Road. Pilot is located 10 miles northwest of Wendover on the Union Pacific.

Pilot Peak was a landmark for emigrants crossing the salt flats of Utah on their way to California. The peak was named by John C. Frémont in 1845, after the first emigrant group, the Bartleson-Bidwell Party, came through in 1841.

The first mine on Pilot Peak was the Pilot Peak mine, owned by F. H. Darling. In July 1878, Walter Brown discovered small silver deposits and organized the Pilot Peak Mining District. Darling owned the Thistle and American Flag mines. With extreme confidence, Brown also filed for a mill site, but little activity ensued, and if there was any production during the 1870s, it was very small. Mining interest did not return until 1908 when J. C. Hillman, a saloon owner in Cobre, began working some claims, as did William Porter. However, little was produced.

With the completion of the Western Pacific (wp) Railroad in 1907, a stop and signal station named Pilot opened. The railroad built a couple of buildings to house section crews and their families. A school opened in 1910, with Edna Ross serving as the first teacher. The school operated until the 1920s. Other teachers included Alice Watkins, L. G. Hodges, and Margaret Northrup. The Pilot station was phased out in the 1920s, and the section crews moved elsewhere. The wp dismantled the buildings and moved them to other stations on the railroad.

From 1934 to 1938, a number of small mines in the area were worked, including the Badger, Crazy Dutchman, American Flag, and Western Star. Total production from this activity amounted to 636 ounces of silver, 22 ounces of gold, and 833 pounds of copper. There was no other mining activity until the 1980s, when the Pilot Limestone Quarry, which had been discovered in 1960 but not mined by the Utah Construction and Mining Company, was taken over by Continental Lime, Inc. A 400-ton (daily capacity) lime plant, still in operation, was completed in 1989. It produced 103,000 tons of quicklime in 1990.

There is not much left at the various sites. At Pilot, on the railroad, only a couple of concrete foundations and scattered debris mark the site. Only small ore dumps and collapsed workings are left at the mines in Miners Canyon. Evidence of the California Trail exists nearby; wagon ruts and rust marks on the rocks show sections of the trail, which have been marked by members of the Oregon-California Trails Association.

Proctor

DIRECTIONS: *From Wendover, head east on I-80 for 16 miles to the Proctor turnoff. Head south for ½ mile to Proctor, adjacent to railroad tracks.*

Proctor first appeared in 1872 when Frank Proctor (for whom the place is named) discovered silver ore here, leading to the formation of the Proctor Mining district. After a brief rush to the area, the mines were abandoned when the veins ran out. When the Western Pacific Railroad was completed in 1909, Proctor became a stop and signal station for the railroad, leading to a revival of mining interest.

The Silver Standard and Star mines, four miles south of the Proctor siding, were later discovered. The railroad's proximity to the mines led to extensive exploration. The Western Pacific Railroad began construction on the Arnold Loop, with the small town of Proctor as the base for construction workers, but the new route on the loop bypassed Proctor's location. In March 1910, John Cardron announced plans to build a forty-room hotel at Proctor. When he realized that Proctor would not survive after Arnold Loop was completed and the town was bypassed, he quietly cancelled his plans.

The Arnold Loop was completed in 1914, and Proctor was abandoned. Interest in mining faded. The only recorded production from the Proctor district took place from 1917 to 1921, with 38 pounds of copper and 304 ounces of silver produced from the Silver Hoard and Nick Del Duke (Keystone) Mines. Only mine dumps are left, and nothing remains at the Proctor station.

Sage

DIRECTIONS: *From Wells, take U.S. 93 south for 14 miles to the Tobar turnoff. Turn left and travel 4 miles to Tobar. At the Tobar site, take the road parallel to the tracks southeast, then north, for 22 miles to Sage.*

Sage was a siding on the Western Pacific Railroad (now the Union Pacific) between Shafter and Spruce. A small sectionhouse and water tank were built at Sage and only their concrete foundations are left.

Nevada Northern Railroad switch house at Shafter. (Photo by Shawn Hall)

Shafter

(Bews)

DIRECTIONS: *From Wendover, go west on I-80 for 22 miles to the Shafter exit. Go south on the gravel road for 6 miles to Shafter.*

Bews was established as a siding for the Nevada Northern Railway in 1906. It was named after an Englishman, Richard Bews, who established a ranch in 1897 and ran a stage line and freight station. During April 1906, a railroad construction crew of 150 Greeks and Italians camped here. Bews was renamed Shafter, for General W. R. Shafter, a commander in the U.S. Army, during the Spanish-American War, when the Western Pacific Railroad tracks reached this location, crossing the Nevada Northern, in September 1907.

As Western Pacific track-laying crews neared Shafter, many lots were sold in the town. The first store, the Morgan-Spencer Mercantile Company, opened in early 1908. Orsen Spencer also became the first postmaster when the office opened in his store on August 28, 1908. The Western Pacific began regular operations on November 9, 1908.

A community of about forty lived at Shafter for years and both railroads maintained section crews and small depots at Shafter. A school opened in 1909 and remained open until 1933, when the county ran out of money.

Schoolteacher M. J. Williams formed the Shafter Literary Society in October 1932. Society events were reported in the *Nevada State Herald*. When Williams left after the school closed, the society folded. In the early 1930s,

The abandoned right-of-ways of the Nevada Northern Railroad near Shafter. (Photo by Shawn Hall)

Clarence Neasham opened a general store, running it until his death in January 1941. His wife ran the store until 1947.

In February 1950, the operator of the Shafter store, Joe Thomas, was threatened by Dee Gower. Thomas responded by killing Gower with a shotgun. In court, Thomas testified, "I had to shoot him. It was a case of either shoot him or let him get a hold of the gun and kill me," and was found not guilty of the killing.[1]

During the 1950s, Shafter's importance diminished. By September 1953, Joe LaFrance was named postmaster, mainly because he was the only eligible resident. The post office closed on April 19, 1957. Throughout the years, postmasters included Susie Fuller, George Kennan, Charles Dougherty, Stephen Tryman, Albert King, Charles Stackhouse, Grace Neasham, Gertrude Moody, William Thomas, Beatrice Bake, Elnora Frisella, and Aloha Peterson.

Shafter businesses had all closed by 1957, and the town was abandoned after that. The Railway Express Agency closed its Shafter office in March 1959. Until a few years ago, a couple of buildings still stood at Shafter but have since been dismantled. Only concrete foundations now mark the site and a small cemetery is located nearby.

Silver Zone

DIRECTIONS: Silver Zone Pass is located 2 miles southeast of the Shafter exit on I-80. Silver Zone siding (on the Union Pacific) is ½ mile south of the highway.

Silver Zone Pass was part of the Hastings Cutoff of the California Emigrant Trail. The Donner Party passed through in 1846 on the way to their deaths in the Sierra. Signs of the trail are still visible in the area. The name Silver Zone came about after Major Robert Goldman discovered silver nearby in May 1872. In the summer of 1872, a small boom camp formed, and Moffitt and Gassett began running a stage and freight line from Toano.

Active mines included the Silver Zone, Wilson, Currier and Goldman, Poor Men's, Star of the West, Governor Bradley, and Delmonico. A post office opened on August 27, 1872, with Charles Toyer as postmaster. However, the boom went bust by the next summer, and the camp was empty by fall, forcing the post office to close on September 10, 1873. Some mines were worked again in the mid-1880s, including the Golden King (A. P. Shively), Ledger (Shively and Peter Blair), Golden Prize (Lizzie Shively), and Little Treasure (William Riley, N. M. Pratt, and Don Wickizen).

Silver Zone enjoyed a revival in 1907 when a work camp formed for the construction of the Western Pacific Railroad through the pass. T. J. Connelly built a saloon a short distance away from the camp, but it violated the three-mile limit for alcohol consumption set by the Western Pacific. Many workers were arrested, and finally Connelly's license was revoked. When the railroad was completed, the camp was disbanded, and Silver Zone became a siding and section-crew location.

Silver Zone Pass is the highest point on the former Western Pacific (now the Union Pacific) between Oakland and Salt Lake City at 5,875 feet. The pass has been the scene of many railroad accidents. The most serious took place in March 1936 when the boiler of helper engine 19 exploded, killing brakemen Bud Howell and C. E. Dickerdorff. The men were in a caboose just ahead of the locomotive, and were thrown through the roof. The conductor, Fred Black, also in the caboose, was scalded by steam, dying five days later. Three men in the nearby sectionhouse were also scalded, but survived.

In 1942, tungsten was discovered at the Silver Zone and Great Western mines, owned by Lester Hice, Robert Hice, and O. T. McVey. The mines were later sold to the Rare Metals Company of Lovelock, and Robert Hice was hired as foreman. About two hundred units of tungsten were produced before the company left the district. While trains still traverse Silver Zone Pass, there is little left of the settlement except concrete ruins at the railroad siding. At the old mines, a few signs of the short-lived boom camp remain.

Sonar

DIRECTIONS: From Wells, take U.S. 93 south for 14 miles to the Tobar turnoff. Turn left and travel for 4 miles to Tobar. At the Tobar site, take the road parallel to the tracks southeast for 11 miles to Sonar.

Sonar, a signal station on the former Western Pacific Railroad (now the Union Pacific), is located between Ventosa and Spruce. The only known mention of Sonar in historical sources is that Robert Anderson was killed by a train at the station in June 1947. No structures were built at Sonar.

Tobar

(Clover City)

DIRECTIONS: From Wells, go south on U.S. 93 for 14 miles. Turn left and continue for 4 miles to Tobar.

In 1908, Tobar was established as a construction camp for the Western Pacific Railroad. A substantial depot was built, and a small town began to form. During construction, the owner of the Rag Saloon, which was housed in a canvas tent, put up a sign that simply said "To Bar." The two words were put together, and the new town had a name, Tobar.

Although Tobar was essentially a railroad town, it also was the center of a planned dry-farming community. The first dry farmers were Gover, Fred, and Ernest Wood, and Sidney Curtiss. By 1910, there were sixteen homesteads around Tobar. By 1911, there were about seventy-five people and twenty dwellings in the town and surrounding area. Due to demand, a school, later moved to Tobar in 1913, was built at the Munson Ranch near Tobar. A post office opened on December 20, 1911, with Mack Backstead as postmaster.

In 1912, the railroad began selling land at Tobar for $4 to $11 per acre; these prices attracted even more people to Tobar. In June 1912, the *Tobar Eye-Opener* was supposed to begin publication under the guidance of local attorney Frank Spear. However, no issues have ever been located, and it seems likely that the newspaper was never actually published.

Tobar, besides becoming a dry-farming area, also became the main shipping point for ore from mines at Warm Creek and Spruce Mountain and produce from Clover Valley. During 1913, the Tobar settlement greatly expanded with A. B. Hoaglin promoting the local farming area. Hoaglin also platted a townsite and built a two-story hotel, called the "White Elephant" by local residents.

Advertisements in newspapers throughout the country attracted many people to Tobar, but the promotional material contained false information. The brochures heralded Tobar as the home of the "big red apple," even though

there were no orchards in the area. The promotional campaign also claimed that fifty thousand acres would be under cultivation, and that Tobar would soon have a population of three thousand. However, no one stated where the water to irrigate fifty thousand acres was coming from.

Hoaglin was charged with mail fraud for trying to sell public land, but was acquitted. Hoaglin left Tobar for Canada, but later returned. During his absence, his brother stayed to carry on the land promotion.

In July 1915, the Hoaglin brothers opened the Chicago Store, a complete grocery store. Two other stores, the Golden Rule and United, also opened in 1915. By the end of 1915, Tobar had fourteen businesses, relying on patronage from the Tobar Flat farmers.

On Tobar Flat, a number of hamlets had formed, each containing ten to twenty-five people. The population of the Tobar area was five hundred, four hundred of whom lived on farms. Half of the local residents were from northern Utah. Most of these people were former railroad workers with an average age of thirty-nine. Three thousand acres had been cultivated, but droughts beginning in 1915 foreclosed any future the Tobar farms had.

By 1916, Tobar began to decline. The Chicago store was destroyed by fire in March and was not rebuilt. A short-lived newspaper, the *Tobar Times* (A. L. Covert, publisher), started publication on July 22, 1916, but folded during August. Subscribers who had paid for a year's subscription were upset with Covert, and he quietly left town without reimbursing subscribers. Another paper, the *Tobar Sentinel*, was published for a short period in 1916, edited by the elderly Sunday-school teacher.

Concrete foundations in Tobar. (Photo by Shawn Hall)

The problems at the dry farms continued. Besides the extended drought that began in 1915, an invasion of jackrabbits worsened the situation. Only one inch of rain fell at Tobar in 1916; the rabbits ate what few plants grew. One farmer commented that the best crop he had was two boxes of arrowheads. Many families moved away, and those who stayed had to seek employment in nearby mines to make ends meet.

A boost for the town took place when the railroad built a fifty thousand–gallon water tank and some sectionhouses, but farmers continued to leave. By the end of 1917, most of the dry farms had been abandoned.

Under a new campaign in 1918, the Tobar post office was renamed Clover City in an effort to portray the area in a more lush, positive light. Tobar's streets were regraded and Elko Valley Estates was formed. Two lots for $395 were advertised, but there were too many jackrabbits around for people to take farming seriously, and the efforts failed. Local boosters could not convince people that this was a good farming area when there was no water or rain. By 1920, dry farming ended in Tobar. Only six of the original homesteads were occupied, and those homesteaders worked elsewhere, not on their own farms.

The town of Tobar struggled to survive; its main source of income was from ore and cattle shipments. A new store, the Sawyer Mercantile Company, opened in March 1920. The completion of U.S. 93 led to cattle being shipped by truck, and that development, taking business away from the railroad, combined with a depression of metal prices slowing ore shipments, meant that Tobar's days were numbered. On January 18, 1921, the post office was renamed Tobar. In September 1923, the Tobar Lumber Company, which had been opened during Tobar's early days by E. E. Glaser, was moved to Wells and renamed the Western Hardware and Lumber Company.

By the end of the 1920s, only the station, school, Clover Valley Store, and post office remained open in Tobar. There were many abandoned homes and businesses, including the real estate office. During the 1930s, the remnants of Tobar served mostly railroad workers and their families. The school, in disrepair, was closed and sold by the county for $10 in February 1937.

The Tobar post office closed on September 17, 1942. Postmasters had included John Kenney, Anna Rutherford, Lizzie Bissell, Ethel Carady, Edith Ling, Frances Merrill, Mary Bassford, Eldora and Clarence Barton, and Laura Higley. In 1946, the Western Pacific abandoned the depot, and the last remaining business, the Clover Valley Store, closed. In October 1948, Hal Bricker of Wells bought the school and moved it to Wells. One by one, the other buildings were sold and moved.

By 1950, only the water tank, depot, ore loading chute, cattle pens, and sectionhouses were left. In 1952, all of the remaining railroad buildings were sold and moved. The Tobar depot was moved to Battle Creek, where it served as a boardinghouse for a mining operation. The station stood until August 1995, when a brush fire destroyed it, thwarting plans to move it to Elko to serve as the office of the Elko Chamber of Commerce. When the water tank was dismantled later in 1952, only foundations were left at Tobar. Tobar made the news again in 1969 when on June 19, a carload of bombs for Vietnam exploded one mile west of Tobar, leaving a huge crater and injuring conductor T. M. Johnson and brakeman Freeman Stephens.

Today at Tobar, extensive foundations and collapsed cellars show the layout of the once bustling town, but not much else is left. One mile south of the townsite are the concrete walls of large homesteads from the 1910s, and a few other smaller homestead ruins are scattered on the flat below the Tobar townsite.

Ventosa

DIRECTIONS: *Located 5 miles southeast of Tobar (see above) on the Union Pacific.*

Ventosa was a stop on the Western Pacific Railroad, the next depot southeast of Tobar. Ventosa was mainly a shipping point for Spruce Mountain ore, and a siding was built to load the ore. A school, with G. E. Brown as teacher, was started at Ventosa in 1912 and remained open until the 1920s. Other teachers were Ella Nelson and Esther McCanse.

From the 1910s through the 1940s, about ten people lived at Ventosa, most

Western Pacific depot foundation at Ventosa. (Photo by Shawn Hall)

working for the railroad. In 1929, a railroad spur from Ventosa to Spruce Mountain was planned but the rise of trucks for shipping put an end to this plan.

Ventosa was in the news in August 1950 when thirty-two freight cars derailed due to a broken drawbar. The derailment started a fire, destroying the cars, at a loss of $250,000. The depot and section buildings were sold and removed in the early 1950s. Only concrete foundations are left at Ventosa today.

Wendover

(Eastline) (West Wendover)

DIRECTIONS: *Located on I-80 on the Nevada-Utah border.*

Wendover has a split personality, with half of the town in Nevada and the other half in Utah. Wendover came into existence when the Western Pacific Railroad was completed in 1908. A settlement began to form at Wendover, the main attraction being the Bonneville Salt Flats in Utah, which were used as early as 1911 for automobile land speed–record attempts. The first business in Wendover was the Cobblestone Service Station, built by Bill Smith and a man named Eckstein. On June 17, 1914, Wendover was the site of the final connection of the first transcontinental telephone line. A 1994 monument in Wendover commemorates this achievement.

The Western Pacific built the Overland Hotel for passengers and railroad workers; the hotel burned in December 1922 at a loss of $100,000. Reese Foulks, a Western Pacific worker, was killed, and three other people were burned. In 1926, Joe Conely opened the Tri-State Mercantile Store on the Nevada side of Wendover.

Gambling was legalized in Nevada in 1931, creating an economic opportunity for the Nevada side of Wendover. Bill Smith's Stateline Hotel was the first legal casino in Wendover. The Smith family still runs casinos in Wendover, making it the oldest family-owned gaming operation in Nevada. Contrary to public misconception, West Wendover is not named West because of its geographical location, but instead in honor of Fred West, who came to the town in 1936, bought out Joe Conely, and opened the A-1 Service and Motel. These were the only two businesses located on the Nevada side of Wendover.

During World War II, Wendover boomed. The population went from about 125 to as high as 20,000 due to the formation of the Wendover Air Base, a training base for bomber pilots. Bob Hope visited the base and called it a "leftover Alcatraz with tents." At its peak, the base had 250 barracks, a three hundred–bed hospital, service clubs, two theaters, a gymnasium, a chapel, a band, and a camp newspaper, the *Salt Tablet*. Because of the pressure to train new pilots as quickly as possible, accidents were common, with as many as twenty men being killed in a day.

While thousands of men received training at Wendover, the most famous group to train at Wendover was the 509th Composite Group, commanded by Paul Tibbets Jr., which dropped two atomic bombs on Japan in August 1945 to end World War II. The base was deactivated in 1948, and the town of Wendover shrank to less than one hundred people, although the base is still occasionally used by the military.

By 1960, only the A-1 Service and Motel, Stateline Hotel, and Hide-a-Way Club were in business on the Nevada side of Wendover. During the 1970s, developers turned Wendover into a gambling spot for tourists and Utah residents. Today, Wendover is a substantial town. A number of casinos have joined the older ones, and Wendover Will, a sixty-four-foot neon cowboy, looks over the town. West Wendover became Elko County's fourth incorporated city in 1991, and the town continues to grow, as does the casino business.

The boom on the Nevada side of Wendover, compared to the slump on the Utah side, has created friction between residents of the two sides of town. This is particularly true with regard to the public schools, but the problems are being worked out. There is an interesting museum at the air force base on the Utah side, but it is open only occasionally.

Notes

Northwestern Elko County

1. Edna Patterson, Louise Ulph, and Victor Goodwin, *Nevada's Northeast Frontier* (Reno, Nevada: University of Nevada Press, 1969).
2. *Tuscarora Times-Review,* April 24, 1886.

North Central Elko County

1. *Tuscarora Times-Review,* October 1, 1884.
2. Carol Hendershot, "Dinner Station," *Northeastern Nevada Historical Society Quarterly* 3 (summer 1985): 67.
3. *Elko Independent,* August 5, 1899.
4. *Elko Free Press,* November 5, 1887.
5. *Wells Progress,* May 23, 1926.

Northeastern Elko County

1. *Wells Progress,* November 30, 1936.
2. Ibid., April 2, 1909.
3. Marguerite Patterson Evans, "Letters from Contact," *Northeastern Nevada Historical Society Quarterly* (winter 1988): 12.
4. Ibid.
5. *Nevada State Herald,* December 21, 1900.

Southwestern Elko County

1. *Nevada State Herald,* October 23, 1954.
2. *Elko Independent,* October 15, 1907.

3. *Elko Daily Free Press,* October 11, 1952.

4. *Elko Independent,* June 19, 1869.

5. *Elko Weekly Post,* September 4, 1880.

6. Bill Nelson, "J. M. Capriola Company," *Northeastern Nevada Historical Society Quarterly* (summer 1983): 81.

7. C. I. Walther, "Ice Harvesting in Elko," *Northeastern Nevada Historical Society Quarterly* (spring 1992): 11.

8. Gayle Puccinelli, "The Luther Jones Murder Case," *Northeastern Nevada Historical Society Quarterly* (winter 1975): 9.

9. Compiled by Howard Hickson, with additions by author.

10. *Wells Progress,* June 23, 1960.

11. Ibid.

12. *Elko Independent,* May 12, 1900.

13. *Elko Chronicle,* advertisements appearing during 1870.

Southeastern Elko County

1. *Elko Daily Free Press,* February 16, 1950.

Bibliography

Books

Aitchison, Pat Morse. *Morse Family Treasures.* Salt Lake City, Utah: Circulation Service, Inc., 1990.

Anderson, Ruth. *Memoirs of Leona Reynolds.* Carson City, Nevada: Bicentennial Commission, 1976.

Angel, Myron, ed. *Thompson and West's History of Nevada, 1881.* Berkeley: Howell-North Books, 1958.

Armstrong, Robert. *Nevada Printing History, A Bibliography of Imprints and Publications, 1881–1890.* Reno, Nevada: University of Nevada Press, 1981.

———. *A Preliminary Union Catalog of Nevada Manuscripts.* Reno, Nevada: University of Nevada Library Association, 1967.

Asay, Jeff. *Western Pacific Timetables and Operations, A History and Compendium.* Crete, Nebraska: J-B Publishing Company, 1983.

Ashbaugh, Don. *Nevada's Turbulent Yesterday.* Los Angeles: Westernlore Press, 1963.

Bancroft, Hubert. *History of Nevada, Colorado and Wyoming, 1540–1888.* San Francisco: The History Company, 1890.

Bartlett, R. A. *Great Surveyors of the American West.* Norman, Oklahoma: University of Oklahoma Press, 1962.

Basso, Dave. *Nevada Historical Marker Guidebook.* Boise, Idaho: Falcon Hill Press, 1979.

———. *Nevada Lost Mines and Hidden Treasures.* Sparks, Nevada: Dave's Printing and Publishing, 1974.

Beebe, Lucius. *The Central Pacific & the Southern Pacific Railroads.* Berkeley: Howell-North Books, 1962.

Beebe, Lucius, and Charles Clegg. *U.S. West: The Saga of Wells Fargo.* New York: E. P. Dutton and Company, 1949.

Bell, Charles. *Nevada Official Centennial Magazine*. Las Vegas, Nevada: Charles Bell Publishing, 1964.

Bowman, Nora. *Only the Mountains Remain*. Caldwell, Idaho: Caxton Printers, 1958.

Carillo, F. V., and J. G. Price. *The Mineral Industry of Nevada*. Washington, D.C.: Government Printing Office, 1988.

Carlson, Helen. *Nevada Place Names: A Geographical Dictionary*. Reno, Nevada: University of Nevada Press, 1974.

Cline, Gloria Griffin. *Exploring the Great Basin*. Norman, Oklahoma: University of Oklahoma Press, 1963.

Cloud, Barbara. *The Business of Newspapers on the Western Frontier*. Reno, Nevada: University of Nevada Press, 1992.

Couch, Bertrand, and Jay Carpenter. *Nevada's Metal and Mineral Production, 1859–1940*. Reno, Nevada: University of Nevada, 1941.

Darrah, Elliott W. *Reviewing Nevada's Legacy*. Sepulvada, California: The Sagebrush Press, 1964.

Davis, Sam. *The History of Nevada*. Los Angeles: Elms Publishing Company, 1913.

Denevi, Don. *Tragic Train, The City of San Francisco*. Seattle: Superior Publishing Company, 1977.

———. *The Western Pacific*. Seattle: Superior Publishing Company, 1978.

Douglas, I. H. *Geology of the Tecoma District*. Reno: Nevada Bureau of Mines and Geology, 1984.

Douglass, William A. *Basque Sheepherders of the American West*. Reno, Nevada: University of Nevada Press, 1985.

Dunn, Hal, and Duane Feisel. *Nevada Trade Token Place Names*. Carson City, Nevada: Hal Dunn, 1973.

Egan, Howard. *Pioneering the West, 1846–1878*. Richmond, Utah: Howard Egan Estate, 1917.

Elliott, Russell, and Helen Poulton. *Writings on Nevada: A Selected Bibliography*. Reno, Nevada: University of Nevada Press, 1963.

Emmons, William Harvey. *A Reconnaissance of Some Mining Camps in Elko, Lander and Eureka Counties, Nevada*. Washington, D.C.: Government Printing Office, 1910.

Ferguson, Henry. *The Mining Districts of Nevada*. Reno: Nevada Bureau of Mines, 1944.

Fletcher, Fred Nathaniel. *Early Nevada*. Reno, Nevada: A. Carlisle and Company, 1929.

Florin, Lambert. *Ghost Towns of the West*. Seattle: Superior Publishing Company, 1971.

Folkes, John. *Nevada Newspapers*. Reno, Nevada: University of Nevada Press, 1964.

Fox, Theron. *Nevada Treasure Hunters Ghost Town Guide*. San Jose, California: Harlan-Young Press, 1961.

Frickstad, Walter, and Edward Thrall. *A Century of Nevada Post Offices*. Oakland, California: Pacific Rotoprinting Company, 1958.

Friends of the Nevada Northern Railway. *Nevada Northern Railway and the Copper Camps of White Pine County, Nevada*. Salt Lake City, Utah: Taylor Publishing Company, 1991.

Galloway, John. *The First Transcontinental Railroad*. New York: Simmons-Boardman, 1950.

Gammett, James, and Stanley Paher. *Nevada Post Offices.* Las Vegas, Nevada: Nevada Publications, 1989.

Goodwin, Victor. *The Humboldt, Nevada's Desert River and Thoroughfare of the American West.* Washington, D.C.: Government Printing Office, 1966.

Granger, Arthur Earle, et al. *Geology and Mineral Resources of Elko County.* Reno, Nevada: Nevada Bureau of Mines, 1957.

Hanks, Edward. *A Long Dust in the Desert.* Sparks, Nevada: Western Printing and Publishing, 1967.

Hanley, Mike. *Owyhee Trails, the West's Forgotten Corner.* Caldwell, Idaho: The Caxton Printers, 1975.

Harris, Robert. *Nevada Postal History.* Santa Cruz, California: Bonanza Press, 1973.

Haws, Adelaide. *Valley of Tall Grass.* Caldwell, Idaho: Caxton Printers, 1950.

Higgins, James, Eric Moody, and Lee Mortensen. *A Preliminary Checklist of the Manuscript Collections at the Nevada Historical Society.* Reno, Nevada: Nevada Historical Society, 1974.

Higgs, Gerald. *Lost Legends of the Silver State.* Salt Lake City, Utah: Western Epics, 1976.

Hill, J. M. *Notes on Some Mining Districts in Eastern Nevada.* Washington, D.C.: Government Printing Office, 1916.

Hitt, Douglas. *The Original Ghost Town Directory.* Carson City, Nevada: Sanale Vending and Distribution, 1970.

Holbrook, Marjorie. *History of Metropolis, Nevada.* Privately published, 1986.

Howard, Robert West. *The Great Iron Trail.* New York: S. P. Putnam and Sons, 1883.

Johnson, Robert Neil. *California-Nevada Ghost Town Atlas.* Susanville, California: Cy Johnson and Son, 1970.

Jones, R. B. *Directory of Nevada Mining Operations Active During 1985.* Reno, Nevada: Nevada Bureau of Mines, 1986.

Kneiss, Gilbert. *Bonanza Railroads.* Palo Alto, California: Stanford University Press, 1941.

Koontz, John. *Political History of Nevada.* Carson City, Nevada: State Printing Office, 1960.

Kraus, George. *High Road to Promontory.* Palo Alto, California: American West Publishing Company, 1969.

LaPointe, Daphne, Joseph Tingley, and Richard Jones. *Mineral Resources of Elko County, Nevada.* Reno, Nevada: Nevada Bureau of Mines, 1991.

Larrison, Earl. *Owyhee: The Life of a Northern Desert.* Caldwell, Idaho: Caxton Printers, 1957.

Lavender, David. *The Great West.* Palo Alto, California: American Heritage Publishing Company, 1965.

Laxalt, Robert. *In a Hundred Graves: A Basque Portrait.* Reno, Nevada: University of Nevada Press, 1972.

———. *Nevada: A Bicentennial History.* New York: W. W. Norton and Company, 1977.

Leigh, Rufus Wood. *Nevada Place Names: Their Origin and Significance.* Salt Lake City, Utah: Deseret News Press, 1964.

Lincoln, Francis Church. *Mining Districts and Mineral Resources of Nevada.* Reno, Nevada: Nevada Newsletter Publishing Company, 1923.

Lingenfelter, Richard, and Karen Gash. *The Newspapers of Nevada: A History and Bibliography, 1854–1979*. Reno, Nevada: University of Nevada Press, 1984.

Loofbourow, Leon. *Steeples Among the Sage*. Oakland, California: University of the Pacific, 1964.

Mack, Effie Mona. *Nevada*. Glendale, California: Arthur H. Clark, 1936.

Marshall, Howard, and Richard Ahlborn. *Buckaroos in Paradise: Cowboy Life in Northern Nevada*. Washington, D.C.: Government Printing Office, 1980.

McClellan, E. C. *Elko County: Location and Site and a Full Description of Its Agricultural, Mineral, and Quarry Resources and Climate and Rainfall*. Elko, Nevada: Independent Job Print, 1891.

McDonald, Douglas. *Nevada Lost Mines and Buried Treasures*. Las Vegas, Nevada: Nevada Publications, 1981.

McElrath, Jean. *Aged in Sage*. Reno, Nevada: University of Nevada Press, 1964.

———. *Tumbleweeds, 1940–1967*. Reno, Nevada: University of Nevada Press, 1971.

McKinney, Whitney. *A History of the Shoshone-Paiutes of the Duck Valley Indian Reservation*. San Francisco: The Institute of the American West, 1983.

Mitchell, James. *Gem Trails of Nevada*. Glendale, California: Gem Guides Book Company, 1991.

Moody, Eric. *An Index to the Publications of the Nevada Historical Society, 1907–1971*. Reno, Nevada: Nevada Historical Society, 1977.

Murbarger, Nell. *Ghost of the Glory Trail*. Palm Desert, California: Desert Magazine Press, 1956.

———. *Sovereigns of the Sage*. Palm Desert, California: Desert Magazine Press, 1958.

Myrick, David. *Railroads of Nevada. Volume 1, Northern Railroads*. Berkeley: Howell-North Books, 1963.

Nevada Department of Economic Development. *Nevada Community Profiles*. Carson City, Nevada: State Printing Office, 1964.

Nevada Writers Project. *Nevada*. Reno, Nevada: Binfords and Mort, 1940.

Nielson, Norm. *Tales of Nevada*. Vol. 1. Reno, Nevada: Tales of Nevada, 1989.

———. *Tales of Nevada*. Vol. 2. Reno, Nevada: Tales of Nevada, 1993.

O'Bryan, Frank. *Overland Chronicle: Emigrant Diaries in Western Nevada Libraries*. Reno, Nevada: Nevada Historical Society.

Owens, Preston. *Wes Helth: A Man for All Reasons*. Provo, Utah: Brigham Young University Family History Services, 1990.

Paher, Stanley. *Nevada, An Annotated Bibliography*. Las Vegas, Nevada: Nevada Publications, 1980.

———. *Nevada Ghost Towns and Mining Camps*. Las Vegas, Nevada: Nevada Publications, 1973.

———. *Nevada Official Bicentennial Book*. Las Vegas, Nevada: Nevada Publications, 1976.

———, ed. *Nevada Towns and Tales*. Las Vegas, Nevada: Nevada Publications, 1981.

Paris, Beltran, with William A. Douglass. *Beltran: Basque Sheepman of the American West*. Reno, Nevada: University of Nevada Press, 1979.

Patterson, Edna. *Sagebrush Doctors*. Salt Lake City, Utah: Art City Publishing, 1972.

———. *This Land Was Ours*. Salt Lake City, Utah: Art City Publishing, 1973.

————. *Who Named It?* Elko, Nevada: Elko Independent, 1965.

Patterson, Edna, Louise Ulph, and Victor Goodwin. *Nevada's Northeast Frontier.* Reno, Nevada: University of Nevada Press, 1969.

Penfield, Thomas. *A Guide to Treasure in Nevada.* Carson City, Nevada: Carson Enterprises, 1974.

Reed, Flo. *Bygone Days of Nevada Schools.* Privately published, 1991.

Ruby Valley Memories. Privately published, n.d.

Sawyer, Byrd. *Gold and Silver Rushes of Nevada.* San Jose, California: Harlan-Young Press, 1971.

Schilling, John. *The Nevada Mineral Industry, 1980.* Reno, Nevada: Nevada Bureau of Mines and Geology, 1980.

————. *The Nevada Mineral Industry, 1981.* Reno, Nevada: Nevada Bureau of Mines and Geology, 1981.

————. *The Nevada Mineral Industry, 1985.* Reno, Nevada: Nevada Bureau of Mines and Geology, 1985.

————. *The Nevada Mineral Industry, 1990.* Reno, Nevada: Nevada Bureau of Mines and Geology, 1990.

Scott, Kenneth. *Calvacade of Time.* Elko, Nevada: Elko Independent, 1982.

Scrugham, James. *Nevada, a Narrative of the Conquest of a Frontier Land: Comprising the Story of Her People from the Dawn of History to the Present Time.* Chicago: The American Historical Society, 1935.

Shawe, F. R., R. G. Reeves, and V. E. Kral. *Iron Deposits of Nevada.* Part C, *Iron Ore Deposits of Northern Nevada.* Reno, Nevada: Nevada Bureau of Mines and Geology, 1962.

Smith, Raymond. *Saloons of Old and New Nevada.* Reno, Nevada: Silver State Printing, 1992.

Stapley, Linda. *Together in My Name: A Centennial Tribute to the Little Church of the Crossroads, Lamoille, Nevada.* Elko: Elko Independent, 1990.

Stevens, Horace. *The Copper Handbook.* Vols. 2–10. Washington, D.C.: Government Printing Office, 1908.

Truett, Velma. *On the Hoof in Nevada.* Los Angeles: Gehrett-Truett-Hall, 1950.

University of Nevada. *Metal and Non-metal Occurences in Nevada.* Reno, Nevada: University of Nevada, 1932.

Vanderbilt, Paul. *Guide to the Special Collections of Prints and Photographs in the Library of Congress.* Washington, D.C.: Government Printing Office, 1955.

Vanderburg, William O. *Placer Mining in Nevada.* University of Nevada Bulletin 30, no. 4. Reno: University of Nevada, 1936.

Vanderburg, William O., and Alfred Smith. *Placer Mining in Nevada.* Reno, Nevada: University of Nevada, 1932.

Van Meter, David. *G. S. Garcia: A History of the World Famous Saddlemaker.* Reno, Nevada: Avail Publishing, 1984.

Weed, Walter. *The Copper Handbook.* Vol. 2. Washington, D.C.: Government Printing Office, 1912.

————. *The Mines Handbook and Copper Handbook, 1916–1926.* Washington, D.C.: Government Printing Office, 1927.

Western States Historical Publishers. *Nevada, the Silver State.* Carson City, Nevada: Western States Historical Publishing, 1970.

Winchell, Bessie. *Now and Then.* San Francisco: Bonanza Publishing, 1986.

Works Progress Administration. *Inventory of the County Archives of Nevada, No. 4 Elko County.* Washington, D.C.: Works Progress Administration, 1938.

Wren, Thomas. *The State of Nevada: Its Resources and People.* New York: Lewis Publishing Company, 1904.

Articles

Aguirre, Angela. "It Began in Elko." *Northeastern Nevada Historical Society Quarterly* (fall 1982): 43–62.

Aldrich, Ethel. "Elko County's First Courthouse." *Northeastern Nevada Historical Society Quarterly* (winter 1977): 3–15.

Badt, Gertrude. "Milton Benjamin Badt." *Northeastern Nevada Historical Society Quarterly* (summer 1978): 90–114.

Bowen, Marshall. "Bitter Times: The Summers of 1915 and 1916 on Northeast Nevada's Dry Farms." *Northeastern Nevada Historical Society Quarterly* (winter 1993): 3–26.

———. "Elko County's Dry Farming Experimental Station." *Northeastern Nevada Historical Society Quarterly* (spring 1979): 36–41.

Braithwaite, Debra. "Double Gallows." *Northeastern Nevada Historical Society Quarterly* (fall 1973): 3–17.

Branscomb, Mary. "Tom Short: Ruby Valley." *Northeastern Nevada Historical Society Quarterly* (summer 1995): 59–81.

Earl, Phillip. "The Montello Robbery." *Northeastern Nevada Historical Society Quarterly* (summer): 3–20.

Edgar, Bob. "Case 945." *Northeastern Nevada Historical Society Quarterly* (fall 1973): 19–28.

Evans, Marguerite Patterson. "Letters from Contact." *Northeastern Nevada Historical Society Quarterly* (winter 1988): 3–15.

Goodwin, Victor. "Beachey: Nevada-California-Idaho Stagecoach King." *Nevada Historical Society Quarterly* (spring 1967).

Harper, Doug. "Fifty Years Too Soon." *Northeastern Nevada Historical Society Quarterly* (fall 1974): 3–19.

Harris, Leona Gilbertson. "Journey into the Past: Island Mountain School, 1926." *Northeastern Nevada Historical Society Quarterly* (spring 1989): 31–56.

Hendershot, Carol. "Bing Crosby and Elko: A Mutual Admiration Society." *Northeastern Nevada Historical Society Quarterly* (summer 1984): 67–93.

———. "Dinner Station." *Northeastern Nevada Historical Society Quarterly* (summer 1985): 63–81.

Henley, Brigadier General David. "Elko County's 'Navy.'" *Northeastern Nevada Historical Society Quarterly* (fall 1989): 87–105.

Hickson, Howard. "Dirt Runways." *Northeastern Nevada Historical Society Quarterly* (summer 1970): 1–3.

———. "Hardly a High School." *Northeastern Nevada Historical Society Quarterly* (winter 1974): 3–26.

————. "Jiggs and Mound Valley." *Northeastern Nevada Historical Society Quarterly* (summer 1988): 59–73.

————. "Wells, Nevada: A Pictorial History." *Northeastern Nevada Historical Society Quarterly* (winter 1986): 3–21.

————. "Where's the Beef." *Northeastern Nevada Historical Society Quarterly* (fall 1990): 81–83.

Meade, Sharon. "Elko Independent." *Northeastern Nevada Historical Society Quarterly* (winter 1985): 3–12.

Morandi, David. "The Old Elko County Library." *Northeastern Nevada Historical Society Quarterly* (summer 1986): 83–85.

Murphy, E. C., Jr. "The Murphy Story: Starr and Secret Valley." *Northeastern Nevada Historical Society Quarterly* (fall 1992): 73–94.

Nelson, Bill. "J.M. Capriola Company." *Northeastern Nevada Historical Society Quarterly* (summer 1983): 79–90.

Nelson, George. "Grandpa Nelson: Nathan Nelson, 1816–1903." *Northeastern Nevada Historical Society Quarterly* (spring/summer 1982): 3–25.

Oakberg, Helen Olmsted, and Suverkrup, Annette Leighton. "Dr. A.C. Olmsted Family." *Northeastern Nevada Historical Society Quarterly* (winter 1994): 28–35.

Patterson, Edna. "Kate St. Clair: One of Nevada's Great Women." *Northeastern Nevada Historical Society Quarterly* (fall 1992): 137–144.

Powell, Charles Stewart. "Depression Days in Tobar." *Northeastern Nevada Historical Society Quarterly* (fall 1978): 126–141.

Puchinelli, Gayle. "The Luther Jones Murder Case." *Northeastern Nevada Historical Society Quarterly* (winter 1975): 3–11.

Reynolds, Leona. "Memories of Currie, Nevada." *Northeastern Nevada Historical Society Quarterly* (spring 1975): 3–16.

Robertson, Opal Curieux. "William and Catherine Johnson Family, North Fork Pioneers: Lillian M. Johson." *Northeastern Nevada Historical Society Quarterly* (summer 1991): 51–75.

Sheerin, Chris. "Newton Hunt Crumley." *Northeastern Nevada Historical Society Quarterly* (winter 1979): 3–15.

Smith, Mary Urriola. "Memories of Jack Creek, 1925–1935." *Northeastern Nevada Historical Society Quarterly* (spring 1990): 31–44.

Steninger, Dan. "Elko Daily Free Press." *Northeastern Nevada Historical Society Quarterly* (spring 1981): 47–59.

Strode, Nevada Boies. "Horace and Etta Agee." *Northeastern Nevada Historical Society Quarterly* (winter 1972): 17–32.

Tatomer, William. "Tobar." *Northeastern Nevada Historical Society Quarterly* (winter 1978): 3–12.

Walther, C. I. "Ice Harvesting in Elko." *Northeastern Nevada Historical Society Quarterly* (winter 1992): 3–19.

Wetzel, Barbi. "Pioneer Hotel." *Northeastern Nevada Historical Society Quarterly* (spring 1985): 35–45.

Whittaker, Leslie. "Elko Flouring Mill." *Northeastern Nevada Historical Society Quarterly* (spring 1981): 61–67.

Wright, Christy. "Carlin's Ice Harvest." *Northeastern Nevada Historical Society Quarterly* (winter 1978): 14–22.

Newspapers and Periodicals

Business Talks, Tuscarora (September 1908–November 1908).
Commonwealth, Carlin (September 8, 1909–February 21, 1912).
Commonwealth, Deeth (February 28, 1912–October 28, 1914).
Daily Argonaut, Elko (January 3, 1898–February 6, 1899).
Elko Chronicle (January 5, 1870–December 4, 1870).
Elko Enterprise (December 1, 1916–February 9, 1917).
Elko Free Press (January 5, 1883–December 31, 1994).
Elko Independent (June 19, 1869–December 31, 1994).
Elko Weekly Post (September 11, 1875–April 30, 1881).
Gold Circle Miner, Midas (April 11, 1908).
Gold Circle News, Midas (September 26, 1908).
Gold Circle Porcupine, Midas (May 20, 1914).
Gold Creek News (December 24, 1896–December 10, 1897).
Metropolis Chronicle (September 15, 1911–December 15, 1913).
Mountain City Mail (November 17, 1938–February 23, 1939).
Mountain City Times (January 21, 1898–May 13, 1898).
Nevada Democrat, Carlin (February 23, 1917–April 13, 1917).
Nevada Silver Tidings, Elko (January 2, 1897–July 15, 1899).
Nevada State Herald, Wells (March 19, 1897–April 14, 1933).
Northeastern Nevada Historical Society Quarterly (1971–1996).
Rio Tinto News.
Ruby Valley News (1975–1992).
Tobar Times (July 22, 1916).
Tuscarora Mining News (September 21, 1907–December 7, 1907).
Tuscarora Mining Review (May 23, 1877–December 30, 1877).
Tuscarora Times (March 24, 1877–December 1877).
Tuscarora Times-Review (January 3, 1878–December 26, 1903).
Wells Progress (June 26, 1936–December 31, 1980).

Dates of newspapers are not necessarily actual publication dates but rather dates of available issues that were reviewed.

Index